SCiENCE to GCSE

Stephen Pople
Michael Williams

Oxford University Press

Oxford University Press, Walton Street, Oxford OX2 6DP

Oxford   New York
Athens   Auckland   Bangkok   Bombay
Calcutta   Cape Town   Dar es Salaam   Delhi
Florence   Hong Kong   Istanbul   Karachi
Kuala Lumpur   Madras   Madrid   Melbourne
Mexico City   Nairobi   Paris   Singapore
Taipei   Tokyo   Toronto

and associated companies in
Berlin   Ibadan

Oxford is a trademark of the Oxford University Press

First published 1995
Reprinted 1995, 1996

A CIP record for this book is available from the British Library.

Typeset in Univers 45 Light

Printed in Italy by G. Canale & C. S.p.A. - Borgaro T.se - TURIN

ISBN 0 19 914635 7 (bookshop edition)
     0 19 914634 9 (school edition)
     0 19 914686 1 (hardback edition)

Acknowledgements

*The publisher would like to thank the following for their kind permission to
reproduce the following photographs:*

AEA Technology p 192; Allsport pp 158, 166; Ancient Art & Architecture p 96;
Bruce Coleman Photo Library /D Spears p 16, /T Bucholz p 19, /J Shaw p 22;
Colorsport pp 148, 164; GeoScience Features pp 76 (all), 88 (both); Holt Studios
p 53; Raymond Irons p 71; J Allan Cash pp 45, 78, 98, 99, 104, 118, 121, 145, 152,
169, 186; Patricia Moffett p 70; Oxford Scientific Films /A Walsh p 49, /G Kidd
p 54, /P Parks p 57 (both), /S Rowner p 59, /B Kent p 69, /U Walz p 150; Performing
Arts Library p 181; Science Photo Library pp 28, 36 (all), 37, 126, 179, /Dr K Schiller
p 27, /CNRI p 30, 43, /D Scharf p 34, 44, /H Morgan p 40, /Dr G Settles p 42,
/R Follwell p 64, 65 (left), /V Fleming p 65 (right), 195, /Dr J Burgess p 117,
/H Schneebeli p 130, /A Bartel p 141, /S Fraser p 156, /R Ressmeyer p 160, /J Yeats
p 164, /G Tompkinson p 174, /D Parker p 183, /P Aprahamian p 190, /M Dohrn
p 196, /J Sandford p 201, /NASA p 199, 203, /Royal Observatory Edinburgh p 202;
Spectrum Colour Library pp 118, 177; Zefa Picture Library pp 60 (all), 90, 92.

Additional photography by Chris Honeywell.

Cover photograph courtesy of Zefa Picture Library.

*The publisher would also like to thank
the following for their kind permission
to reproduce examination questions:*

Midland Examining Group; Northern
Examinations and Assessment Board;
Southern Examining Group; University
of London Examinations and
Assessment Council.

The illustrations are by:

Chris Duggan, Jones Sewell,
Patricia Moffett, Pat Murray,
Mike Ogden, Oxford Illustrators,
Steve Scanlan, Pat Thorne,
Borin Van Loon, and Pamela Venus.

Introduction

If you are working towards GCSE Science (double or single award), then this book is designed for you. It explains the science concepts that you will meet, and helps you find what you need to know. The topics are covered in double-page units which we have called *spreads*. Some spreads cover the basic ideas, others are more advanced. The more advanced spreads are marked with the symbol ♦ in the top left corner and on the contents list.

Contents Here, you can see how the spreads are arranged.

Test and check Try answering these questions when you revise. At the end of each question, there is a number telling you which spread to look up if you need to check information or find out more.

Spreads 1.1 and 1.2 These tell you how to plan and carry out an investigation, interpret and evaluate your results, and decide how valid your conclusions are.

Spreads 2.1 to 4.39 These are grouped into three sections, matching Attainment Targets 2, 3, and 4 of the National Curriculum.

Section summaries These tell you the main points covered in each section, and the particular spreads which deal with them.

GCSE questions These are taken from papers supplied by the GCSE examination boards. A single question may cover topics from more than one area of science.

Answers to questions on spreads Here, you will find brief answers to *all* the questions in the spreads, not just the numerical ones. But try the questions before you look at the answers!

Answers to GCSE questions Brief answers to all the GCSE questions are given here.

Scientific units Here, you will find the main units of measurement, their abbreviations, and the prefixes (such as 'kilo' and 'milli') which are used to form larger or smaller units.

Index Use this if you have a particular scientific word or term which you need to look up.

To be a good scientist, you need to carry out investigations. This book should help you to understand the scientific ideas which support your investigations. We hope that you will find it useful.

Stephen Pople
Michael Williams

Contents

Test and check

Can you answer the following? The spread number in brackets tells you where to find the information.

1 What eight features do animals and plants have in common? *(2.1)*

2 Which part of a cell is the 'control centre'? *(2.1)*

3 How do plant cells and animal cells differ? *(2.1)*

4 How do plants obtain their food? What is the process called? *(2.2)*

5 How do plants and animals get their energy? What is the process called? *(2.2)*

6 On what factors does the rate of photosynthesis depend? What is meant by a limiting factor? *(2.3)*

7 What do guard cells do? *(2.3)*

8 Why do plants need minerals? How do these get into the roots and up through the plant? *(2.3)*

9 Where do plants store the food they make? *(2.3)*

10 Where in a flower are the male sex cells and the female sex cells? *(2.4)*

11 How can pollen be transferred from one flower to another? *(2.4)*

12 In a flower, what happens after fertilization? *(2.4)*

13 What are the three main jobs done by your skeleton? *(2.5)*

14 Why do muscles work in pairs? *(2.5)*

15 What is the central nervous system? What does it do? *(2.5)*

16 What happens to food in the gut? *(2.6)*

17 What are the five main types of nutrient in food? *(2.6)*

18 How is digested food absorbed by your blood? *(2.7)*

19 What unit is used to measure amounts of food energy? *(2.7)*

20 What is the difference between aerobic and anaerobic respiration? *(2.7)*

21 Why do your cells make ATP? *(2.7)*

22 How would you test for starch, glucose, fat, and protein? *(2.7)*

23 Can you describe five important jobs done by the blood? *(2.8)*

24 What is the difference between arteries and veins? *(2.8)*

25 Why does the heart need to work as two separate pumps? *(2.8)*

26 What job is done by the lungs? *(2.9)*

27 Can you describe some of the jobs done by the liver? *(2.9)*

28 What do the kidneys do? *(2.9)*

29 How often do a woman's ovaries release an ovum? *(2.10)*

30 How is an ovum fertilized? What happens to it if it is fertilized? *(2.10)*

31 What happens if the ovum is not fertilized? *(2.10)*

32 In the uterus, how does a developing baby get its food and oxygen? *(2.11)*

33 Why should a woman avoid smoking when she is pregnant? *(2.11)*

34 In the body, where are hormones made? What do they do? *(2.12)*

35 What is the difference between a sensory nerve cell and a motor nerve cell? *(2.12)*

36 Some nerve fibres have a fatty coating. What is this for? *(2.12)*

37 What is a reflex action? *(2.12)*

38 In a plant, what does auxin do? *(2.12)*

39 What is homeostasis? Can you give three examples of homeostasis in the human body? *(2.13)*

40 Where in the body are nephrons and what do they do? *(2.13)*

41 What effect does insulin have on the liver? *(2.13)*

42 Can you describe three ways in which the body can control its temperature? *(2.13)*

43 What are germs? How can they spread from one person to another? *(2.14)*

44 How does your body defend itself against germs? *(2.14)*

45 How can you help the body defend itself against germs? *(2.14)*

46 What are your white blood cells for? *(2.15)*

47 Where are antibodies made? What do they do? *(2.15)*

48 How does your skin help protect you against disease? *(2.15)*

49 What does the mucus in your nose and windpipe do? *(2.15)*

50 Can you give three examples of hormones being taken as drugs? Are any of these harmful? *(2.15)*

51 Can you use a key to identify a plant or animal? *(2.16)*

52 What feature do vertebrates have in common? *(2.16)*

53 What are the five main groups of vertebrates? *(2.16)*

54 Can you give two examples of inherited characteristics? *(2.17)*

55 Where is information about your inherited characteristics stored? *(2.17)*

56 Can you give an example of how the environment can affect a characteristic? *(2.17)*

57 Can you give an example of selective breeding? *(2.17)*

58 What are alleles? *(2.18)*

59 If an allele is recessive, what does this mean? *(2.18)*

60 What is the difference between a genotype and a phenotype? *(2.18)*

61 What are gametes? How does the number of chromosomes in a gamete compare with that in other cells? *(2.18)*

62 What is meiosis? What does it produce? *(2.18)*

63 If one person has XX chromosomes in their cells and another XY, what are their sexes? *(2.18)*

64 What is mitosis? What does it produce? *(2.19)*

65 What is DNA? Where is it found, and what job does it do? *(2.19)*

66 How does DNA make copies of itself? *(2.19)*

67 What is the difference between sexual and asexual reproduction? *(2.19)*

68 What is the difference between being homozygous for a characteristic and being heterozygous? *(2.20)*

69 What is the difference between the F$_1$ generation and the F$_2$ generation? *(2.20)*

70 What is cloning? For plants, how is it done, and what is it used for? *(2.20)*

71 Can you give an example of a genetic disease? *(2.20)*

72 Why is the theory of natural selection sometimes called the survival of the fittest? *(2.21)*

73 How, in time, does a species become adapted to its environment? *(2.21)*

74 What are mutations? How can they be caused? *(2.21)*

75 Can you name one living factor and one non-living factor that can affect a population of animals or plants? *(2.22)*

76 Can you give an example of how an animal or plant is adapted to its environment? *(2.22)*

77 Humans grow crops. How can this affect other populations of plants and animals? *(2.23)*

78 Can you describe five different types of pollution caused by humans? *(2.23)*

79 Could you carry out a line transect and a belt transect? *(2.24)*

80 Could you use a quadrat to estimate the number of dandelion plants in a field? *(2.24)*

81 Could you use a capture-recapture technique to estimate the number of woodlice in a small yard? *(2.24)*

82 What is the greenhouse effect, and what is its most likely cause? *(2.25)*

83 Why is the ozone layer important, and how is it being damaged? *(2.25)*

84 What are the possible causes and effects of acid rain? *(2.25)*

85 What problems are caused by forest destruction? *(2.25)*

86 Can you give an example of a food chain? *(2.26)*

87 Why are most food chains only three or four organisms long? *(2.26)*

88 What is a pyramid of biomass? *(2.26)*

89 What are decomposers? What do they do? *(2.26)*

90 How can carbon atoms in the atmosphere end up in the body of an animal? How are they returned to the atmosphere? *(2.27)*

91 How can nitrogen atoms in the atmosphere end up in the body of an animal? How are they returned to the atmosphere? *(2.27)*

92 What is a trophic level? *(2.28)*

93 When plant or animal matter decomposes, what factors affect its rate of decay? *(2.28)*

94 What part do microbes have to play in the treatment of sewage? *(2.28)*

95 What useful products come from a sewage treatment works? *(2.28)*

96 How can increasing food production cause environmental damage? *(2.28)*

Test and check

Can you answer the following? The spread number in brackets tells you where to find the information.

1 What differences are there between a solid, a liquid, and a gas? *(3.1)*

2 What are the main properties of metals, ceramics, plastics, glasses, and fibres? *(3.1)*

3 What is meant by a change of state? *(3.2)*

4 When ice melts, what happens to its particles? *(3.2)*

5 When water evaporates, what happens to its particles? *(3.2)*

6 Why does a steel bar expand when it is heated? *(3.2)*

7 What is the difference between an element and a compound? *(3.3)*

8 What does the reactivity series tell you about different metals? *(3.3)*

9 What is the difference between a mixture and a compound? *(3.4)*

10 What is a solute? What is a solvent? What is a solution? *(3.4)*

11 How would you separate sand from salt? *(3.4)*

12 How would you separate copper(II) sulphate from water? *(3.4)*

13 How would you separate salt from water? *(3.4)*

14 How would you separate the different inks in a mixture? *(3.4)*

15 Can you describe four differences between mixtures and compounds? *(3.5)*

16 In what ways are solutions different from suspensions? *(3.5)*

17 What are colloids? *(3.5)*

18 What are composite materials? Can you give five examples? *(3.5)*

19 What gas is given off when an acid reacts with a metal? *(3.6)*

20 How does an acid affect litmus indicator? *(3.6)*

21 How does an alkali affect litmus indicator? *(3.6)*

22 If a solution has a pH of 1, what does this tell you about it? *(3.6)*

23 If a solution has a pH of 7, what does this tell you about it? *(3.6)*

24 If a base neutralizes an acid, what is produced? *(3.6)*

25 In the periodic table, in what ways are elements in the same group similar? *(3.7)*

26 What three types of particle make up an atom? *(3.8)*

27 What is an ion? *(3.8)*

28 What is the difference between ionic bonding and covalent bonding? *(3.8)*

29 What is a molecule? *(3.8)*

30 What do you understand by an ionic crystal, molecular crystal, and giant molecule? *(3.9)*

31 What is the structure of graphite? Why does graphite conduct electricity? *(3.9)*

32 What is the difference in chemical structure between wet clay and baked clay? *(3.9)*

33 What are metallic bonds? *(3.9)*

34 Why are alloys harder than pure metals? *(3.9)*

35 What is the difference between an exothermic chemical reaction and an endothermic one? *(3.10)*

36 How can you tell whether a chemical reaction has taken place? *(3.10)*

37 What factors affect the rate of a chemical reaction? *(3.10)*

38 If an element burns in oxygen, what is the product? *(3.11)*

39 If a fuel such as methane burns, what are the products? *(3.11)*

40 What is the combustion triangle? *(3.11)*

41 Can you give an example of food oxidation? *(3.11)*

42 If a metal has become corroded, what has happened on its surface? *(3.11)*

43 Why must a chemical equation balance? *(3.12)*

44 What is meant by the relative atomic mass (A_r) of an atom? *(3.12)*

45 What is meant by the relative molecular mass (M_r) of a molecule? *(3.12)*

46 In chemistry, what is meant by a mole? *(3.12)*

47 Can you calculate the masses and/or volumes of products of a given reaction? *(3.12)*

48 Why is gold found in the ground as a pure metal, while iron is only found in compounds? *(3.13)*

49 How is iron produced from iron ore? *(3.13)*

50 What is steel? How is it made? *(3.13)*

51 Why are some metals more difficult to separate from their ores than others? *(3.13)*

52 What metals are produced by electrolysis? *(3.13)*

53 How many uses or products of common salt can you think of? *(3.14)*

54 What is limestone used for? *(3.14)*

55 What is the ionic equation for the neutralization of an acid by an alkali? *(3.15)*

56 What are half-reaction equations? *(3.15)*

57 What are the products of electrolysing concentrated sodium chloride solution in a membrane cell? *(3.15)*

58 How can a layer of copper be electroplated onto an article made of iron? *(3.15)*

59 What type of ion does a Group I metal make? What is the charge on this ion? *(3.16)*

60 Why does potassium form an ion more easily then lithium? *(3.16)*

61 What are the halogens? Why do they form negative ions? *(3.16)*

62 Can you describe three chemical characteristics of metals? *(3.16)*

63 How does chlorine affect wet litmus paper? *(3.17)*

64 Can you give some industrial uses of chlorine? *(3.17)*

65 When an acid reacts with a carbonate, what are the products? *(3.17)*

66 Can you name three transition metals and describe some of their properties and uses? *(3.17)*

67 What is a redox reaction? *(3.18)*

68 How can iron(II) ions be converted to iron(III) ions? *(3.18)*

69 What is a reversible reaction? If the reaction is in equilibrium, what does this mean? *(3.18)*

70 In the manufacture of ammonia, what is meant by percentage yield? *(3.18)*

71 Can you use ideas about bond breaking and making to describe what an exothermic reaction is? *(3.19)*

72 Can you use ideas about bond breaking and making to describe what an endothermic reaction is? *(3.19)*

73 Knowing the bond energies in the reactants and products, can you calculate the energy changes which occur during a reaction? *(3.19)*

74 What are the main fractions in oil? What are they used for? *(3.20)*

75 What are the two main gases in air? What are they used for? *(3.20)*

76 If a hydrocarbon is unsaturated, what does this mean? *(3.21)*

77 What is formed when a large hydrocarbon molecule is cracked? *(3.21)*

78 What is the structural formula of ethane? *(3.21)*

79 What is a polymer? How is polythene made? *(3.21)*

80 What kind of polymer is nylon 66? How is it made? *(3.21)*

81 How are nylon fibres made? *(3.21)*

82 How is ammonia made by the Haber process? Can you write the equation for the reaction? *(3.22)*

83 What is Nitram? How is it made? *(3.22)*

84 What three substances are combined to produce NPK fertilizers? *(3.22)*

85 How many separate chemical plants are there in a factory making NPK fertilizer? *(3.22)*

86 What is meant by environmental costs? *(3.22)*

87 Can you describe four methods of preserving food and explain why they work? *(3.23)*

88 Can you give three examples of ways in which enzymes are useful? *(3.23)*

89 What happens during fermentation? *(3.23)*

90 What is meant by weathering? Can you describe two causes of weathering? *(3.24)*

91 Why can frost crack pieces of rock? *(3.24)*

92 Where did the gases in the Earth's early atmosphere come from? *(3.24)*

93 Which gas was most abundant in the Earth's early atmosphere? Why is there much less of this gas in the present atmosphere? *(3.24)*

94 What is the water cycle? *(3.25)*

95 What is the rock cycle? *(3.25)*

96 What are the three main types of rock in the Earth's crust? How are they each formed? *(3.26)*

97 Why do earthquakes and volcanoes mainly occur at plate boundaries? *(3.27)*

98 How are oceanic ridges formed? *(3.27)*

99 How can surface rocks become magma deep underground? *(3.27)*

100 What evidence is there that part of the Earth's core is liquid? *(3.27)*

Test and check

Can you answer the following? The spread number in brackets tells you where to find the information.

1 Which materials are the best conductors of electricity? *(4.1)*

2 What happens when like charges are brought close? *(4.1)*

3 How does a switch stop a current flowing? *(4.1)*

4 Can you draw a simple circuit with a battery and two bulbs a) in series b) in parallel? What are the advantages of the parallel arrangement? *(4.2)*

5 Why do heating elements get hot, while copper connecting wires do not? *(4.3)*

6 What does 'kW h' stand for? What does it measure? *(4.3)*

7 Can you describe some uses of logic gates? *(4.4)*

8 Can you write truth tables for AND, OR, and NOT gates, and explain what they mean? *(4.4)*

9 Why do automatic control systems need feedback? *(4.5)*

10 What is the special feature of a bistable? *(4.5)*

11 What is the difference between an analogue and a digital display? *(4.5)*

12 What is Ohm's law? What type of materials obey this law? *(4.6)*

13 What equation links voltage, current, and resistance? *(4.6)*

14 What equation links power, voltage, and current? *(4.6)*

15 What happens when like poles of two magnets are brought close? *(4.7)*

16 Why would the core of an electromagnet be made of iron rather than steel? *(4.7)*

17 How many uses of electromagnets can you describe? *(4.7)*

18 What produces the turning effect in an electric motor? *(4.8)*

19 What is an alternator? How does it work? *(4.8)*

20 What do AC and DC stand for? What is the difference between them? *(4.8)*

21 What are transformers used for? *(4.8)*

22 With mains circuits, why are switches and fuses fitted in the live wire? *(4.9)*

23 What colours are used for the live, neutral, and earth wires in a mains plug? *(4.9)*

24 How do two-way switches work? *(4.9)*

25 What is the advantage of a ring main? *(4.9)*

26 How could you increase the voltage output of a simple generator? *(4.10)*

27 What equation links the output and input voltages of a transformer? *(4.10)*

28 Why is mains power transmitted across country at very high voltage? *(4.10)*

29 What equation links charge, current, and time? *(4.11)*

30 What does a battery's voltage tell you about the energy it delivers? *(4.11)*

31 What is Fleming's left hand rule? *(4.11)*

32 How are X-rays produced? *(4.11)*

33 How many different types of energy can you list? Can you give an example of each type? *(4.12)*

34 What is the law of conservation of energy? *(4.12)*

35 In what ways can heat travel? *(4.13)*

36 Why are wool and fur good insulators? *(4.13)*

37 If a power station has an efficiency of 35%, what does this mean? *(4.14)*

38 Can you explain the difference between a non-renewable and a renewable energy source? Can you give an example of each type? *(4.14)*

39 Can you explain how the energy in petrol originally came from the Sun? *(4.15)*

40 What is internal energy? *(4.16)*

41 What equation links heat input and temperature rise? *(4.16)*

42 Why does heat energy become less useful when it spreads out? *(4.16)*

43 What unit is used to measure force? *(4.17)*

44 What are the forces on a parachutist descending at steady speed? How do they compare? *(4.17)*

45 How do you calculate pressure? *(4.17)*

46 What is absolute zero on the Celsius scale? *(4.18)*

47 What is absolute zero on the Kelvin scale? *(4.18)*

48 What is the link between the pressure, volume, and temperature of a fixed mass of gas? *(4.18)*

49 How do you calculate the moment of a force? *(4.19)*

50 What is the law of moments? *(4.19)*

51 What features make one thing less likely to topple over than another? *(4.19)*

52 What is Hooke's law? *(4.20)*

53 What is meant by the elastic limit of a material? *(4.20)*

54 What is the difference between a vector and a scalar? *(4.20)*

55 How do you calculate average speed? *(4.21)*

56 Can you give two ways in which friction is useful and two ways in which it is a nuisance? *(4.21)*

57 When a car has to slow down, what is meant by the 'thinking distance'? *(4.21)*

58 How is velocity different from speed? *(4.22)*

59 How do you calculate acceleration? *(4.22)*

60 What is the equation linking force, mass, and acceleration? *(4.22)*

61 If two objects push or pull on each other, how do the forces compare? *(4.22)*

62 How is momentum calculated? *(4.22)*

63 What is the law of conservation of momentum? *(4.23)*

64 What is the acceleration of free fall on Earth? *(4.23)*

65 What is centripetal force? *(4.23)*

66 Can you name a machine which is a) a force magnifier b) a movement magnifier? *(4.24)*

67 How do you calculate work done? *(4.24)*

68 How do you calculate power? *(4.24)*

69 How do hydraulic machines work? *(4.25)*

70 How do you calculate gravitational potential energy? *(4.25)*

71 How do you calculate kinetic energy? *(4.25)*

72 What causes sound waves? *(4.26)*

73 Why cannot sound travel through a vacuum? *(4.26)*

74 How could an echo be used to calculate the speed of sound? *(4.26)*

75 What happens inside your ear when sound waves are received? *(4.27)*

76 Comparing sound waves, how are loud sounds different from quiet sounds? How are high sounds different from low sounds? *(4.27)*

77 What is the difference between longitudinal waves and transverse waves? Can you give an example of each? *(4.28)*

78 What equation links the speed, frequency, and wavelength of waves? *(4.28)*

79 What are harmonics? *(4.28)*

80 Can you give an example of resonance? *(4.28)*

81 How does a flat mirror form an image? *(4.29)*

82 Why do light rays bend when they enter glass? What is the effect called? *(4.29)*

83 How do optical fibres work? *(4.29)*

84 How is the image formed in a camera? How is the eye similar to a camera? *(4.30)*

85 What happens to white light when it passes through a prism? *(4.31)*

86 Can you list the different types of waves in the electromagnetic spectrum? *(4.31)*

87 What primary colours must be added to make white? *(4.32)*

88 What colour(s) does a red filter transmit? What colour(s) does it absorb? *(4.32)*

89 What is diffraction? When are waves diffracted most? *(4.33)*

90 What is interference of waves? *(4.33)*

91 What is the difference between polarized and unpolarized light? *(4.33)*

92 What are the three main types of nuclear radiation? How are they different? *(4.34)*

93 What is meant by radioactive decay? *(4.35)*

94 What is meant by the half-life of a radioactive isotope? *(4.35)*

95 What is fission? *(4.35)*

96 How can radioactivity be used to estimate the age of rocks? *(4.35)*

97 What keeps the Earth in orbit around the Sun? *(4.36)*

98 Why do we get seasons? *(4.36)*

99 Why do we see different phases of the Moon? *(4.36)*

100 What is a galaxy? Why are humans never likely to visit other galaxies? *(4.37)*

101 What is a comet's orbit like? Where does a comet have its highest and lowest speeds? *(4.38)*

102 What causes tides? *(4.38)*

103 Why is the Moon's surface covered with craters, but not the Earth's? *(4.38)*

104 How were the Sun and planets formed? *(4.39)*

105 What will happen to the Sun when all its hydrogen fuel has been used up? *(4.39)*

106 What evidence is there for the big bang and an expanding Universe? *(4.39)*

1·1 How to investigate

This spread should help you to
- *plan a scientific investigation*
- *obtain your evidence*
- *analyse your results and reach conclusions*
- *check your findings*

The right-hand side of each page shows one student's thoughts about her investigation.

Planning

- **Decide on a problem to investigate**
  In the example shown on the right, the student has decided to investigate how quickly sugar dissolves in water.

- **Write down your hypothesis**
  You may already have an idea of what you expect to happen in your investigation. This idea is called your **hypothesis**. It may not be right! It is just an idea, though it may be based on work in science which you have done before. The aim of your investigation is to test your idea.

- **Decide what variables you are dealing with**
  Things like temperature, particle size, mass, and colour are all called **variables**. They are things you can measure or observe, but they can *change* from one situation to another.

  In your investigation, you have to decide what the variables are, which ones you will keep fixed, and which you will change.

  To make sense of your results, you need to change just one variable at a time, and find out how it affects one other. If lots of variables change at once, it won't be a fair test. For example, if you want to find out how particle size affects dissolving, it wouldn't be fair to compare big, brown sugar crystals in hot water with small, white ones in cold water.

- **Decide what equipment you need, and in what order you will do things**
  First, read **Getting your evidence** on the next page. To help in your planning, you may need to carry out a trial run of the experiment.

- **Prepare tables for your results**
  First, read **Getting your evidence.**

I will investigate how quickly sugar dissolves in water.

Sugar is made up of molecules. These stick together to make bigger particles (sugar crystals). In icing sugar, the particles are very tiny. In caster sugar, they are a bit bigger. In ordinary sugar, they are a bit bigger again.

If the particles are small, the water can get in contact with all the sugar more quickly. So I think that small particles will dissolve more quickly than big ones.

I also think that sugar particles will dissolve more quickly in hot water. The water molecules will be moving faster, so they will bump into sugar molecules more often.

The main variables I will be dealing with are:
  time for the sugar to dissolve
  particle size
  temperature

Other variables are the amount of sugar, amount of water, the type of sugar (brown or white), and whether I stir it or not. I will use the same amounts of sugar and water each time. I will use white sugar. And I will stir gently, because that separates the particles. If the particles are in a heap, the water cannot reach them properly.

Items needed:
  ordinary sugar, caster sugar, icing sugar
  beaker
  thermometer

First, I will find out how temperature affects dissolving. I will use ordinary sugar each time, so that particle size is fixed. I will dissolve the sugar in water at different temperatures. When I do this, I will measure the temperature with a thermometer, and the time for dissolving with a stopwatch.

Next, I will see how particle size affects dissolving. I might be able to measure the size of the sugar crystals with a microscope. If not, I will just call them 'small', 'medium', and 'large'.

Getting your evidence

- **Make your measurements and observations, and record your results**

  First, decide what readings you will take, how many of them, and over what range. For greater accuracy, you may want to repeat measurements.

Reaching conclusions

- **Look for patterns in your results**

  One way of doing this is to plot a graph, showing how one variable changes with another.

  Some measurements are difficult to make accurately, so the points on your graph may be scattered. Draw a ***line of best fit*** through them. This is a straight line or smooth curve which passes close to as many points as possible.

- **Present your conclusions**

  What links did you find between any of the variables? How would you explain these links?

Assessing your findings

- **Compare your conclusions and hypothesis**

  Do your results support your original idea?

- **Assess your methods**

  How sure are you of your findings? Would you expect to get the same results if you repeated the investigation? Could your methods be improved?

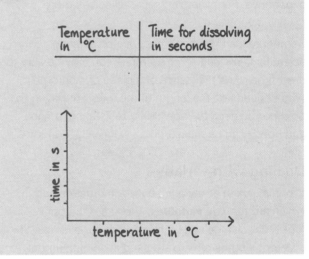

There seems to be a link between time for dissolving and temperature. As the temperature gets higher, the time for dissolving gets....

This is why I think there is a link. When the temperature rises, the water molecules move faster, and .....

Measuring the time accurately was difficult. It was hard to tell when all the sugar had dissolved. Also, I would like to measure the particle size more accurately.

Investigating further

This spread should help you to:
- carry out investigations in which you use your scientific knowledge
- identify and measure variables
- use graphs to help you reach conclusions
- assess the reliability of your findings

The left-hand side of each page describes some of the aspects you should consider in a more advanced investigation. The right-hand side shows one student's thoughts about her investigation.

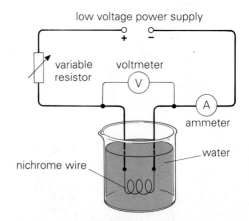

low voltage power supply

Starting with science

Sometimes, a hypothesis is based on everyday experience. For example: 'sugar dissolves more quickly if you stir it'.

Sometimes, a hypothesis depends on existing scientific knowledge. For example, you may be able to predict how the resistance of a piece of nichrome wire depends on the length of the wire. However, to do this, you need to know what 'resistance' means and how it can be measured.

Dealing with variables

When planning an investigation, you must decide which are the **key variables**. These are the ones which will change and be measured. For example, if different lengths of wire are used in an experiment, then length is one of the key variables.

Having identified the key variables, you must decide how to measure them and over what range.
In the nichrome wire experiment:
- What should the highest voltage and current values be? (Safety is a factor here.)
- What lengths of wire will you use?

As well as the key variables, there may be other variables to consider. You may not need to measure them, but you might have to control them. In the nichrome wire experiment, you might want to keep the temperature of the wire steady.

Some variables are difficult to control. For example, in growth experiments, some plants may be in more shade than others. You must take factors like this into account when deciding how reliable your results are.

I will investigate how the resistance of a nichrome wire depends on its length. I know from earlier work that resistance can be calculated with this equation:

$$\text{resistance (in } \Omega) = \frac{\text{voltage (in V)}}{\text{current (in A)}}$$

I think I can predict how the resistance will vary with length. If the length of wire is doubled, the current (flow of electrons) has to be pushed between twice as many atoms. So I would expect the resistance to double as well.

In my circuit, I shall start with 50 cm of thin nichrome wire, put a voltage of 6 V across it, and measure the current through it. (I will do a trial run first, using an ammeter that can measure several amperes. I may be able to change to a more sensitive meter for my main experiment.)

From my voltmeter and ammeter readings, I will calculate the resistance. Then, I will take more sets of readings, shortening the wire by 5 cm each time until it is only 10 cm long.

In my experiment, my key variables will be voltage, current, and length. From data books, I know that the resistance of nichrome changes with temperature, so temperature is another variable which I must control. A large beaker of cold water should keep the temperature of the nichrome steady.

Uncertainties

No measurement is exact. There is always some **uncertainty** about it. For example, you may only be able to read a voltmeter to the nearest 0.1 V.

Say that you measure a voltage of 3.3 V and a current of 1.3 A. To work out the resistance, you divide the voltage by the current on a calculator and get....

This should be recorded as 2.5 Ω. With the uncertainties in the voltage and current readings, you cannot justify any more figures than this.

Uncertainties mean that the points on a graph will be scattered. So you need to draw a straight or smoothly curved line of best fit. Before you do this:

• Decide whether the line goes through the origin.
• Decide whether any readings should be rejected. Some may be so far out that they are probably due to mistakes rather than uncertainties. See if you can find out why they occurred.

From the way points scatter about a line of best fit, you can see how reliable your readings are. But for this, you need plenty of points on the graph.

Trends and conclusions

Graphs help you see trends or patterns in your data.

The simplest form of graph is a straight line through the origin. A graph of resistance against wire length might be like this. If so, it means that if the length doubles, the resistance doubles.... and so on. Resistance and length are in **direct proportion**.

If you think that your graph supports your original hypothesis, then explain your reasons.

In reaching your conclusions, remember that there are uncertainties in your readings, and variables which you may not have allowed for. So your results can never prove your hypothesis. You must decide how far they support it. Having done this, see if you can suggest other ways of getting more evidence.

I have calculated the resistance of each length of nichrome wire. Now I shall use these values to plot a graph of resistance against length.

Length goes along the bottom axis because it is the _independent_ variable – it is the variable which I _chose_ to change. Resistance goes up the side axis because it is the _dependent_ variable. Its value depends on the length of wire chosen.

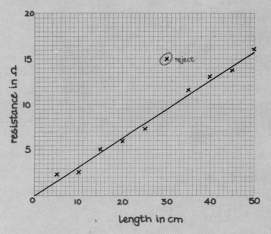

The points on my graph are a little scattered, but I think that the line of best fit is a straight line.

This line ought to go through the origin. If the wire has no length, its resistance should be zero.

I have rejected one point, on my graph. In my table, the current reading for that point seems far too low. I probably misread the ammeter.

As the graph is a straight line through the origin, the resistance of the nichrome wire is in direct proportion to its length. This agrees with my original hypothesis because...

I would like more evidence that the graph really is a straight line. To improve my investigation, I need a more accurate method of measuring resistance. I might get some ideas from reference books...

2·1 Looking at life

By the end of this spread, you should be able to:
- *describe the features which are common to living things*
- *describe the differences between animal cells and plant cells*

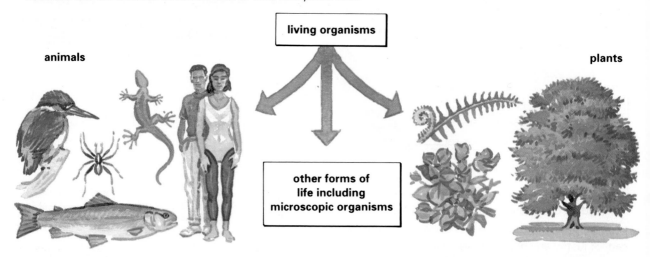

animals   living organisms   plants

other forms of
life including
microscopic organisms

Features of life

Animals and plants are ***living organisms***. They have these features in common:

Feeding Animals and plants need food. Animals must take in food. Plants take in simple materials like water and carbon dioxide gas. They use these, and the energy in sunlight, to make their own food.

Respiration (releasing energy from food) Animals and plants need energy to stay alive, grow, and move. Usually, they get their energy from chemical reactions between food and oxygen.

Excretion (getting rid of waste products) Animals and plants produce waste materials which they must get rid of. For example, you excrete when you breathe out 'used' air, or go to the toilet.

Growth Animals and plants grow bigger. They may also grow new parts to replace old or damaged ones.

Movement Animals and plants can move, though animals usually make bigger and faster movements than plants.

Reproduction Animals and plants can produce more of their own kind. For example, humans have children.

Sensitivity Animals and plants react to the outside world. For example, they may be sensitive to light or a change in temperature. Animals usually react much more quickly than plants.

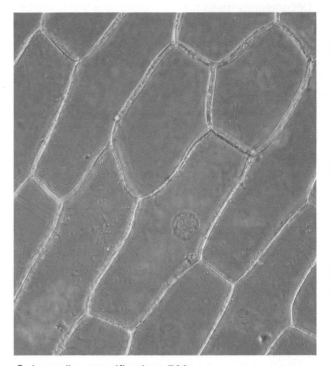

Onion cells: magnification x700

Cells Animals and plants are made from tiny, living units called cells. Respiration takes place in cells. So do all the other chemical reactions needed for life. Living organisms grow by ***cell division***. A cell grows and splits to form two new cells. Then these cells grow and split.... and so on.

Animal cells

Animal cells exist in many shapes and sizes. But they all have several features in common:

Nucleus This controls all the chemical reactions that take place in the cell. It contains, thread-like **chromosomes** which store the chemical instructions needed to build the cell.

Cell membrane This is a thin skin which controls the movement of materials in and out of the cell.

Cytoplasm In this jelly, the cell's vital chemical reactions take place. New substances are made, and energy is released and stored. Sometimes, cytoplasm contains tiny droplets of liquid called **vacuoles**.

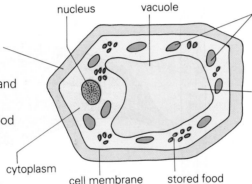

stored food

vacuole

Plant cells

Plant cells also have a **cell membrane**, **cytoplasm**, and **nucleus**. But they have certain features which make them different from animal cells:

Cell wall Plant cells are surrounded by a firm wall made of **cellulose**. This holds plant cells together and gives them much of their strength. For example, wood is mainly cellulose.

nucleus   vacuole

cytoplasm

cell membrane   stored food

Chloroplasts These contain a green substance called **chlorophyll**. This absorbs the energy in sunlight. Plants need the energy to make their food.

Cell sap This is a watery liquid in a large vacuole. Pressure from the liquid keeps the cell firm, rather like a tiny balloon. If a plant loses too much liquid from its cells, the pressure falls and the plant wilts.

Groups of cells

Complicated organisms like you and me are made of billions of cells. Different groups of cells have different jobs to do. Groups of similar cells are called **tissue**. A collection of tissues doing a particular job is called an **organ**. Eyes are organs, so are muscles.

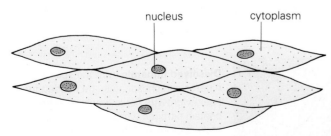

nucleus   cytoplasm

To make a muscle contract, these muscle cells shorten

1 In what ways are living things different from non-living things?
2 In what ways are animals different from plants?
3 Animals and plants show *sensitivity*. Give an example to explain what this means.
4 Give *three* ways in which plant cells are similar to animal cells.
5 Give *three* ways in which plant cells are different from animal cells.
6 What are *chloroplasts* and what do they contain?
7 What job is done by the *nucleus* of a cell?
8 What is meant by *respiration*? Where in the body of an animal or plant does it take place?
9 What is *tissue*? What is the name for a collection of tissues doing one particular job?

2·2 Making and using food

By the end of this spread, you should be able to:
- explain how plants make their food
- explain why animals and plants respire
- name the gases involved in making and using food

Living things need food. It supplies them with materials for growth, and energy for maintaining life. Animals have to find their food. But plants make their own.

Photosynthesis

Plants take in carbon dioxide gas from the air, and water from the soil. They use the energy in sunlight to turn these into food such as glucose sugar. The process is called **photosynthesis**.

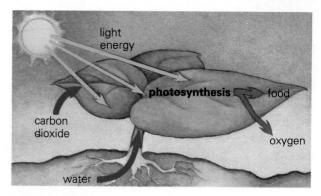

This equation summarizes what happens during photosynthesis:

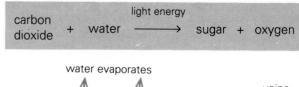

carbon dioxide + water $\xrightarrow{\text{light energy}}$ sugar + oxygen

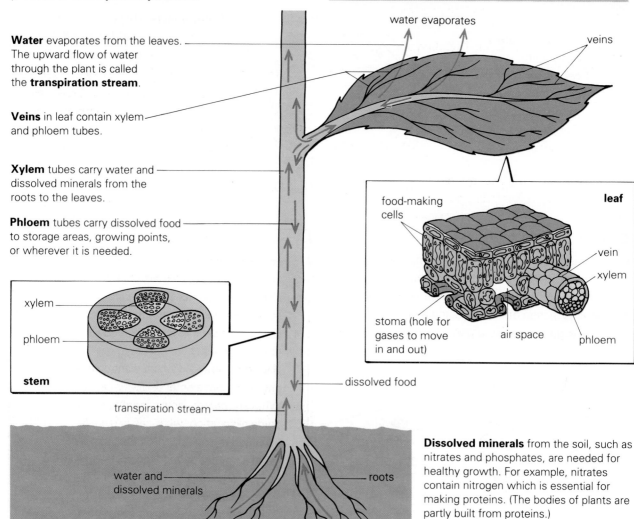

Water evaporates from the leaves. The upward flow of water through the plant is called the **transpiration stream**.

Veins in leaf contain xylem and phloem tubes.

Xylem tubes carry water and dissolved minerals from the roots to the leaves.

Phloem tubes carry dissolved food to storage areas, growing points, or wherever it is needed.

water evaporates

veins

food-making cells

leaf

vein

xylem

stoma (hole for gases to move in and out)

air space

phloem

xylem

phloem

stem

dissolved food

transpiration stream

water and dissolved minerals

roots

Dissolved minerals from the soil, such as nitrates and phosphates, are needed for healthy growth. For example, nitrates contain nitrogen which is essential for making proteins. (The bodies of plants are partly built from proteins.)

To absorb the energy in sunlight, plants have a green chemical called chlorophyll in their leaves.

During photosynthesis, plants make oxygen as well as food. They need some of this oxygen. But the rest comes out of their leaves through tiny holes called **stomata** (each hole is called a **stoma**). The same holes are also used for taking in carbon dioxide.

When plants make their food, they can store it in their leaves and roots to be used later on. Some is stored in the form of **starch**. By eating plants, animals can use this stored food.

Respiration

Plants and animals get energy from their food by a chemical process called **respiration**. It is rather like burning, but without any flames. Usually, the food is combined with oxygen:

food + oxygen → carbon dioxide + water + *energy*

Carbon dioxide and water are the waste products. For example, the air you breathe out contains extra carbon dioxide and water vapour produced by respiration.

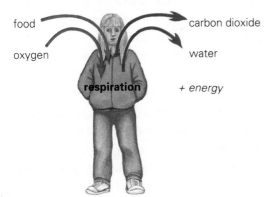

Gases in balance

Respiration takes place all the time. So plants and animals need a steady supply of oxygen.

During daylight hours, plants make oxygen by photosynthesis. They make more than they need for respiration, so they put their spare oxygen into the atmosphere.

At night, photosynthesis stops. So plants must take in oxygen - just like animals. However, they use less oxygen during the night than they give out during the day.

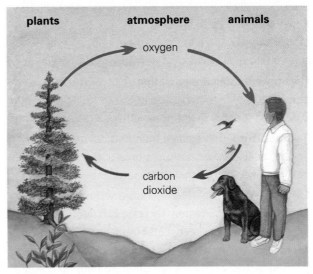

Overall, plants take in carbon dioxide and give out oxygen, while animals take in oxygen and give out carbon dioxide. Between them, they keep the gases in the atmosphere in balance.

1 During photosynthesis, what gas is
   a) used up b) made?
2 What else do plants make during photosynthesis?
3 Why does photosynthesis usually stop at night?
4 Why do plants need minerals from the soil?
5 Where do gases enter and leave a plant?
6 What is a *transpiration stream*?
7 During respiration, what gas is usually
   a) used up
   b) made?
8 Animals are using up oxygen all the time. Why does the amount of oxygen in the atmosphere not go down?

Plant processes

By the end of this spread, you should be able to:
- *explain how the rate of photosynthesis can change and what happens to the substances made*
- *explain how materials are transported in a plant*

Photosynthesis factors

The *rate* of photosynthesis depends on these factors:

Light intensity If the light is brighter, then photosynthesis may speed up. However, very bright sunshine can damage plants.

Water supply If a plant cannot get enough water, then photosynthesis slows down.

Carbon dioxide concentration This is the percentage of carbon dioxide in the air (usually about 0.03%). If it rises, then photosynthesis may speed up.

Temperature If this rises, then photosynthesis may speed up. (However, temperatures above about 40 °C can damage the plant so that photosynthesis stops.)

On a dull day, a rise in temperature will not make photosynthesis go faster. The rate is limited by the amount of light available. Light intensity is a **limiting factor**. However, when it is bright, temperature is a limiting factor. Without a temperature rise, no amount of extra light can speed up photosynthesis. The graph below illustrates these results. It shows how light intensity affects the rate of photosynthesis at two different temperatures.

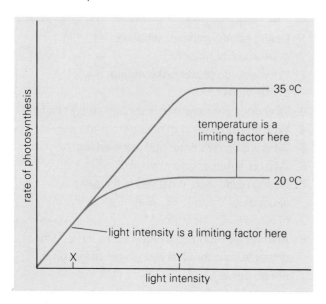

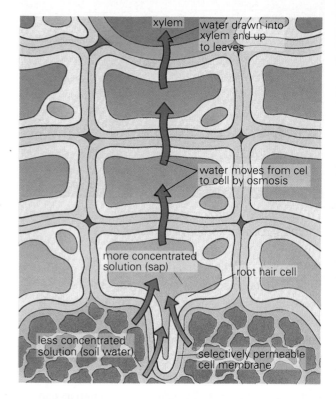

Materials on the move

Dissolved minerals in the soil enter roots by a process called **diffusion** (see Spread 3.2). The same effect makes dyes spread when dropped into water.

In a plant, the mixture of water and dissolved minerals is called **sap**. If the amount of dissolved material is increased, then scientists say that the *solution* is more *concentrated* (see Spreads 3.4 and 3.12).

In roots, sap passes from cell to cell as follows. Cell membranes are **selectively permeable** – they allow some materials through but not others. Water passes through, but some dissolved materials do not. This causes a flow from cells where the solution is less concentrated to those where it is more concentrated. The process is called **osmosis**. (It is pressure from osmosis which keeps cells firm.) Dissolved minerals can also be pumped from cell to cell by chemical reactions. This is called **active transport**.

Sap is drawn up through a plant as water evaporates from the leaves through the stomata (tiny holes). The plant controls the water loss by changing the size of the stomata. To reduce the hole size, **guard cells** either side of each stoma swell up by osmosis.

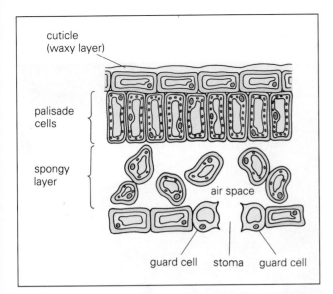

cuticle (waxy layer)
palisade cells
spongy layer
air space
guard cell   stoma   guard cell

Photosynthesis mainly takes place in the **palisade cells** of a leaf. These are near the upper surface, where sunlight can reach them. Beneath them, there are air spaces so that carbon dioxide, oxygen, and water vapour can pass between cells and air by diffusing across the cell membranes. The guard cells control the flow of gases in or out of the leaf.

Food in store

During daylight hours, when a leaf makes plenty of glucose, some is turned into starch and stored in the leaf. Later, it is turned back into glucose and carried (in water) to other parts of the plant. There, it can be stored as starch or used to make other materials.

Many plants need to build up a store of food so that they can survive the winter. Often, we eat their food stores. For example, carrots are swollen roots.

Like other seeds, the broad bean seed below contains a store of food. It must rely on this until its shoot grows out of the ground and can make more food by photosynthesis.

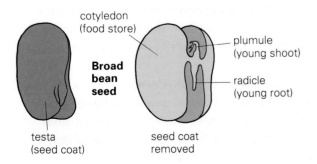

cotyledon (food store)
plumule (young shoot)
Broad bean seed
radicle (young root)
testa (seed coat)
seed coat removed

Making new materials

Plants are complicated chemical factories. They turn incoming materials into a whole range of new materials which are needed for food or new growth. Photosynthesis is the first step in the process. It produces **glucose** and other types of sugar. Sugars are made from carbon, hydrogen, and oxygen. Substances like these are called **carbohydrates**.

The chart shows some of the materials made in a plant, and how minerals are vital for many of them.

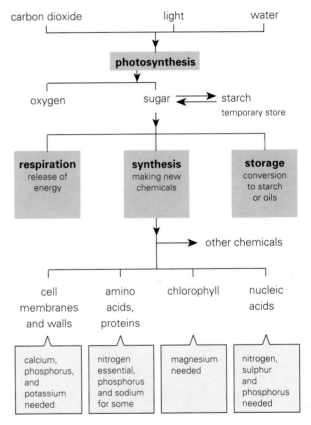

1 Look at the graph on the opposite page. a) If the plant is at 20 ºC and the light intensity is increased beyond Y, what will happen to the rate of photosynthesis? b) At X, light intensity is a limiting factor. What does this mean?
2 By what process does water move from one cell to another in the roots of a plant?
3 What do guard cells do? How do they work?
4 Describe *three* things that can happen to sugar made in a leaf by photosynthesis.

Reproducing with flowers

By the end of this spread, you should be able to:
- explain what the different parts of a flower do
- describe how seeds are formed and scattered
- describe how seeds grow

Some plants produce flowers. They have flowers so that they can reproduce themselves. Flowers contain the tiny male and female cells which, when combined, grow into seeds.

Flowers

Parts of a flower

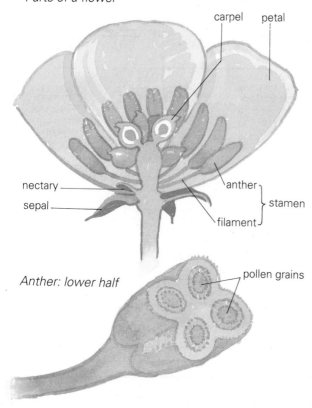

Anther: lower half

Some flowers contain **male sex cells**. Some contain **female sex cells**. But many contain both types.

Stamens hold the grains of **pollen** which contain the male sex cells. Pollen is released when the **anther** ripens and splits open.

Carpels have a space inside called an **ovary**. In the ovary are tiny **ovules**, each containing a female sex cell. When the tip of a carpel is ripe, it is ready to receive grains of pollen.

Pollination

Before a male sex cell can combine with a female sex cell, pollen grains must be transferred to the tip of a carpel. This process is called **pollination**.

Self-pollination means that pollen is transferred from stamens to carpels on the *same plant*.

Cross-pollination means that pollen is transferred from stamens to carpels on *another plant* of the same type. There are different ways in which this can happen:

Insect-pollinated plants Insects, such as bees, carry pollen on their bodies as they move from flower to flower. The insects are attracted to the flowers by their scent or bright colours. They search for the sugary nectar inside.

Wind-pollinated plants Pollen is carried by the wind from one plant to another. The flowers are not usually brightly coloured, but they have parts which hang out in the wind.

Cross-pollination gives a wider variety of young plants than self-pollination. This helps in the struggle for survival. To prevent self-pollination, flowers often have stamens and carpels which ripen at different times.

Fertilization

When a pollen grain sticks to a ripe carpel, a pollen tube may grow out of the grain and down to an ovule. A nucleus from a male sex cell can pass down this tube and combine with the nucleus of the female sex cell. If this happens, the cell has been **fertilized**.

Seeds and fruits

A complete ovary after fertilization is called a **fruit**. In the ovary, each fertilized cell grows by cell division to form a **seed**. This has a thick coat for protection.

Plants try to scatter their seeds over a large area so that some may survive to grow into new plants. The scattering of seeds is called **dispersal**. Different plants use different methods. Here are some of them:

- Seeds have hooks so that they can be carried by animals.
- Fruits are eaten by animals. The seeds come out with the droppings.
- Seeds are shaped so that they can be carried by the wind.
- Seeds are in pods. These pop open when dry and flick out the seeds.

Germination

If a seed absorbs water, and the temperature and air conditions are right, it may begin to grow. Scientists say that the seed **germinates**.

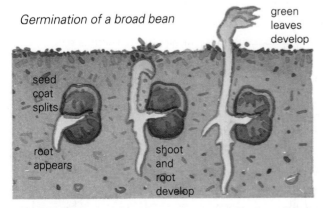

Germination of a broad bean

green leaves develop

seed coat splits

root appears

shoot and root develop

When a seed germinates, a tiny shoot grows upwards, and a root grows downwards. The root and shoot are sensitive to the direction of gravity. The shoot may also be sensitive to light. For example, when it comes out of the soil, it may bend towards the light. Growth in a particular direction, because of light, gravity, or other influence is called a **tropism**.

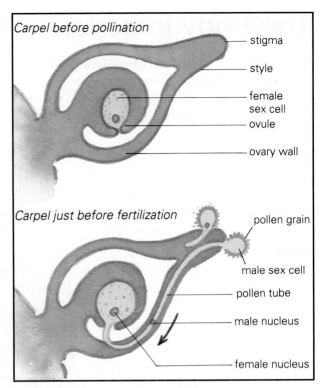

Carpel before pollination
- stigma
- style
- female sex cell
- ovule
- ovary wall

Carpel just before fertilization
- pollen grain
- male sex cell
- pollen tube
- male nucleus
- female nucleus

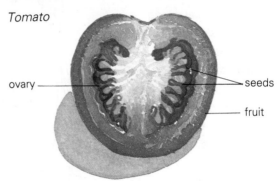

Tomato
- ovary
- seeds
- fruit

1 Which part of a flower contains a) the female sex cells b) the male sex cells?
2 What is the difference between *self-pollination* and *cross-pollination*?
3 Describe *two* ways in which cross-pollination can take place.
4 Why are some flowers brightly coloured?
5 Once pollen grains have stuck to a carpel, how does fertilization take place?
6 In a flower, what do the ovaries become after fertilization?
7 In what ways do plants disperse their seeds?
8 What is meant by *germination*?
9 Why do seeds need a thick coat?
10 Give an example of a *tropism*.

The body in action

By the end of this spread, you should be able to:
- *describe the jobs done by the skeleton*
- *describe how muscles move the body*
- *explain how the body is controlled*

The skeleton

Your body is supported by a framework of rigid bones called a **skeleton**. This has several important jobs to do:

Support The skeleton allows you to stand upright on the ground. It also supports vital organs inside your body.

Protection The skeleton protects many organs:

The **skull** protects the brain. The **ribs** form a cage which protects the heart and lungs. The **vertebral column** (backbone) protects the spinal cord.

Movement Many parts of the skeleton are jointed so that you can move bits of your body. The movements are made by muscles fixed to the skeleton.

Some joints just allow small movements. For example, your back can bend a little because the vertebrae have **cartilage** (gristle) discs sandwiched between them. The discs also absorb jolts.

Bone contains living cells, surrounded by hard minerals for strength. Calcium is the main mineral used. Bone is also reinforced by tough **collagen** fibres which give it even more strength.

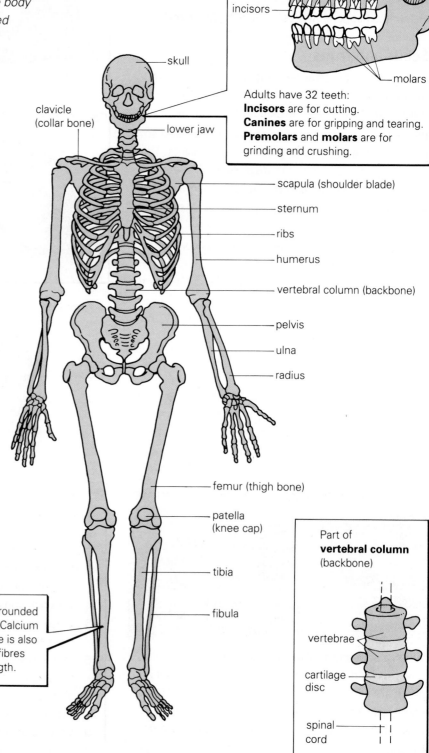

Adults have 32 teeth:
Incisors are for cutting.
Canines are for gripping and tearing.
Premolars and **molars** are for grinding and crushing.

premolars
canine
incisors
molars

skull
clavicle (collar bone)
lower jaw
scapula (shoulder blade)
sternum
ribs
humerus
vertebral column (backbone)
pelvis
ulna
radius
femur (thigh bone)
patella (knee cap)
tibia
fibula

Part of **vertebral column** (backbone)

vertebrae
cartilage disc
spinal cord

Joints and muscles

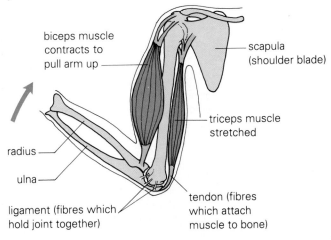

Raising arm

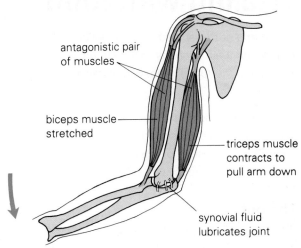

Lowering arm

Many joints are like hinges or swivels. The joints in your arms are like this. Muscles move joints by contracting (getting shorter). However, a muscle cannot lengthen itself. It has to be pulled back to its original shape. That is why muscles are often arranged in **antagonistic pairs**. One muscle pulls the joint one way, the other pulls it back.

Sense and control

Your body is controlled by the **central nervous system** (the brain and spinal cord). This is linked to all parts of the body by **nerves**. Signals called **nerve impulses** travel along these nerves. The central nervous system uses them to sense what is happening inside and outside the body and to control the actions of muscles and organs. For example, if you see a wasp on your hand, your eyes send signals to your brain. This sends signals to muscles, making them contract so that your hand moves.

Signals sent to the central nervous system come from **sensor cells**. The table below shows some of the things these cells respond to:

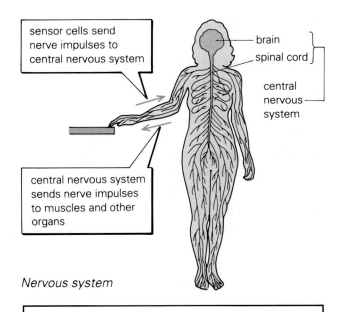

Nervous system

Sensors cells in...	respond to
eyes	light
ears	sound
nose	chemicals in air
tongue	chemicals in food
skin	touch, pressure, heat, pain

1 Which parts of the human body are protected by a) the skull b) the ribs c) the vertebral column?
2 The vertebrae have cartilage discs sandwiched between them. What do these discs do?
3 Apart from protection, what other jobs are done by the skeleton?
4 What is the main mineral in bone? What else gives bone its strength?
5 What are a) tendons b) ligaments?
6 Why do muscles work in pairs?
7 You hear a loud noise and it makes you jump. Use your ideas about the nervous system to explain how a loud noise makes you jump.

Dealing with food

By the end of this spread, you should be able to:
* *describe what happens to food in the body*
* *describe the foods needed for a balanced diet*

When you eat food, much of it ends up, dissolved, in your blood. This carries food to all the cells of your body. The cells use it for energy, and for making the materials needed for living and growing.

The gut

When you swallow food, it moves down a long tube called the **alimentary canal** or **gut**. This runs from the mouth to the anus. Two important things happen to food as it passes along the gut:

Food is digested This means that it is broken down into simpler substances which will dissolve. The chemicals which do this are called **enzymes**. Enzymes are **catalysts**: they speed up chemical reactions without being used up themselves.

Digestion mainly takes place in the stomach and small intestine. But it begins in the mouth. As you chew, an enzyme called **amylase** in your saliva starts to break down any starch into a type of sugar called **glucose**.

Digested food is absorbed into the blood Once food has dissolved, it can pass into the blood. This mainly happens in the small intestine. Its walls are lined with tiny blood tubes which carry the digested food away.

Undigested matter passes into the large intestine. Here most of its water is reabsorbed by the body. This leaves a semi-solid waste (faeces) which comes out of the anus when you go to the toilet.

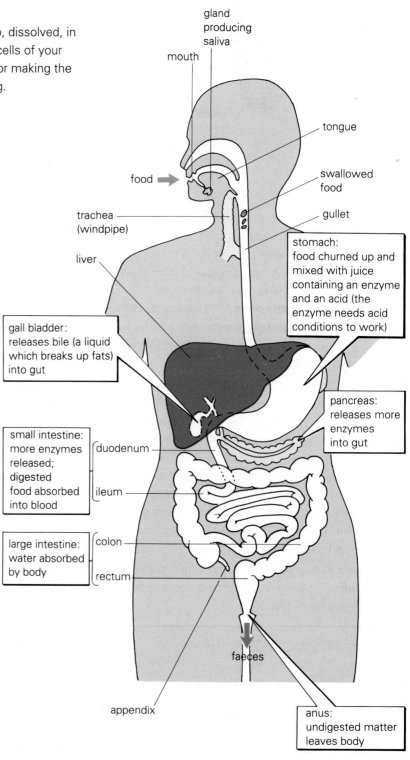

gland producing saliva

mouth

tongue

food

swallowed food

gullet

trachea (windpipe)

liver

stomach:
food churned up and mixed with juice containing an enzyme and an acid (the enzyme needs acid conditions to work)

gall bladder:
releases bile (a liquid which breaks up fats) into gut

pancreas:
releases more enzymes into gut

small intestine:
more enzymes released; digested food absorbed into blood

duodenum

ileum

large intestine:
water absorbed by body

colon

rectum

appendix

faeces

anus:
undigested matter leaves body

Nutrients

The useful substances in our food are called **nutrients**. The five main types of nutrient are shown in the table below.

A balanced diet is one which supplies the right amounts of *all* the nutrients. A poor diet can lead to health problems (see Spread 2.14).

Nutrients	Examples		
Carbohydrates Supply about 50% of our energy	*Sugars* Jam, cakes, sweets, glucose, sweet fruits *The body breaks down sugars and starches into simple sugars like glucose. Some may be converted into fats.*	*Starches* Potatoes, rice, bread, flour	*Cellulose* Vegetables, cereal foods *Cellulose cannot be used by the body as a nutrient, but it provides bulk (dietary fibre or 'roughage') to help food pass through the system more easily.*
Fats Supply about 40% of our energy	Butter, margarine, lard, meat *Fats can be stored by the body; they provide a reserve supply of food.*		
Proteins Supply materials for growth	Meat, eggs, fish, milk, cheese, bread *The body breaks down proteins into amino acids which it can use to build new body tissues*		
Minerals Needed for some body tissues and some chemical reactions	Minerals needed by the body include: Calcium *(for teeth and bones)* – from cheese, milk, vegetables Iron *(used in making blood)* – from liver, eggs, bread Sodium *(for muscle movements)* – from salt		
Vitamins Needed to speed up some chemical reactions	Vitamins needed by the body include: **Vitamin A** – from green vegetables, carrots, liver, butter. *a shortage of vitamin A weakens your vision in the dark* **Vitamin B$_1$** (thiamine) – from yeast, bread, meat, potatoes, milk. **Vitamin B$_2$** (riboflavine) – from fresh milk, liver, eggs. **Vitamin C** – from blackcurrants, green vegetables, oranges. *a shortage of vitamin C causes a disease called scurvy* **Vitamin D** – cod liver oil, margarine, eggs. *a shortage of vitamin D causes rickets (soft bones)* *Your skin makes vitamin D when exposed to sunlight*		

1 Food is *digested*. What does this mean?
2 Where does digestion mainly take place?
3 What are *enzymes*?
4 What happens to food in the stomach?
5 What happens to food after it has been digested?
6 What happens to undigested food?
7 What are the five main types of nutrient?
8 Which nutrients supply us with most of our energy?
9 Why does the body need a) proteins b) calcium? Name some foods which can suppy a) and b).
10 Why does the body need vitamins?
11 The body cannot digest fibre (cellulose). Why is it still important in our diet?

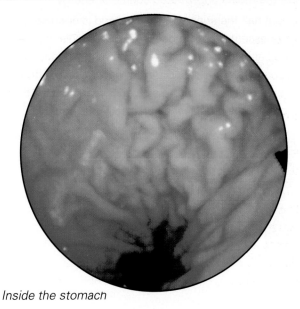

Inside the stomach

Food and energy

By the end of this spread, you should be able to:
- *describe how food gets into the blood*
- *explain the difference between aerobic and anaerobic respiration, and the job done by ATP*

Digestion and absorption

During digestion, food is broken down into substances which will dissolve. These are then absorbed by the blood. This mainly happens in the small intestine.

The inner surface of the small intestine is covered with million of tiny bumps called *villi*. These contain a network of blood capillaries. Together, the villi have a huge surface area for absorbing food into the blood. The blood flows to the liver where there may be further processing of the food.

Villi also absorb undigested droplets of fat. These pass into tiny tubes containing a liquid called *lymph*. Lymph drains into the blood elsewhere in the body.

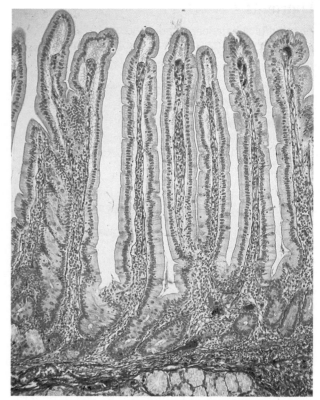

Section through villi: magnification x80

Energy values

Some foods give us more energy than others. Scientists normally measure amounts of food energy in *kilojoules (kJ)* (see Spread 4.12). The energy available is the same as if the food were burnt. The chart below gives some typical energy values. Fats are the most concentrated source of energy.

About half the energy from your food is needed to drive essential body processes – like circulating the blood and keeping you warm. The rest is needed for moving your muscles. Different people have different energy requirements. An active 18-year-old uses 50% more energy per day than an inactive 50-year old.

crisps
cheese (Cheddar)
sugar
bread
potatoes (boiled)
cabbage

1000   2000
Energy in kJ per 100 g

Aerobic and anaerobic respiration

The body's main 'fuel' is glucose sugar, produced by digestion. Its energy is released during respiration. This equation summarizes what normally happens:

glucose + oxygen → carbon dioxide + water + *energy*

This type of respiration is called **aerobic respiration** ('aerobic' means 'using oxygen').

During vigorous exercise, the lungs, heart, and blood system cannot always deliver oxygen fast enough for aerobic respiration. Fortunately, your muscles can work for short periods without oxygen. They can still release some energy from glucose, but the chemical reactions are incomplete and the glucose is turned into *lactic acid*:

glucose → lactic acid + *energy*

This is an example of **anaerobic respiration** ('anaerobic' means 'without oxygen'). In humans, it is only possible for a minute or so because the build up of lactic acid soon stops the muscles working. However, after a rest, when extra oxygen has been breathed in, the lactic acid is changed into glucose, carbon dioxide, and water.

Energy from cells

Respiration takes place in the cells of your body. But it involves a long and complicated series of chemical reactions. If, say, your muscle cells need energy quickly to produce movement, the respiration reactions would be too slow. To overcome this problem, cells do not use the energy from respiration directly. Instead, they use it to make a substance called **ATP** (adenosine triphosphate). ATP acts as a temporary energy store. It can release that energy very quickly whenever it is needed.

Cells contain tiny structures called **mitochondria**. Respiration takes place and ATP is made inside these.

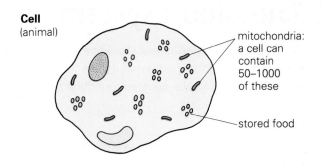

Cell (animal)

mitochondria: a cell can contain 50–1000 of these

stored food

Food tests

Foods can be tested to find out which nutrients they contain. There are some simple examples below:

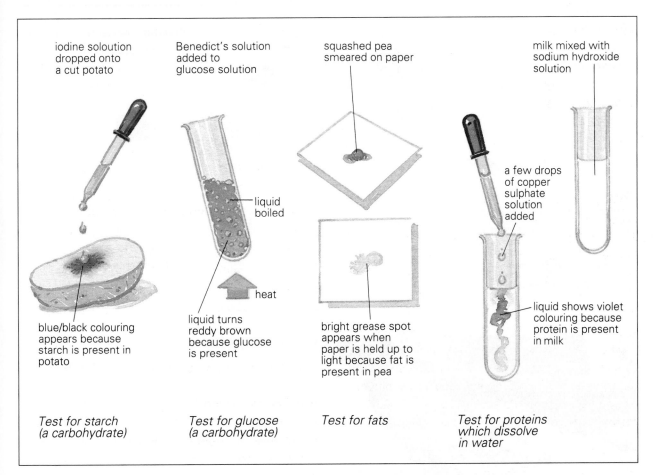

iodine soloution dropped onto a cut potato

Benedict's solution added to glucose solution

squashed pea smeared on paper

milk mixed with sodium hydroxide solution

liquid boiled

heat

a few drops of copper sulphate solution added

blue/black colouring appears because starch is present in potato

liquid turns reddy brown because glucose is present

bright grease spot appears when paper is held up to light because fat is present in pea

liquid shows violet colouring because protein is present in milk

Test for starch (a carbohydrate)

Test for glucose (a carbohydrate)

Test for fats

Test for proteins which dissolve in water

1 Use the chart on the opposite page to estimate how much energy is stored in a 100 g of a) crisps b) bread c) Cheddar cheese.
2 Crisps give you far more energy than boiled potatoes. Why is it *not* a good idea to eat crisps instead of boiled potatoes with your meals?
3 What are *villi* and what do they do?
4 Why is your respiration sometimes *anaerobic*? How is this different from *aerobic* respiration?
5 Where is *ATP* made? What is it used for?
6 How would you test a piece of bread to find out whether it contained a) starch b) protein?

The blood system

By the end of this spread, you should be able to:
- *explain what blood is and what it does*
- *describe how blood is pumped round the body*

Blood

Blood is a mixture of **red cells**, **white cells**, and **platelets**, in a watery liquid called **plasma**.

There are hundreds of times more red cells than white. It is the red cells which give blood its red colour.

Jobs done by the blood

- Bringing oxygen, water, and digested food (such as glucose) to the cells of the body.
- Taking carbon dioxide and other waste products away from the cells.
- Distributing heat to all parts of the body.
- Carrying **hormones** round the body. (Hormones are chemicals which control how different organs work.)
- Carrying substances which help fight disease.

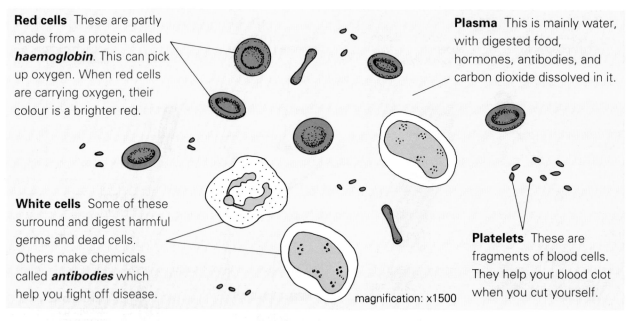

Red cells These are partly made from a protein called **haemoglobin**. This can pick up oxygen. When red cells are carrying oxygen, their colour is a brighter red.

Plasma This is mainly water, with digested food, hormones, antibodies, and carbon dioxide dissolved in it.

White cells Some of these surround and digest harmful germs and dead cells. Others make chemicals called **antibodies** which help you fight off disease.

Platelets These are fragments of blood cells. They help your blood clot when you cut yourself.

magnification: x1500

False colour photo of red blood cells in a capillary: magnification x1800

Circulating blood

The heart pumps blood round the body through a system of tubes.

Arteries Blood leaves the heart at high pressure through wide tubes called arteries.

Capillaries The arteries divide into narrower tubes. These carry the blood to networks of very fine tubes called capillaries. Every living cell in the body is close to a capillary. Water and dissolved substances can pass between cells and capillaries through the thin capillary walls.

Veins Blood from the capillaries drains into wider tubes called veins. It returns to the heart at low pressure. Some veins contain one-way valves to stop the blood flowing backwards.

The heart

The heart is really two separate pumps in one. One pump sends blood through capillaries in the lungs, where it absorbs oxygen. The other pump takes in this oxygen-carrying blood and pumps it round the rest of the body. The cells use up the oxygen.

Circulation of the blood

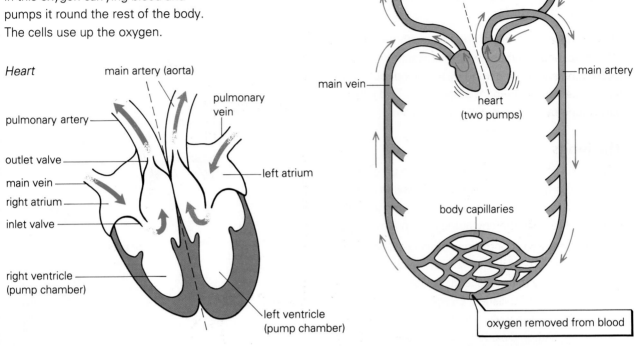

Heart

Each pump has two valves. These let blood through in one direction only. Between the valves is a chamber called a **ventricle**. When muscles around the chamber contract, it gets smaller, and blood is pushed out through the outlet valve. When the muscles relax again, more blood flows into the ventricle through the inlet valve.

The muscle contractions are called **beats**. They are set off by nerve impulses produced in the heart itself. However the beat rate can be changed by the nervous system. If you are exercising, your heart beats faster so that your muscles get oxygen more quickly.

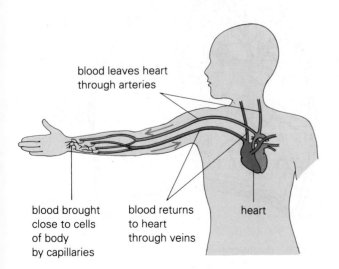

1   *Veins* and *arteries* carry blood. Which of these carry blood a) away from the heart b) back to the heart?
2   What are *capillaries*? What job do they do?
3   Why do the cells of the body need to be close to a supply of blood?
4   What is the liquid part of blood called?
5   Which blood cells help your body fight disease?
6   Which blood cells carry oxygen? What substance is used to carry oxygen?
7   Where does blood absorb oxygen?
8   Why does the heart need valves?
9   Describe what happens to blood as it leaves the pulmonary artery and circulates round the body, back to where it started.

Lungs, liver, and kidneys

By the end of this spread, you should be able to:
- *describe the jobs done by the lungs, liver and kidneys*
- *explain how these organs affect the blood.*

Blood supplies the cells of the body with the things they need, and it carries away their waste products. Many substances are carried by the blood, but they have to be kept in the right proportions. This job is partly done by the lungs, liver, and kidneys.

The lungs

When cells of the body respire, they use up oxygen. At the same time, they make carbon dioxide and water. The job of the lungs is to put oxygen into the blood, and remove the unwanted carbon dioxide.

The lungs are two spongy bags of tissue. They are filled with millions of tiny air spaces, called *alveoli*. These have very thin walls, and are surrounded by a network of blood capillaries. Oxygen in the air can seep through these walls and into the blood. At the same time, carbon dioxide (and some water) can seep from the blood into the air.

As you breathe in and out, some of the old air in your lungs is replaced by new, and the *exchange* of oxygen and carbon dioxide takes place.

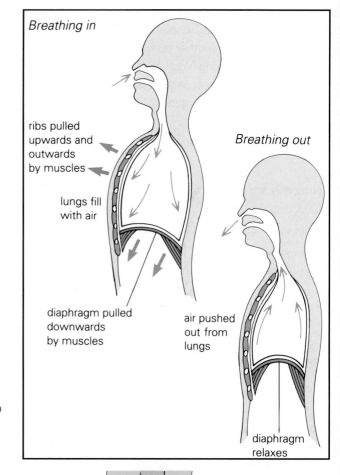

Breathing in

ribs pulled upwards and outwards by muscles

Breathing out

lungs fill with air

diaphragm pulled downwards by muscles

air pushed out from lungs

diaphragm relaxes

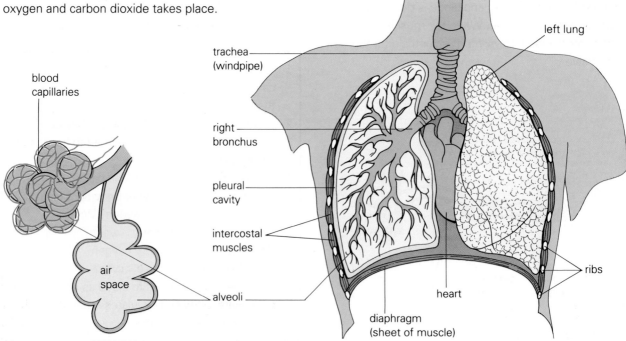

blood capillaries

trachea (windpipe)

left lung

right bronchus

pleural cavity

intercostal muscles

air space

alveoli

heart

diaphragm (sheet of muscle)

ribs

Liver

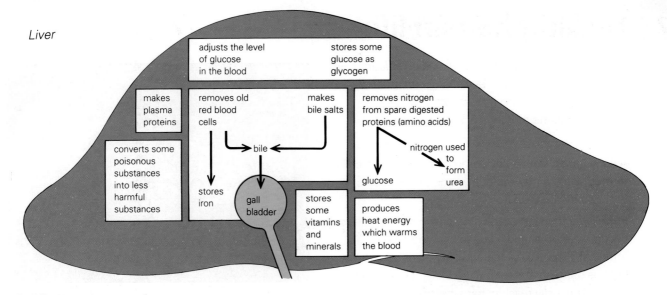

The liver

The liver is the largest organ in the body. It is a complicated chemical factory with many jobs to do. One of these is to keep you blood topped up with the right amount of 'fuel', **glucose**, for your body cells.

The kidneys

The kidneys 'clean' your blood by filtering it. First, they remove water and other substances. Then they put some of these back so that the proportions are correct. Unwanted water and other substances collect in your bladder as **urine**.

The kidneys are called organs of **excretion** because they remove unwanted substances from your body. The lungs work as organs of excretion as well.

Kidney

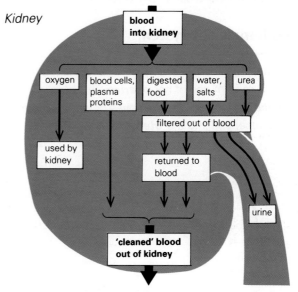

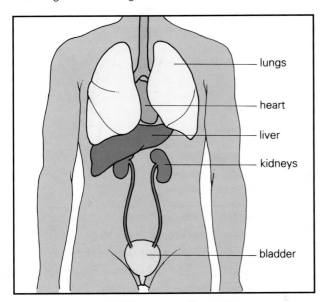

1   In the lungs:
    a) what substance is taken into the body?
    b) what substance is removed from the body?
2   Why are the tiny air spaces in the lungs surrounded by blood capillaries?
3   What makes your lungs expand when you breathe in?
4   Name *three* things which the liver stores.
5   Descibe *two* other jobs done by the liver.
6   What job is done by the kidneys?
7   What happens to waste substances removed by the kidneys?
8   Why are the kidneys called organs of *excretion*?
9   Give another example of an organ of excretion.

Making human life

By the end of this spread, you should be able to:
- explain the meaning of ovulation, menstruation, menstrual cycle, and fertilization
- describe some methods of birth control.

A baby grows from a tiny cell in its mother. This cell is formed when an **ovum** (egg) inside the mother is fertilized by a **sperm** from the father.

Puberty is the start of the time when a girl is able to become a mother and a boy to become a father. It often happens around the age of twelve to fourteen, but it is quite normal for it to be earlier or later than this. Girls usually reach puberty before boys.

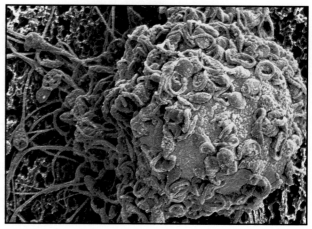

Sperms cluster round an ovum: magnification x500

The female sex system

Ovulation About every 28 days, a woman releases an ovum from one of her **ovaries**. This is called **ovulation**. The tiny ovum moves down the **oviduct** (egg tube) and into the **uterus** (womb).

Lining growth Near the time of ovulation, the lining of the uterus thickens, and a network of blood capillaries grows in it. The uterus is now ready to receive and nourish a fertilized ovum.

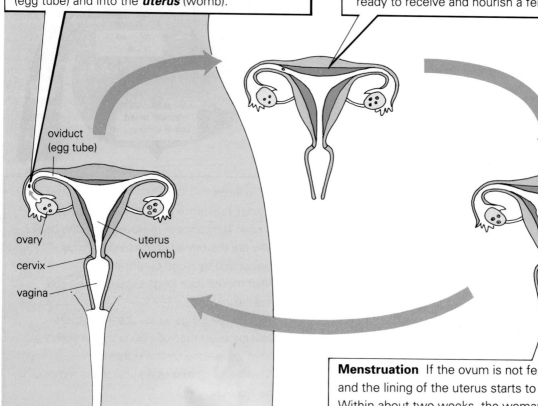

oviduct (egg tube)

ovary

cervix

vagina

uterus (womb)

Menstruation If the ovum is not fertilized, it dies, and the lining of the uterus starts to break up. Within about two weeks, the woman has her **period**: blood and dead cells pass out through the vagina. This is called **menstruation**.

The 28-day cycle of ovulation, lining growth, and menstruation is called the **menstrual cycle**.

The male sex system

A man makes sperms in his **testicles**.

Before sperms leave his body, they are mixed with a liquid which comes from glands. Sperms and liquid are called **semen**.

Semen leaves the penis through the same tube as urine.

Fertilization

When a man and woman have sex, the man's penis goes stiff and is placed in the woman's vagina. When the man **ejaculates**, a small amount of semen is pumped from his penis. The semen contains millions of sperms. Some pass into the uterus. And some reach the oviducts, where they may meet an ovum. Only one sperm can fertilize the ovum. After fertilization, an extra 'skin' forms round the ovum to keep out other sperms.

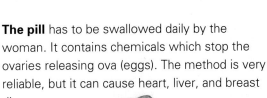

glands make liquid for semen

bladder
sperm duct
front of pelvis
prostate gland
penis
anus
testicles: sperms are made here
blood pressure in this tissue stiffens penis

Birth control

Parents like to give their children the best possible chance in life. For this reason, they may decide to limit the number of children they have. Here are some methods of **contraception** (birth control):

The condom is a thin rubber cover which is put over the man's penis. It traps sperms. A condom is more reliable if used with a **spermicide**. This is a cream containing chemicals which kills sperms.

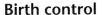

The diaphragm is a rubber cover which is put over the woman's cervix. It too stops sperms reaching the uterus. Like a condom, it is best used with a spermicide.

The pill has to be swallowed daily by the woman. It contains chemicals which stop the ovaries releasing ova (eggs). The method is very reliable, but it can cause heart, liver, and breast disease.

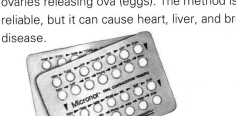

The rhythm method The couple avoids having sex near the time of the month when ovulation is likely. The method is not very reliable, but it can be used by people who think it is wrong to use other kinds of birth control.

1 Explain what each of the following means:
   ovum   ovulation   menstrual cycle
2 About how often is an ovum released?
3 What happens to an ovum after it is released, if it is not fertilized?
4 What must happen to an ovum for it to be fertilized?
5 Where are sperms produced?
6 Some methods of contraception are called *barrier* methods because they stop sperms reaching the uterus. Which of the methods shown on this page are barrier methods?
7 What are the disadvantages of a) the pill b) the rhythm method?

Growing to be born

By the end of this spread, you should be able to:

- *describe how a fertilized human egg develops into a baby*
- *describe how a baby is born*
- *describe some of the factors that can affect the health of an unborn baby.*

Actual sizes

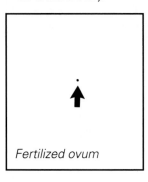

Fertilized ovum

Embryo

...at 4 weeks

...at 7 weeks

From egg to embryo

An ovum (egg) is a single cell. So is a sperm. When a sperm fertilizes an ovum, the nucleus of the sperm joins with the nucleus of the ovum to become a single nucleus. This now has a full set of chemical instructions to 'build' a baby by cell division.

The fertilized ovum divides over and over again as it passes down the oviduct (egg tube) and into the uterus. As more and more cells are produced, they form a tiny **embryo**. This sinks into to the thick lining of the uterus. The embryo now starts to develop into a baby. The woman is **pregnant**.

The growing embryo

After six weeks, the embryo has a pumping heart, and a brain. It lies in a 'bag' of watery liquid which protects it from jolts and bumps.

The embryo cannot eat and breath, so it must get all the substances it needs from its mother's body. It does this through an organ called the **placenta** which grows into the uterus lining. The embryo is linked to the placenta by an **umbilical cord**.

In the placenta, a thin membrane (sheet) separates the embryo's blood from the mother's. The two blood systems do not mix. But dissolved materials can pass from one to the other across the membrane.

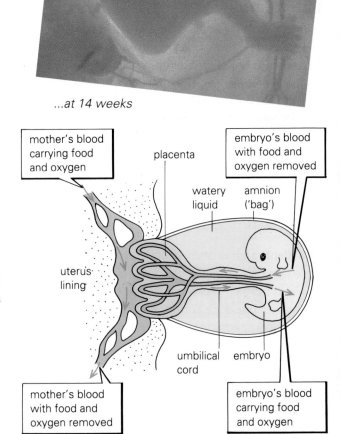

...at 14 weeks

mother's blood carrying food and oxygen

placenta

embryo's blood with food and oxygen removed

watery liquid

amnion ('bag')

uterus lining

umbilical cord

embryo

mother's blood with food and oxygen removed

embryo's blood carrying food and oxygen

Through the placenta, the embryo gets food and oxygen from its mother. Also, carbon dioxide and other waste products are taken away.

Birth

Once an embryo begins to look like a tiny baby, it is called a **foetus**. Birth usually happens about 9 months after fertilization.

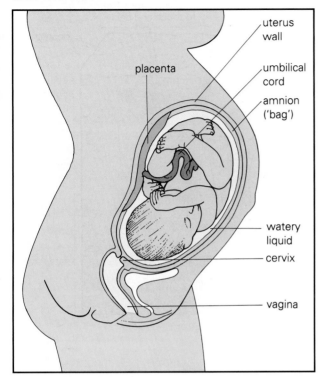

A few days before birth, the baby normally turns so that its head is by the **cervix** (the uterus entrance). As birth approaches, muscles in the walls of the uterus begin to make rhythmic contractions and the cervix starts to open. When the opening is wide enough, the baby's head passes into the vagina. At about this time, the 'bag' bursts and the watery liquid runs out.

1 Why must an ovum be fertilized before it can develop into a baby?
2 How is an unborn baby protected from jolts and bumps?
3 Explain what these are: *placenta*, *umbilical cord*.
4 How does an unborn baby get its food and oxygen?
5 How does an unborn baby get rid of its waste products?
6 How does the position of an unborn baby change a few days before birth? Why?
7 Why is it important that a pregnant mother does not drink alcohol or smoke?

Powerful contractions push the baby from the uterus and out of the mother. Shortly after the birth, more contractions push out the placenta (the 'afterbirth').

The baby gives a loud cry as its lungs fill with air for the first time. From now on, it must take in its own oxygen and food. Soon after birth, the umbilical cord is clipped and cut. Later, the remains of the cord will shrivel away to leave the navel ('belly button').

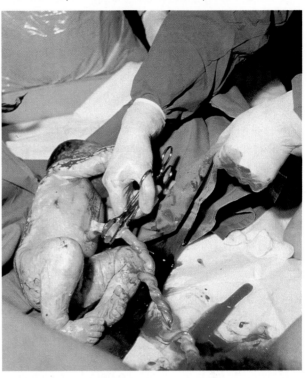

A healthy baby

Care of a baby must start long before it is born. There are many things which can threaten the health of an unborn child:

Smoking Pregnant mothers who smoke tend to have smaller babies than non-smokers. Babies born underweight have more of a struggle for survival.

Alcohol If a pregnant mother drinks alcohol, this can affect the development of her baby. Also, the baby may be premature (born too early).

AIDS Some diseases can be passed from a mother to her unborn baby. AIDS is one example.

German Measles (rubella) If a mother catches German Measles during the first twelve of pregnancy, it can cause deafness, blindness, and heart disease in the baby. That is why girls are given injections to stop them catching German Measles later.

Nerves and hormones

By the end of this spread, you should be able to:
• explain how nerve impulses and hormones co-ordinate the actions of different organs

In living things, the different organs must work together at the right rate and in the right order. This process is called **co-ordination**. Your body has two methods of sending messages between organs: **nerve impulses** and chemical messengers called **hormones**.

Nerve cells in action

Nerves are made up of bundles of **nerve cells**. The impulses they carry are tiny pulses of electricity.

Sensory nerve cells carry information from **receptors** (sensor cells) to the central nervous system. On the right, you can see some of the receptors in the skin.

Motor nerve cells carry instructions from the central nervous system to muscles or other organs. The organs they control are called **effectors**.

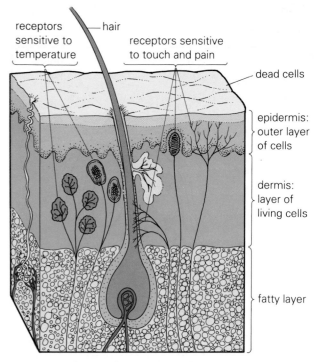

Structure of your skin

Reflex actions

You do some things without having to think about them. For example, if something flashes in front of your eyes, you blink. The response is quick and automatic. Its job is to protect the body from pain or harm. Actions like this are called **reflex actions**. Other examples include coughing and sneezing.

The brain is not involved in all reflex actions. The diagram below shows the path of the impulses if you touch something hot. The path is called a **reflex arc**.

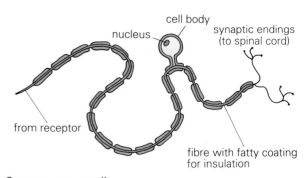

Sensory nerve cell

Hormones in humans

Using nerve impulses, the central nervous system has second-by-second control of the body. Hormones cause changes which are often much slower – growth for example.

Hormones are made in the **endocrine glands** and released in tiny amounts into the blood (see Spread 2.8). Their release may be triggered by nerve impulses or by other hormones. Some hormones are *specific*: they only affect certain cells. For example, **insulin** affects cells in the liver. The table on the next page lists some of the hormones in the human body.

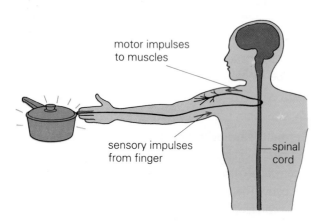

Hormone	Where made	Main effects
HGH (human growth hormone)	pituitary gland	stimulates growth
ADH (anti-diuretic hormone)	pituitary gland	makes nephrons in kidneys reabsorb more water
thyroxin	thyroid gland	speeds up heat production
insulin	glands in pancreas	makes liver turn glucose into glycogen for storage
adrenalin	adrenal glands	speeds up heart and breathing
oestrogen, progesterone	ovaries (female)	female sexual development, uterus changes in menstrual cycle
testosterone	testes (male)	male sexual development

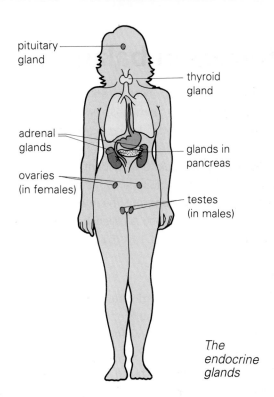

The endocrine glands

- The pituitary gland is the **manager gland**. It releases hormones which stimulate other glands to release their hormones.
- **Adrenalin** is often called the 'fight or flight' hormone. More is released if something scares you. It prepares the body for a rapid output of energy so that you can face the danger or escape.
- For more on ADH and insulin, see Spread 2.13.
- For more on oestrogen and progesterone, see Spread 2.15.

1 What job is done by
   a) sensory nerve cells b) motor nerve cells?
2 Give *three* examples of reflex actions.
3 How do hormones reach the organs that they control?
4 Name *two* hormones made in the pituitary gland and decribe the effects they have.
5 Where is adrenalin made? Why is it sometimes called the 'fight or flight' hormone?
6 How does auxin make a plant shoot grow towards the light?

Plant hormones

Plants do not have a nervous system. They use only hormones for co-ordination. The hormones are carried with the dissolved food in the phloem tubes.

Auxin is a hormone which stimulates plant growth. The diagram below shows how scientists think auxin may make a shoot grow towards the light. Auxin tends to collect on the side of the shoot away from the light. This side grows more than the other, so the shoot starts to bend over.

Artificial auxins are used as weed killers. They make weeds grow too quickly so that they run out of materials and food.

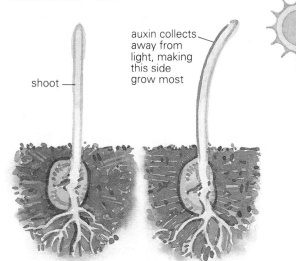

shoot

auxin collects away from light, making this side grow most

Bodies in balance

By the end of this spread, you should be able to:
* *explain how water balance, blood sugar level, and temperature are maintained in the body.*

In your body, temperature, amount of water, and many other factors must be kept steady. Your **internal environment** must be in **balance**. Maintaining this balance is called **homeostasis**. The systems which control it work automatically.

Water balance

You lose about 2 litres of water per day in urine and sweat. This is mainly replaced by water in your food and drink, though some water is made during respiration (see Spread 2.2).

Your kidneys filter your blood and produce urine (see Spread 2.9). They contain millions of tiny **nephrons** like the one below. Liquid (mainly water) is absorbed from the blood, then most of this water (plus other useful substances) is *reabsorbed* by the blood.

The amount of water in the blood is controlled by adjusting the amount of water reabsorbed. This is done using a hormone called **ADH**, made in the pituitary gland. ADH causes more water to be reabsorbed. If you sweat a lot or drink very little, the amount of water in your blood drops. The pituitary gland senses this and responds by making more ADH.

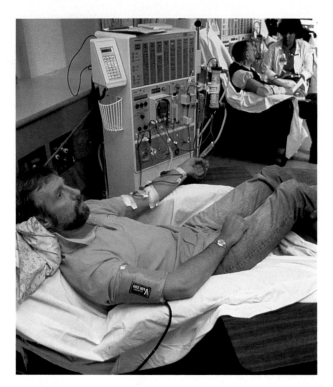

People whose kidneys do not work properly must have their blood 'cleaned' regularly by a **renal dialysis machine** like the one above. In the machine, the blood is pumped through a membrane tube. Excess water is pushed out through the membrane and unwanted dissolved substances diffuse across it into a liquid on the other side.

Controlling blood sugar

Your body's 'fuel' is a sugar called glucose. It is made when food is digested, and carried in the blood to the tissues and organs which need it. In your liver, glucose can be changed into glycogen, stored, and converted back into glucose when needed. **Insulin** is the hormone which makes the liver change glucose into glycogen. It comes from glands in the pancreas.

Too much glucose is harmful. The diagram on the right shows how the blood sugar (glucose) level is automatically adjusted if someone has just eaten a big meal and their blood sugar level is too high.

People with **diabetes** do not produce enough insulin. They must control their own glucose level by carefully monitoring their food intake and injecting themselves with calculated doses of insulin.

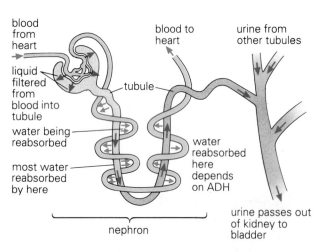

blood from heart

blood to heart

urine from other tubules

liquid filtered from blood into tubule

tubule

water being reabsorbed

most water reabsorbed by here

water reabsorbed here depends on ADH

urine passes out of kidney to bladder

nephron

The kidneys contain millions of nephrons like this

Temperature control

The internal temperature of your head, chest, and abdomen is called your core temperature. It must be kept close to 37 °C for the tissues and organs of the body to work properly.

Respiration releases heat. The heat is carried round the body by the blood and mainly lost through the skin. Sensors in the brain are constantly checking blood temperature to make sure that the body is not gaining or losing too much heat. On the right, you can see some of the factors affecting heat gains and losses, and how adjustments are made.

Feedback

In the system below, information on blood sugar (glucose) level is fed back to the liver, so that its glucose output can be adjusted. This is an example of *feedback*. Feedback is a feature of all automatic control systems (see Spread 4.5), including the body's water balance and temperature control systems.

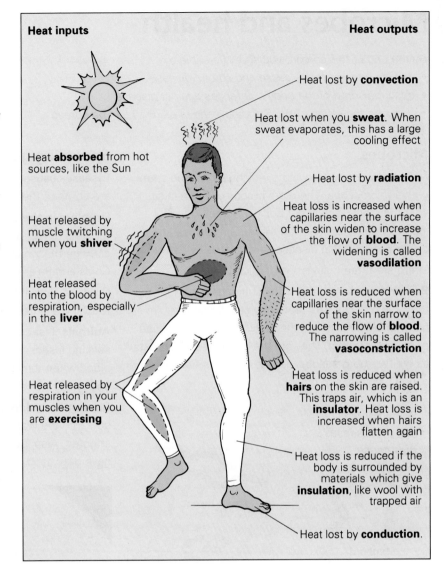

Heat inputs

Heat **absorbed** from hot sources, like the Sun

Heat released by muscle twitching when you **shiver**

Heat released into the blood by respiration, especially in the **liver**

Heat released by respiration in your muscles when you are **exercising**

Heat outputs

Heat lost by **convection**

Heat lost when you **sweat**. When sweat evaporates, this has a large cooling effect

Heat lost by **radiation**

Heat loss is increased when capillaries near the surface of the skin widen to increase the flow of **blood**. The widening is called **vasodilation**

Heat loss is reduced when capillaries near the surface of the skin narrow to reduce the flow of **blood**. The narrowing is called **vasoconstriction**

Heat loss is reduced when **hairs** on the skin are raised. This traps air, which is an **insulator**. Heat loss is increased when hairs flatten again

Heat loss is reduced if the body is surrounded by materials which give **insulation**, like wool with trapped air

Heat lost by **conduction**.

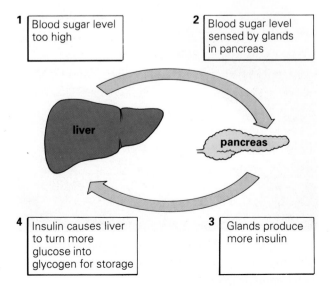

1 Blood sugar level too high

2 Blood sugar level sensed by glands in pancreas

liver

pancreas

4 Insulin causes liver to turn more glucose into glycogen for storage

3 Glands produce more insulin

1 In what ways does the body a) gain water b) lose water?

2 What job is done by nephrons?

3 What is the effect of the hormone ADH?

4 Why do some people need to use a renal dialysis machine? What does the machine do?

5 What is the effect of the hormone insulin?

6 Explain how the body's blood sugar level is decreased if it starts to rise.

7 How does the blood flow near the surface of your skin change if your body is a) too hot b) too cold?

8 Apart from a change in blood flow, how else can the body lose more heat when its temperature starts to rise?

Microbes and health

By the end of this spread, you should be able to:
- explain how microbes cause and spread disease
- describe some of the body's defences against disease
- describe the effect of AIDS and how the virus (HIV) can be spread

Microbes

Microbes are tiny organisms which can only be seen with a microscope. There are billions of them in air, soil, and water, and in our bodies. Some do useful jobs, but some are harmful. Harmful microbes are called *germs*. Most diseases are caused by germs. There are three main types of microbe:

Bacteria are living cells. If the conditions are right, they can multiply very rapidly by cell division. If harmful bacteria invade the body, they attack tissues or release poisons. They are the cause of sore throats as well as more serious diseases such as whooping cough, cholera, and typhoid.

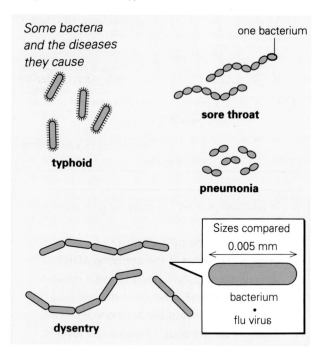

Some bacteria and the diseases they cause

one bacterium

sore throat

typhoid

pneumonia

Sizes compared
0.005 mm

bacterium
•
flu virus

dysentry

Viruses are much smaller than bacteria. Harmful viruses can invade living cells and upset the way they work. They are responsible for diseases such as flu, chicken-pox, and colds.

Fungi include moulds such as those which grow on old bread. Some skin diseases are caused by fungi, for example: athlete's foot and ringworm.

Spreading germs

Diseases caused by germs are called **infections**. Here are some of the ways in which they can spread:

Droplets in the air When you cough or sneeze, droplets of moisture are sprayed into the air. They carry germs which are breathed in by other people. Colds and flu are spread in this way.

Contact Some diseases can be picked up by touching an infected person. Measles is one example.

Animals Insects can leave germs on food. Blood-sucking insects such as mosquitoes put germs in the blood when they bite. Malaria is spread in this way, by one type of mosquito.

Contaminated food Sewage is full of germs. If it gets into the water supply, food and drink may be affected. Also, people may contaminate food if they have dirty hands which are covered with germs.

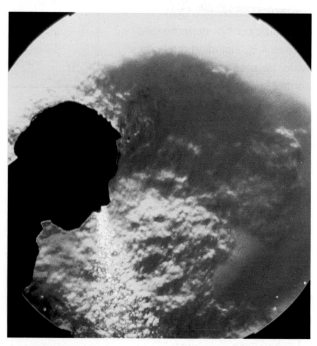

A violent sneeze. To take this photograph, a special technique was used so that air disturbances are seen as different shades and colours.

Fighting disease

Your skin stops some germs from entering the body. However your body has an **immune system** for fighting invaders which do get in. Its 'soldiers' are your white blood cells. Some digest germs. Others make chemicals called **antibodies** which kill them.

Different antibodies are needed for different germs. But fortunately your immune system has a memory. Once it has made antibodies of one type, it can make more of them very quickly if there is another invasion. Once you have had, say, chicken-pox, you are unlikely to get it again. You have become **immune** to the disease. Unfortunately it is almost impossible to become immune to flu and colds. The germs keep changing, and there are many different types.

The body can be given extra help to fight disease:

Antibiotics are medicines which kill bacteria. However, they have no effect on viruses.

Vaccines contain dead or harmless germs which are similar to harmful ones. They are often given by injection. They make the immune system produce antibodies, so that the body's defences are ready if the proper disease ever attacks.

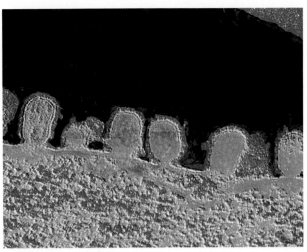

False colour photograph of flu viruses leaving an infected cell: magnification x27 000

Healthy living

To help your health, you need to eat sensibly, take plenty of exercise, and avoid health risks:

Poor diet People can run short of vitamins because they do not eat enough fruit and vegetables. Too little fibre in the diet can cause constipation and bowel disease. Too much fat makes you overweight and may lead to heart disease.

Smoking Smoking causes heart attacks, blocked arteries, lung cancer, and breathing difficulties.

Alcohol Years of heavy drinking can damage the liver, heart, and stomach.

Drugs Drugs make people feel excited or relaxed. But some are addictive: the body becomes dependent upon them. Many addicts die before they are 30.

Solvents Sniffing solvents is very dangerous. The vapours damage the lungs and brain.

▬ AIDS ▬

AIDS stands for **Acquired Immune Deficiency Syndrome**. It is a disease for which there is no known cure.

AIDS is caused by a virus called **HIV**. People with the virus are **HIV positive**. However, it may be many years before the full disease develops.

HIV attacks white blood cells, so the immune system stops working. AIDS sufferers lose their defence against even mild diseases. Minor illnesses can kill them.

There are only three ways in which AIDS can be passed from one person to another:

- by sexual contact
- by blood-to-blood contact
- from an infected mother to her unborn child.

If a man wears a condom while having sex, this reduces the chances of HIV passing between him and his partner.

---

1 Give *three* ways in which germs can be passed from one person to another.
2 Why is it important to wash your hands after going to the toilet?
3 How does your body deal with invading germs?
4 What are *vaccines* and what do they do?
5 List some of the things you should do (or *not* do) if you want to stay as healthy as possible.
6 How does AIDS affect the immune system?
7 There are only three ways in which HIV can be passed on. What are they?

Health matters

By the end of this spread, you should be able to:
- *describe the body's defences against disease*
- *discuss the effects and uses of hormones*
- *explain why smoking, alcohol, drugs, and solvents can damage your health*

The immune system in action

Below, you can see how your immune system uses white blood cells called **phagocytes** and **lymphocytes** to deal with invading germs (harmful microbes):

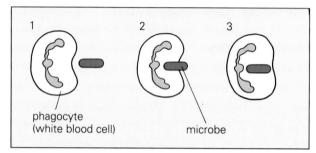

Phagocytes engulf and digest microbes – for example, the germs which get into your blood when you cut yourself.

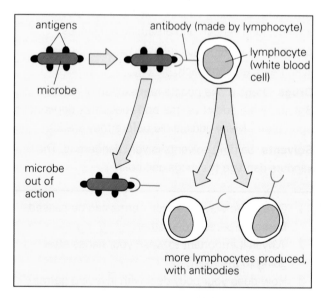

Lymphocytes detect chemicals called **antigens** on microbes. The antigens stimulate the lymphocytes into making and releasing **antibodies**. These chemicals stick to the antigens. They put the microbes out of action or make them easier for phagocytes to digest. When antigens are detected, your body makes lots of lymphocytes, all with the same antibodies. Some are stored, in case the same disease attacks again.

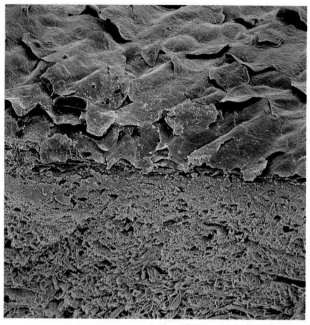

Two layers of human skin: magnification x200

Natural barriers

As part of its defences, your body has natural barriers to keep out dirt and germs. For example:

Your skin has an outer layer of dead cells. Oils in this layer keep it flexible and waterproof, and also help kill germs. The dead cells gradually wear away, but they are replaced by new cells growing just beneath.

Dust and germs in the air you breathe in are trapped by a sticky **mucus** on membranes lining the nose and trachea (windpipe). Tiny hairs called **cilia** make movements which carry the mucus, germs, and dust to the back of the mouth. There, they are swallowed. They pass out of the body with other waste matter.

1 What are a) antigens b) antibodies?
2 How does each of the following help protect your body against disease? a) skin b) mucus on the membranes in your nose c) phagocytes
3 Chemicals which act like hormones are sometimes taken as drugs. Give *two* examples of this. Describe what problems can arise in each case.
4 Give *two* examples of substances which are addictive. What does *addictive* mean?

More on hormones

Hormones are chemical messengers, released into the blood by the endocrine glands (see Spread 2.12). They control how different organs work.

The menstrual cycle (see Spread 2.10) Every month, the ovaries release two hormones: *oestrogen* and *progesterone*. These make the uterus lining repair itself and thicken, ready for a fertilized ovum (egg). If the ovum is not fertilized, the hormone level drops and menstruation starts (the uterus lining breaks up). But if the woman becomes pregnant, her ovaries go on releasing progesterone. This stops menstruation and the release of more ova.

The contraceptive pill (see Spread 2.10) This contains chemicals which act like oestrogen and progesterone. They stop menstruation and the release of ova. However the chemicals may increase the risk of heart and liver disease and breast cancer.

Fertility drugs If a couple cannot have a family, this may be because the woman's ovaries are not releasing ova. The release is normally triggered by hormones. Fertility drugs are chemicals which work like these hormones. However, they can make the ovaries release several eggs at once. This can lead to multiple births – such as twins or triplets.

Growth Some hormones stimulate body growth. *Anabolic steroids* are drugs which act like these hormones. Sensible body-builders do not use these drugs. But those who do risk heart, liver, and kidney damage, and uncontrolled behaviour.

Cattle are sometimes injected with hormones to make them put on weight or give more milk. However, these hormones can end up in our bodies and no one is sure what their long-term effects might be.

Health hazards

Cigarette smoke This contains tar, nicotine, and poisonous gases which irritate and damage the lungs. Tar has chemicals in it which can cause cancer. Nicotine is a poison which damages the heart, blood system, and nerves. Smokers become *addicted* to it. They find it very difficult to give up.

Alcoholic drinks The alcohol in these is a chemical called *ethanol*. Small amounts slow people's reactions. Too much makes them drunk. Years of heavy drinking can cause liver, brain, and heart disease.

Solvents These are used in glues, paints, and cleaning fluids. Some people sniff the fumes, but this can damage the heart and cause heart attacks.

Drugs Some drugs are medicines. But others are taken to make people feel happier, or more lively or aggressive. Some of these, such as *heroin*, are very addictive. Addicts want regular injections. But dirty needles cause infections, and shared needles can transmit diseases such as AIDS.

The variety of life

By the end of this spread, you should be able to:
- *explain how living things on Earth can be classified by their common features*
- *use a key to identify some organisms*

Scientists think that all living things on Earth are related. To show how closely they are related, they try to put them into groups with similar features. They start by grouping them into **kingdoms**. You can see these in the chart on the opposite page.

Humans belong to a large group of animals called the **chordates**. The chordates shown on the chart are known as **vertebrates** because they all have backbones. Here is some information about them:

Fish live in water. They have gills for breathing, scales, and fins.

Amphibians have moist skin. They have lungs, and can live in water and on land. They usually lay their eggs in water.

Reptiles have dry, scaly skin. Most live on land. They lay eggs with a tough leathery skin.

Birds have feathers, and keep a constant body temperature. They lay eggs.

Mammals have hairy skin. They keep a constant body temperature. Most have live young, rather than eggs. The young are fed on milk from the mother.

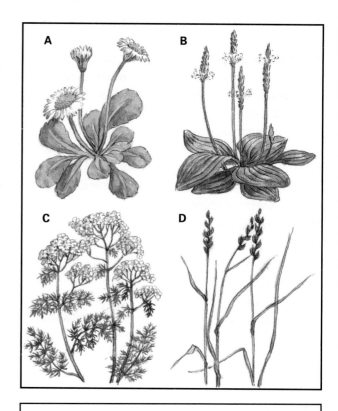

1   In the chart on the right, which animals are *vertebrates*? What do they have in common?
2   Which of the chordates lay eggs?
3   What features do all birds have in common?
4   Where would humans be on the chart? Why?
5   Use the key below to identify the plants above.

Using keys

To help people identify organisms, scientists sometimes construct charts called **keys**. The example on the right is called a **branching key**. You can use it to find the names of the plants in the pictures at the top of the page. For each plant, read the descriptions, follow the route which is the best match, and see where you end up!

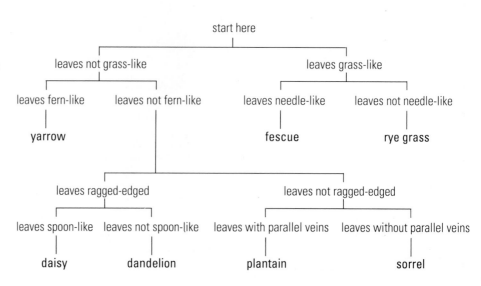

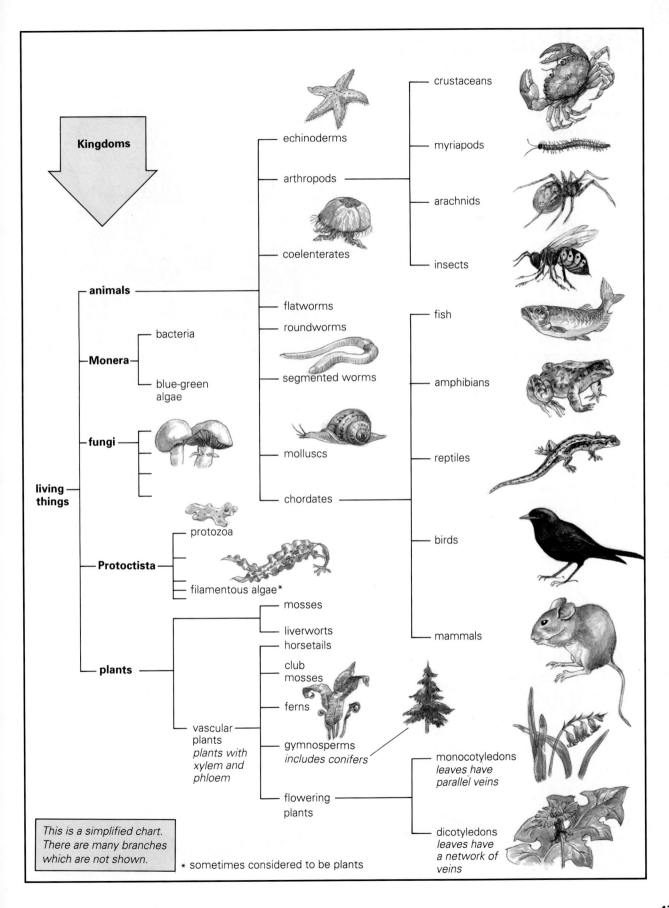

Kingdoms

living things
- **animals**
  - echinoderms
  - arthropods
    - crustaceans
    - myriapods
    - arachnids
    - insects
  - coelenterates
  - flatworms
  - roundworms
  - segmented worms
  - molluscs
  - chordates
    - fish
    - amphibians
    - reptiles
    - birds
    - mammals
- **Monera**
  - bacteria
  - blue-green algae
- **fungi**
- **Protoctista**
  - protozoa
  - filamentous algae*
- **plants**
  - mosses
  - liverworts
  - vascular plants
    plants with xylem and phloem
    - horsetails
    - club mosses
    - ferns
    - gymnosperms
      includes conifers
    - flowering plants
      - monocotyledons
        leaves have parallel veins
      - dicotyledons
        leaves have a network of veins

This is a simplified chart. There are many branches which are not shown.

* sometimes considered to be plants

Pass it on

By the end of this spread, you should be able to:
* *describe how organisms show variation*
* *describe how characteristics depend on genes and on the environment*
* *explain some uses of selective breeding*

Varying features

Your different features are called your **characteristics**. Some, like eye colour, are easy to see. Others, like your blood group, are not so obvious. Many of your characteristics are passed on to you by your parents. They are **inherited**.

No two people are exactly alike. Characteristics like height, weight, and eye and skin colour show **variation**. Identical twins are more alike than most. But even they are not *exactly* alike, as you can see in the photograph.

Continuous variation Humans can be short, or tall, or any height in between. Height shows continuous variation.

Discontinuous variation Some people can roll their tongues, others can't. There is nothing in between. This is an example of discontinuous variation.

All organisms show variation, not just humans.

Genes

A complicated set of chemical instructions is needed to build a human body. Nearly every cell in your body has these instructions. They are stored in the nucleus, in 23 pairs of thread-like **chromosomes**. Small sections of these chromosomes are called **genes**. You have over 100 000 genes altogether. Each gene carries the chemical instructions for a different characteristic.

Genes normally work in pairs. One gene in each pair is inherited from each parent. For example, you may have inherited a gene for black hair from your mother, and a gene for blond hair from your father. Only one of these genes can control your hair colour. A black hair gene is **dominant** over a blond hair gene, so you end up with black hair.

Human cell

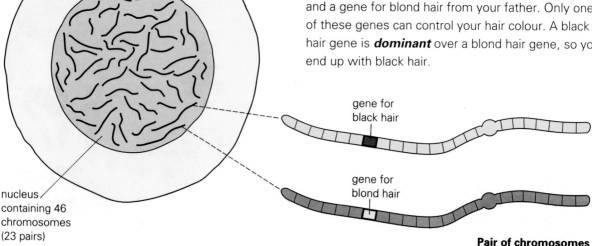

nucleus containing 46 chromosomes (23 pairs)

gene for black hair

gene for blond hair

Pair of chromosomes

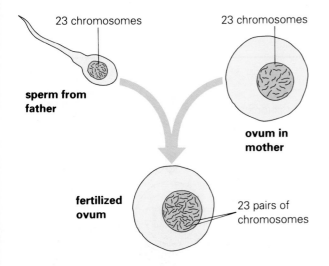

23 chromosomes

23 chromosomes

sperm from father

ovum in mother

fertilized ovum

23 pairs of chromosomes

Each of your parents also inherited *two* genes for each characteristic. However they only passed on *one* of the two to you. It was a matter of chance which one. Unlike other cells, sperms and ova only carry one gene from each pair. But when a sperm combines with an ovum, they make a new cell with a full set of genes. When an ovum is fertilized, millions of gene combinations are possible. That is partly why people can vary so much, even in the same family.

Genes and the environment

Identical twins inherit exactly the same set of genes. Yet one may be heavier than the other because he or she eats more. So, your characteristics depend partly on your genes and partly on your **environment** (your conditions and surroundings).This is true for other organisms as well. For example, two plants may have the same genes. But one may grow better than the other because it has more light, or a better supply of water and minerals from the soil.

---

1 Give *two* examples of *continuous variation*.
2 Give *two* examples of *discontinuous variation*.
3 What are *genes*? Where are they in your body?
4 Genes are in pairs. Where do the genes in each pair come from?
5 What makes 'identical' twins look alike?
6 Why are 'identical' twins not exactly alike?
7 Give *two* examples of the use of selective breeding.
8 Why is it important to preserve rare breeds of animal or rare varieties of plants?

Selective breeding

People often try to breed animals with special characteristics: for example, sheep with plenty of wool, or horses that can run fast. To do this, they select the animals which will be mated. This is called **selective breeding**. The idea is that the offspring ('babies') may inherit the best features of both parents. But chance still affects the result. If two champion racehorses mate, their offspring will not necessarily be a champion.

Selective breeding is also used with plants. For example, one variety of wheat may grow faster than another, or be more resistant to disease. By controlling how the wheat is pollinated, scientists can breed varieties with the characteristics they want. This helps give larger crops (bigger **yields**).

Saving genes

Sometimes, a type of animal or plant may completely die out. It may become **extinct**. Once an organism is extinct, its genes are lost for ever.

Farmers try to preserve rare breeds of farm animal in order to save their genes. If disease strikes a common breed, all the animals might die. However, if a rare breed has genes which make it resistant to the disease, it can be used to improve the first breed.

Dartmoor Greyface Sheep from the Cotswold Farm Park, Gloucestershire.

Genes in action

By the end of this spread, you should be able to:
- *explain how genes are inherited, and the effects which different combinations can produce*
- *describe how sex cells are produced*

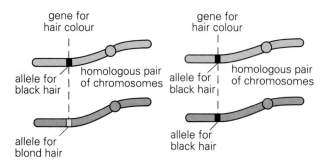

Person A   Person B

The pairs of chromosomes above are from different people:

Chromosomes A are identical in size and shape. They are a **homologous pair**. Genes for the same characteristic (for example, hair colour) are in matching positions along them. However, the gene for hair colour is present in two versions – black and blond. Different versions of a gene are called **alleles**.

Person A will have black hair because the allele for black hair is dominant over that for blond hair. The allele for blond hair is **recessive**.

With some characteristics, neither allele is dominant. Each has an effect. In some animals for example, a brown hair allele and a white hair allele will produce light brown hair.

Chromosomes B are also homologous. Here however, the alleles for hair colour are the same. Both are for black hair, so person B will have black hair.

Phenotypes and genotypes

A characteristic which is seen, like black hair or big muscles, is called a **phenotype**. The combination of alleles which produces it is called a **genotype**. Genotypes are inherited. But phenotypes can depend on conditions and behaviour – for example, how much exercise you take. Identical twins have the same genotypes but different phenotypes.

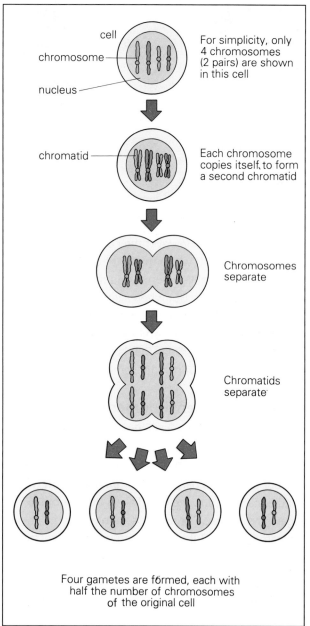

Cell division by meiosis

Cell division – meiosis

When a sperm combines with an ovum, a single cell called a **zygote** is formed. A baby develops from this. Sperms and ova are called **gametes** . Above, you can see how these sex cells are made by cell division. The process is known as **meiosis**. Each gamete receives one allele from each pair in the original cell. But *which* one is a matter of chance.

Inheriting genes

The charts on the right give examples of how genes are inherited. Capital letters stand for dominant alleles, small letters for recessive ones.

In chart 1, the mother has two alleles (HH) for black hair. The father has two alleles (hh) for blond hair. When a sperm and ovum join, there are four possible combinations. All give a zygote with Hh alleles. H is dominant, so the child will have black hair.

In chart 2, both parents have Hh alleles and black hair. Again, there are four possible combinations. Three give black hair. The fourth gives blond hair. So there is a 1 in 4 chance that the child will have blond hair, even though both its parents have black hair.

These are simplified examples. Characteristics are usually controlled by more than one pair of alleles.

Male or female?

In human cells, 22 pairs of chromosomes are homologous. But the 23rd pair do not always match. These are the sex chromosomes. They include genes which control whether someone is male or female. Females have two **X** chromosomes per cell. Males have an X chromosome and a shorter **Y** chromosome.

In males, meiosis produces about equal numbers of X and Y sperms. In females, it produces ova with one X chromosome each. The chart below shows the four possibilities when a sperm combines with an ovum. Two give males and two give females. So there is the same chance of the child being a boy as a girl.

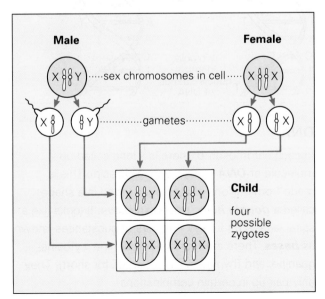

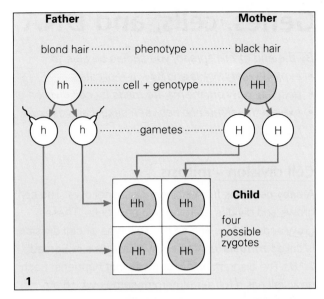

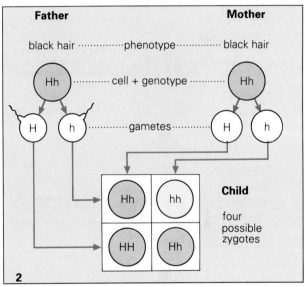

1. What is the difference between a *phenotype* and a *genotype*? Give an example of each.
2. *alleles meiosis zygote homologous pair*
   Which of the above means a) cell division in which gametes are formed b) different versions of a gene c) cell formed when male and female gametes combine.
3. How many chromosomes are there in a) a human gamete b) a human zygote?
4. What is the sex of someone whose sex chromosomes are a) XX b) XY?
5. A mother has blond hair (genotype hh). A father has black hair (genotype Hh). What are the chances of their child having blond hair?

Genes, cells, and DNA

By the end of this spread, you should be able to:
* *explain what DNA is and how it replicates*
* *describe how organisms are made by cell division*
* *explain the difference between sexual and asexual reproduction*

Cell division – mitosis

A baby develops from a single cell as follows. The cell grows and divides, forming two new cells. These grow and divide.... and so on. This type of cell division is called **mitosis** (compare it with *meiosis* in Spread 2.18.) The diagram below shows what happens. Each new cell has a full set of chromosomes which are copies of those in the original cell.

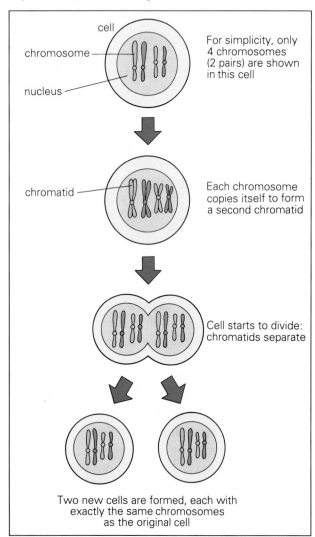

For simplicity, only 4 chromosomes (2 pairs) are shown in this cell

Each chromosome copies itself to form a second chromatid

Cell starts to divide: chromatids separate

Two new cells are formed, each with exactly the same chromosomes as the original cell

Cell division by mitosis

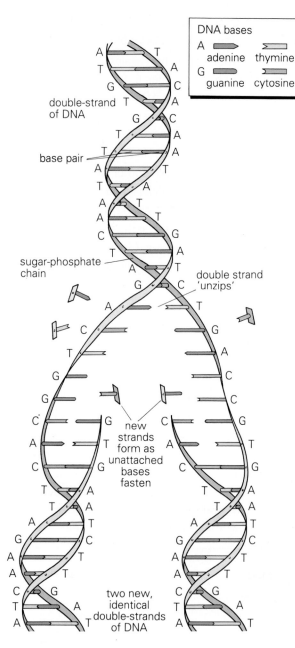

DNA bases

A ⟶ adenine   ⟶ T thymine
G ⟶ guanine   ⟶ C cytosine

double-strand of DNA

base pair

sugar-phosphate chain

double strand 'unzips'

new strands form as unattached bases fasten

two new, identical double-strands of DNA

DNA

In each chromosome, there is a long coiled-up molecule of **DNA** (deoxyribonucleic acid). This is made from millions of atoms, arranged in a shape called a **double helix**, as shown above. It looks like a spiral ladder. Its 'rungs' are pairs of substances known as **bases**. There are four bases: adenine, cytosine, guanine, and thymine (A, C, G, and T for short). They only pair up in certain combinations.

Look at either half of the DNA ladder and you will see that the order of the bases varies. The sequence forms a set of coded instructions for building a complete organism. Genes are different sections of the sequence. The full set of genes in all the chromosomes is called the **genome**.

Translating the code

Cells are largely built from **proteins**. These are made from twenty **amino acids**, linked in different combinations. DNA stores information about which amino acids must be produced in each type of cell. The code works like this:

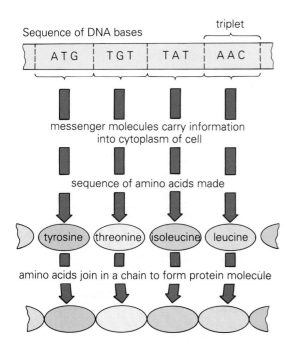

Along a strand of DNA, each sequence of three bases is called a **triplet**. Different amino acids are represented by different triplets. 'Messenger' chemicals carry information to the cytoplasm (the 'factory' part of the cell). There, the proteins are synthesized (made) from incoming materials.

Copying the code

During cell divison, copies of chromosomes are made. This is possible because a DNA molecule can replicate (copy) itself as shown on the opposite page. First, the DNA molecule starts to 'unzip'. Then new 'pieces' of chemicals become attached to the two halves so that two identical molecules of DNA are formed.

Sexual and asexual reproduction

For humans to reproduce, a sperm must combine with an ovum. Reproduction like this, involving male and female gametes, is called **sexual reproduction**. Each baby inherits half its DNA (and therefore half its genes) from each parent. This produces a wide variety of individuals who are different from their parents. At every new generation, the genes are reshuffled.

Flowering plants reproduce sexually (see Spread 2.4). However some also reproduce in another way: they develop parts (such as bulbs and runners) which separate and grow as new plants. This is called **asexual reproduction**. Each new plant is genetically identical to its parent because it is produced only by mitosis. Gametes are not involved.

1 What is the difference between a cell produced by mitosis and one produced by meiosis (see also Spread 2.18)?
2 Where is DNA found? What is it needed for?
3 In DNA, each triplet carries a code for a different amino acid. a) What is a triplet? b) What do amino acids form when they join in a chain?
4 Give an example of a *base pair*.
5 How does a DNA molecule replicate itself?
6 Compared with its parent(s), what would you expect a plant to be like if it had been produced by a) sexual b) asexual reproduction?

More genes in action

By the end of this spread, you should be able to:
- *explain the results of cross-breeding plants*
- *describe what genetic diseases are*
- *discuss cloning and genetic engineering and their uses*

Breeding generations

Remember: P stands for a dominant allele, p for a recessive allele.

Growers often cross-pollinate plants (see Spread 2.4) to produce different characteristics. On the right, a grower crosses a green pod (PP) plant with a yellow pod plant (pp) to produce a new generation of plants with Pp alleles. Then the grower crosses these Pp plants with each other to produce another generation. On average, 3/4 of the new plants have green pods (PP or Pp) and 1/4 have yellow pods (pp).

If alleles are the same (PP for example), then scientists say that the organism is **homozygous** or pure bred for that characteristic. If alleles are different (Pp for example) then the organism is **heterozygous** or **hybrid**. On the right, the grower crosses two pure bred varieties to produce a generation of hybrids. This is the **F₁ generation**. Crossing these plants produces the **F₂ generation**.

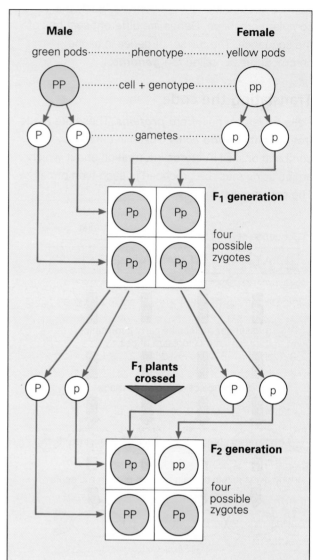

Cloning

When gardeners take cuttings and grow them, the new plants are genetically identical to the original. This is useful if, say, cross-breeding produces a pure bred disease-resistant plant and the grower then wants lots more plants with the same characteristic.

Making genetically identical copies is called **cloning**. Here are three ways of cloning:
- Taking cuttings from plants (as on the left).
- Taking a group of cells and growing these into a larger organism. This is called **tissue culture**.
- Splitting the first small group of cells (for example, when an animal embryo starts to develop).

Genetic diseases

Some diseases are inherited, and caused by faulty genes. **Genetic diseases** in humans include cystic fibrosis, sickle-cell anaemia, and haemophilia.

Sex chromosomes:

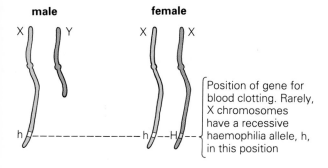

Position of gene for blood clotting. Rarely, X chromosomes have a recessive haemophilia allele, h, in this position

If someone has haemophilia, their blood does not clot properly. The condition is caused by a rare, recessive allele on the X chromosome. Most X chromosomes have a dominant, non-harmful allele in that position. A female has *two* X chromosomes, so the chances of both carrying the harmful allele are slight. However, a male has only one X chromosome, so if this carries the haemophilia allele, the person will have the disease. This means that virtually all haemophilia sufferers are male. However, a mother can be a **carrier**. She can pass the allele on to her children though not being haemophilic herself.

Scientists say that haemophilia is **sex linked** because it affects one sex more than the other. Colour blindness is another sex linked condition which affects mainly males.

---

1. If someone is *homozygous* for hair colour, what does this tell you about their alleles?
2. What is *cloning*? Give an example.
3. Why are males more likely to have haemophilia than females? How can a female be a carrier?
4. How can bacteria be genetically-engineered to produce substances normally made in the human body?
5. A smooth-seed (SS) pea plant is crossed with a wrinkled-seed (ss) pea plant. What are the possible zygotes for the F_1 and F_2 generations? What proportion of each generation would you expect to have wrinkled seeds?

Genetic engineering

Scientists have discovered how to transfer genes from one organism to another. Using enzymes, they can 'cut' pieces from one strand of DNA and insert them into the DNA of a different organism. Techniques like this are called **genetic engineering**.

Some drugs and hormones can be produced by genetic engineering. For example, the diagram below shows how genetically-engineered bacteria can be used to make human insulin. (Diabetics need a supply of insulin because their own bodies do not make it properly.) Similarly, genetically-engineered bacteria can make proteins that can be used as food.

With genetic engineering, it may be possible to replace the harmful genes that cause genetic diseases. However, many people are worried about genetic research. They do not think that human embryos should be used. And they do not like the idea that babies might be 'designed' to order.

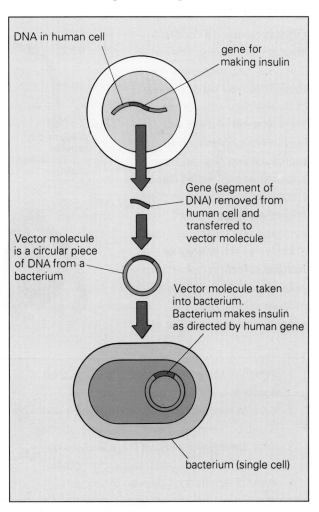

DNA in human cell

gene for making insulin

Gene (segment of DNA) removed from human cell and transferred to vector molecule

Vector molecule is a circular piece of DNA from a bacterium

Vector molecule taken into bacterium. Bacterium makes insulin as directed by human gene

bacterium (single cell)

Evolution

By the end of this spread, you should be able to:
* *describe the theory of natural selection*
* *explain what mutations are and how they occur*

There are over a million different types of living thing on Earth. Each type is called a **species**. Members of one species breed among themselves, but members of different species do not.

In time, as generation follows generation, a species can change. This process is called **evolution**. If members of a species begin to live and breed in separate groups, evolution can take a different course with each group and new species may develop. The chart on the right shows some of the stages in the evolution of today's mammals.

The theory of natural selection

Organisms are in a constant struggle for survival. They must compete with each other for food. They may die of disease or be eaten by other organisms. So only some of them will survive for long enough to reproduce and pass on their characteristics. Charles Darwin (1809-1882) realised that this might help explain how evolution takes place. His idea is known as the **theory of natural selection** (sometimes called 'survival of the fittest'). A modern version of it is described on the opposite page.

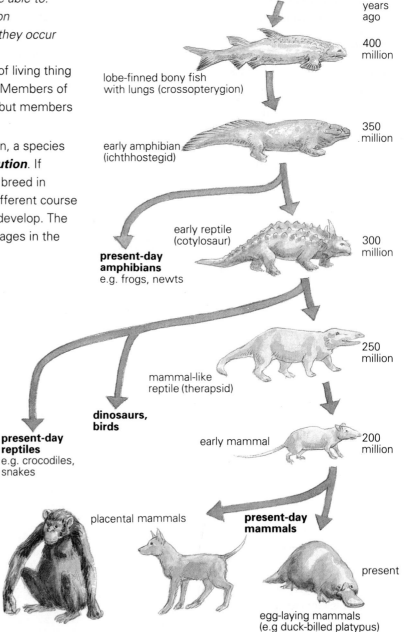

years ago

400 million

lobe-finned bony fish with lungs (crossopterygion)

350 million

early amphibian (ichthhostegid)

present-day amphibians
e.g. frogs, newts

early reptile (cotylosaur)

300 million

250 million

mammal-like reptile (therapsid)

dinosaurs, birds

present-day reptiles
e.g. crocodiles, snakes

early mammal

200 million

placental mammals

present-day mammals

present

egg-laying mammals (e.g duck-billed platypus)

---

1 Which of the groups of animals in the chart above evolved from early reptiles?
2 Give *two* examples of variations which might be found between animals of the same species.
3 Why are some variations more likely to be passed on to later generations than others?
4 What is a *mutation*? Give an example.

5 Describe *two* causes of mutation.
6 In the photographs opposite, which moth is better adapted to its environment? Why?
7 Why, in areas affected by factory soot, are there more dark peppered moths than light ones?
8 Why is it possible for several species to evolve from a single species?

Variation In any species, individuals vary in colour, weight, height, shape, and other features. (Sexual reproduction produces more variations than asexual reproduction.)

Selection Some variations help in the struggle for survival and some do not. So some organisms survive to reproduce and some do not. In this way, nature 'selects' some organisms for survival.

Adaptation The survivors pass on their characteristics to later generations. So the species evolves to cope with its living conditions. It becomes ***adapted*** to its environment.

Natural selection in action

Peppered moths live in woodlands and are eaten by birds. There are light and dark varieties, as on the right. In the 1850s, moths with the allele for dark colouring were rare. But then soot from factories started to blacken tree trunks. By 1895, 98% of the peppered moths in Manchester were dark. Dark moths were less likely to be seen by birds. They survived to reproduce. So the allele for dark colouring was passed on to more and more moths in later generations.

Mutations

Sometimes, genes can change at random. These changes are called ***mutations***. Here are two ways in which they can happen:

- Inaccurate copying of DNA during cell division.
- DNA altered by chemicals or radiation (see 4.34).

Most mutations are harmful, but some may be helpful. The peppered moth's allele for dark colouring was a mutation which turned out to be helpful when the moth's environment changed.

The ***gene pool*** is the complete range of genes and their alleles in a population. Mutations add to the gene pool, so they increase variation.

Living together

By the end of this spread, you should be able to:
- *describe some of the factors which affect living things and their environment*
- *explain how living things are adapted to their environment*

The place where an animal or plant lives is called its **habitat**. It is usually a habitat for other animals and plants as well. All the living things in one habitat are called a **community**. Their **environment** is everything around them which affects their way of life. Together, a community and its environment are known as an **ecosystem**.

Here are some of the factors which affect an organism's environment:

---

1 Explain what these words mean:
   habitat   population   community   predator
2 Give an example of how an animal's environment can change from one part of the day to another.
3 Give an example of how a plant's environment can change from season to another.
4 How do plants compete with each other?
5 If an animal is *adapted to its environment*, what does this mean? Give an example.
6 In the graph on the opposite page a) why does the slug population fall? b) why does it then start to rise again?
7 What would happen to the number of toads if a chemical killed off half of the plants? Why?

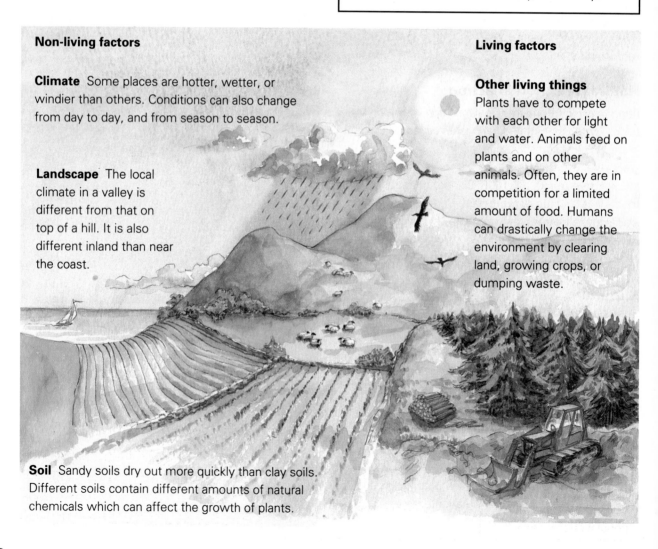

Non-living factors

Climate Some places are hotter, wetter, or windier than others. Conditions can also change from day to day, and from season to season.

Landscape The local climate in a valley is different from that on top of a hill. It is also different inland than near the coast.

Soil Sandy soils dry out more quickly than clay soils. Different soils contain different amounts of natural chemicals which can affect the growth of plants.

Living factors

Other living things Plants have to compete with each other for light and water. Animals feed on plants and on other animals. Often, they are in competition for a limited amount of food. Humans can drastically change the environment by clearing land, growing crops, or dumping waste.

Adapted for living

Over many millions of years, animals and plants have developed special features to help them cope with their way of life. They have become **adapted** to their environment. Here are some examples:

- Dormice and many other small mammals hibernate in the winter months so that they can survive when food is scarce. They go to sleep with their life processes slowed right down.
- Hawks have claws and a beak which are specially shaped for gripping small animals and tearing them apart.
- Many trees lose their leaves in the autumn. This means that they do not need to take up so much water during the months when the ground might be frozen.

Adapted for hunting. The chameleon has a long tongue which it can flick out to catch insects

Changing populations

A group of animals of the same kind is called a **population**. Animals depend on plants or other animals for their food. So a change in one population may affect several other populations.

Animals which feed on other animals are known as **predators**. The animals that they eat are called their **prey**.

Imagine a garden with a stream running through it. This is a habitat for toads, slugs, and plants. The toads feed on the slugs, and the slugs feed on the plants. Normally, the numbers of toads, slugs, and plants will reach a balance. The graphs show what happens if too many toads start to develop. Over a period of time, the balance is restored.

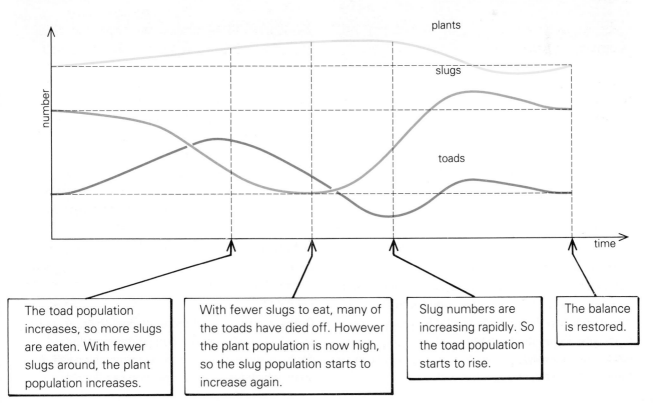

The toad population increases, so more slugs are eaten. With fewer slugs around, the plant population increases.

With fewer slugs to eat, many of the toads have died off. However the plant population is now high, so the slug population starts to increase again.

Slug numbers are increasing rapidly. So the toad population starts to rise.

The balance is restored.

Populations and pollution

By the end of this spread, you should be able to:
- *describe problems caused by the demand for food and materials*
- *describe how human activities cause different types of pollution*

The world's human population is growing. As it does so, it needs more crops, meat, wood, fuels, and minerals. This is causing problems for other populations, and for humans as well:

Using fertilizers To help crops grow, chemical fertilizers are often sprayed onto soil. But they can be washed into lakes and rivers, where they encourage the growth of green, plant-like algae. Microbes feeding on dead algae use up all the oxygen in the water, so fish and other organisms die.

Pesticides These are chemicals sprayed onto crops to kill off insects and other pests. But they can build up in the bodies of birds which feed on the pests. And they can also be washed into lakes and rivers.

Cutting down forests Huge areas of forest are being cut down for timber, or to make space for agriculture or industry. But trees supply the world with some of its oxygen. And they provide shelter for many forms of wildlife. When trees are removed, the soil is easily eroded (worn away), and large areas of ground can be turned into desert, or bog if it is wet.

Digging up land Industry needs fuels and other materials from the ground. For example, huge amounts of limestone (above) are needed for making concrete. And limestone is also used in the manufacture of steel and glass. But mining and quarrying damage the landscape. They can also produce huge heaps of waste materials. Some of these contain poisonous metals which can harm plants.

Fishing Fish is an important food for millions of people. But if too many fish are taken from the sea, there are not enough left to breed. Soon, the fish die out altogether.

Crops Farmers find it more efficient to grow single crops in huge fields. But cutting down hedges destroys the habitats for many forms of wildlife. And pests which feed on the one crop can flourish.

Air pollution

Harmful gases When coal, oil, and petrol are burned, the waste gases include sulphur dioxide and nitrogen oxides. Unless removed, these dissolve in rainwater to form *acid rain*. This corrodes steel, eats into stonework, and damages plants.

Carbon dioxide This is the main gas given off when fuels burn. It traps the Sun's heat and causes *global warming* (the *greenhouse effect*).

Dust Dust from quarries, mines, and factories can cause lung disease.

Smoke This contains particles of soot (carbon) which can blacken buildings.

Pollution
This is anything unwanted which humans put into the environment.

Other pollution

Radiation If an accident happens, radioactive waste from a nuclear power station can contaminate the air, sea, and soil.

Noise Noisy aircraft, or someone else's loud radio, can be very annoying.

Litter Some litter rots away: paper for example. But some does not rot: plastic and glass for example. Litter looks awful, and it can cause injury to animals.

Water pollution

Factory waste Poisonous chemicals are sometimes dumped into rivers or the sea.

Fertilizers and pesticides These can get into lakes and rivers and harm wildlife (see opposite page).

Slurry This farm waste is a mixture of animal droppings and urine. It is used as a fertilizer, but can pollute streams and rivers.

Oil This sometimes spills from tankers. It kills sea-birds and marine life. And it ruins beaches.

Sewage is often dumped at sea. It can be a health hazard.

---

1 A *Using fertilizers and pesticides*
   B *Cutting down forests*
   C *Making larger fields*
   D *Quarrying limestone*
   Give *two* reasons for doing each of the above.
   Then give *two* problems caused by each one.

2 What causes acid rain?
3 What damage does acid rain do?
4 Give *three* examples of how a river might become polluted.
5 Give an example of how our demand for materials might threaten another animal population.

Surveying and estimating

By the end of this spread, you should be able to:
* *survey and estimate populations using transects, quadrats, and capture-recapture techniques.*

Scientists may want to survey an area to find out how the plants or animals are distributed. But the area may be large and the populations difficult to count. If so, parts can be surveyed so that estimates for the whole area can be made. This is called **sampling**.

Transects

Conditions change as you move up a sea-shore. Some areas get covered by the tide, others are drier. Different organisms live in the zone that suits them best. This produces a banding effect called **zonation**.

To study the zonation of seaweed, you could carry out a survey along a straight line or strip. This is called a **transect**.

1 As you move up a sea-shore from the water's edge, there are zones with different organisms living in them. What causes the zonation effect?
2 What survey technique would you use to study a) zonation on a sea-shore b) the population of earwigs on a patch of ground?
3 A field measures 10 m x 10 m. In a survey, the quadrat measures 1 m x 1 m, and there are 8 buttercup plants per quadrat on average. Estimate the buttercup population of the field.
4 In a survey of a small yard, 20 woodlice are found and marked. Two days later, 30 woodlice are found. Of these, 5 are already marked. Estimate the woodlice population of the yard.

flat wrack seaweed (F)

bladder wrack seaweed (B)

serrated wrack seaweed (S)

Line transect Mark a straight line across the ground with string. On a scale drawing, record the different types of seaweed along the line. Alternatively, record the different types of seaweed at regular intervals – say, every 2 metres.

sea ├─S─┼─S─┼─S─┼─SB─┼─B─┼─B─┼─B─┼─BF─┼─F─┼─F─┤ cliff

Belt transect Mark a narrow strip with two pieces of string. Record the seaweed populations in different parts of the strip.

2B   3B

Quadrats

A **quadrat** is a square frame which can be placed on the ground so that plants within its area can be counted. By sampling with a quadrat, you could estimate the number of dandelion plants in a field:

- Drop the quadrat anywhere in the field. Count and record the number of dandelion plants inside the quadrat square.

- Drop the quadrat at random in different parts of the field so that you have ten readings altogether. Use your readings to work out an *average* for the number of plants in the quadrat.

- Work out the total area of the field in m². (For a rectangular field: area = length x width.)

- Work out the area of the quadrat in m².

- To estimate the total number of dandelion plants in the field, use this equation:

$$\frac{\text{estimated}}{\text{number}} = \frac{\text{area of field}}{\text{area of quadrat}} \times \frac{\text{average number}}{\text{in quadrat}}$$

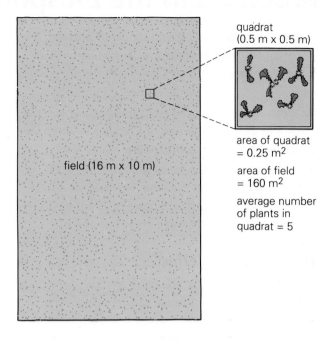

quadrat
(0.5 m x 0.5 m)

area of quadrat = 0.25 m²

field (16 m x 10 m)

area of field = 160 m²

average number of plants in quadrat = 5

estimated number of plants $= \frac{160}{0.25} \times 5 = 3200$

Capture-recapture

Counting animal populations can be a problem because animals can move about and hide. The **capture-recapture** method is one way of overcoming the problem. This is how you would use it to estimate the population of woodlice in a small area such as the back yard of a house:

- Collect all the woodlice you can find in your chosen area. Do this for exactly 10 minutes.

- Mark each woodlouse with a tiny spot of safe marker paint. Count the number of woodlice marked. This is your S_1 total.

- Return the woodlice to where you found them.

- A day or so later, collect woodlice in exactly the same area for 10 minutes again. Some will probably be marked and some will not. Count all the woodlice you collect. This is your S_2 total.

- Count the number of *marked* (recaptured) woodlice in your S_2 sample. This is your S_3 total.

- Return the woodlice to where you found them.

- To estimate the total number of woodlice in the area, use this equation:

$$\text{estimated number} = \frac{S_2}{S_3} \times S_1$$

Handle small animals with care. Replace any stones or leaves which you turned over during your survey.

For example

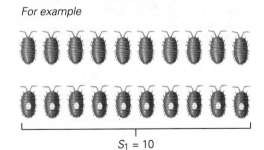

$S_1 = 10$

$S_2 = 12$

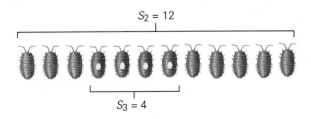

$S_3 = 4$

total number $= \frac{12}{4} \times 10 = 30$

Problems in the biosphere

By the end of this spread, you should be able to:
* *explain how human activity is causing damage in the biosphere.*

On Earth, life exists on the land, in the sea, and in the lower atmosphere. Together, the regions in which life exists are known as the **biosphere**.

The Earth's human population is more than 5000 million, and growing all the time. Humans need food, fuel, and materials for their industries. But their activities are causing damage in the biosphere.

The greenhouse effect

Plants take in carbon dioxide gas from the atmosphere. Animals give out carbon dioxide, and so do burning fuels. But fuel-burning is upsetting the balance. More carbon dioxide is being added to the atmosphere than is being removed.

Methane (natural gas) is another greenhouse gas. It comes from swamps, animal waste, paddy fields, and oil and gas rigs. So keeping cattle, growing food, and drilling for oil and gas can all add to global warming.

Destruction of the ozone layer

High in the atmosphere, there is a band of gases called the ozone layer. It screens us from some of the Sun's ultraviolet rays, which cause skin cancer. Chemical processes in the atmosphere are constantly making and destroying ozone. But some of the gases we produce on Earth are destroying too much. These include **CFCs** (chlorofluorocarbons). They have been used in aerosols, fridges, freezers, and in making foam packaging. However, many manufacturers are now using more 'ozone friendly' gases instead.

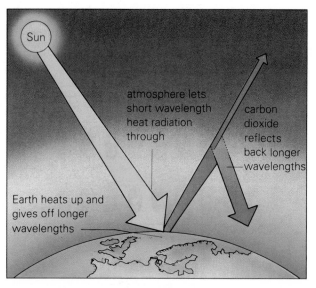

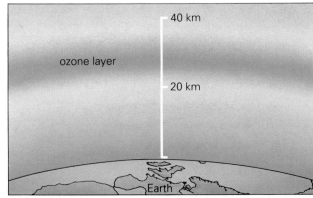

Carbon dioxide acts like the glass in a greenhouse and traps the Sun's heat. With extra carbon dioxide being put into the atmosphere, the Earth may be slowly warming up. Scientists call this **global warming**, or the **greenhouse effect**. Over the next hundred years, average temperatures may rise by only a few degrees, but this could drastically affect world climates:
* Some places may have more rain.
* Some places may have severe droughts.

Acid rain

Rain is naturally slightly acid. Air pollutants such as sulphur dioxide and nitrogen oxides increase its acidity. When these gases dissolve in rainclouds, they form sulphuric and nitric acids. The acid rain attacks stone and steelwork, and can harm plants and water life. Catalytic converters on car exhausts reduce emissions of nitrogen oxides and sulphur dioxide. Desulphurization units can be fitted to coal-burning power stations to reduce sulphur dioxide emissions.

The effects of acid rain

Stream and river pollution

Human activity can upset the ecosystem of a stream or river, and harm animal and plant life:

- Chemical pollution kills water life. The chemicals may also end up in people's drinking water supply.
- If sewage gets into a stream, the nutrients in it encourage the growth of algae. Microbes feeding on dead algae use up all the oxygen, so fish die.
- Fertilizers dissolve in rainwater and can be washed out of the soil (see Spread 2.23). The effect is called **leaching**. Like sewage, fertilizers put unwanted nutrients into a stream.
- Factories and powers stations may discharge warm water into a river. Warm water has less oxygen dissolved in it, so fish are affected. The warmth also encourages the growth of weeds, which can choke the river.

Forest destruction

Rainforests covers 7% of the Earth's land surface. But an area the size of Wales is being destroyed every year. Some is cut down for timber. Some is burnt to clear land for agriculture and industry.

- Destroying forests reduces the number of plants which can take in carbon dioxide and make oxygen.
- Burning timber adds to the greenhouse effect by putting more carbon dioxide into the atmosphere.
- Removing trees removes nutrients which would otherwise be returned to the soil.
- Removing trees exposes soil which is then lost by erosion. The lack of vegetation also affects the amount of water vapour in the air. In time, large areas of land may be reduced to desert.

1 Why are levels of carbon dioxide in the atmosphere rising?
2 Why is global warming called the 'greenhouse effect'?
3 How does the ozone layer protect life on Earth?
4 What causes acid rain? What are its effects?
5 Describe *three* ways in which pollution can harm animal and plant life in streams and rivers.
6 Describe *two* ways in which forest-burning can add to the greenhouse effect.
7 In what other ways can forest destruction damage the environment?

Chains, webs, and pyramids

By the end of this spread, you should be able to:
- *explain what food chains and food webs are*
- *draw pyramids of numbers and biomass*
- *describe what decomposers are and what they do*

Food chains

All living things need food. It supplies them with their energy and the materials they need for building their bodies.

Plants are **producers**. They produce their own food. But animals are **consumers**. They have to get their food by consuming (eating) other living things.

A **food chain** shows how living things feed on other living things. For example, if a blackbird feeds on snails, and these feed on leaves, then the food chain looks like the one on the right.

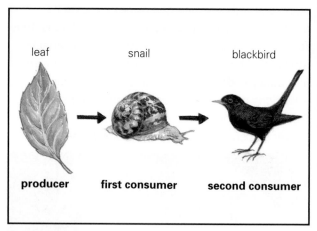

A simple food chain

Pyramid of numbers

In a food chain, only a fraction of the energy taken in by one organism reaches the next. So fewer and fewer organisms can be fed at each stage. For example, it might take 30 000 leaves to feed 300 snails, and 300 snails to feed one blackbird. This can be shown using a **pyramid of numbers** like the one below.

Pyramid of biomass

A leaf is lighter than a snail. So the numbers of leaves and snails do not really give an accurate picture of how much food is being eaten at each stage of the chain. For this, scientists use the idea of **biomass**. In a food chain:

The biomass is the total mass of each type of organism.

The biomasses of the leaves, snails, and bird have been worked out in the table below. Using this information, a **pyramid of biomass** can be drawn.

	A Number	B Mass of each in g	A x B Biomass in g
blackbirds	1	250	250
snails	300	50	15 000
leaves	30 000	20	600 000

(g = gram)

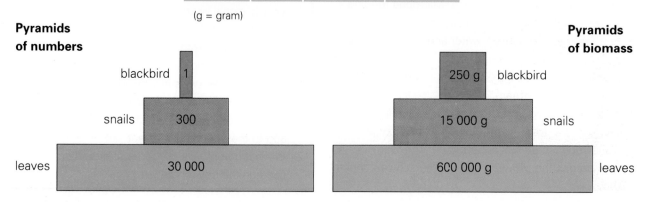

Pyramids of numbers

blackbird 1
snails 300
leaves 30 000

Pyramids of biomass

250 g blackbird
15 000 g snails
600 000 g leaves

Food webs

Many animals eat more than one type of food. So organisms can be part of several food chains. The result is a network of linked food chains called a **food web**. Here is an example:

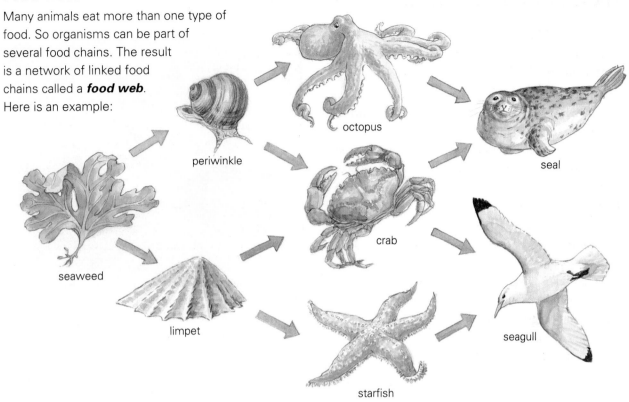

octopus

periwinkle

seal

seaweed

crab

limpet

starfish

seagull

Decomposers at work

Many microbes (bacteria and fungi) feed on the remains of dead plants and animals. They produce enzymes which make the dead things decompose (rot) into a liquid. Then they feed on the liquid.

Microbes which make things rot are known as **decomposers**.

Decomposers are important because:
- they get rid of dead plants and animals
- they put useful chemicals back into the soil.

Materials which rot are called **biodegradable** materials. As well as dead plants and animals, they include things made from plant or animal matter, such as paper, wool, and cotton.

1. What is the difference between a *producer* and a *consumer*? Give an example of each.
2. What are *biodegradable* materials? Give *two* examples?
3. In the food web on this page, what other organisms would be affected if periwinkles were poisoned by chemical waste? Explain what might happen to these organisms.
4. A frog feeds on 250 worms. These feed on 25 000 leaves. Draw the pyramid of numbers.
5. The frog in the last question has a mass of 200 g, a worm 40 g, and a leaf 20 g. Draw the pyramid of biomass. (Hint: start by making a table like the one on the opposite page.)

Recycling atoms

By the end of this spread, you should be able to:
- *explain how atoms of carbon and nitrogen are recycled by living things*

Like everything else, living things are made of **atoms**. These join together in different ways to form different materials in the body. As plants and animals grow and die, most of their atoms are used over and over again.

The carbon cycle

There is a small amount of carbon dioxide in the atmosphere. Plants take in some for photosynthesis, so their bodies are partly carbon. Animals eat plants, so their bodies are partly carbon as well. Respiration puts carbon dioxide back into the atmosphere. So does burning.

As photosynthesis, respiration, and burning take place, carbon atoms are used over and over again. This process is called the **carbon cycle**.

4% carbon
20% carbon
90% carbon

Atoms in living things

Mainly............................ oxygen, carbon, hydrogen
with some...................... nitrogen
and smaller amounts of calcium, phosphorus, others

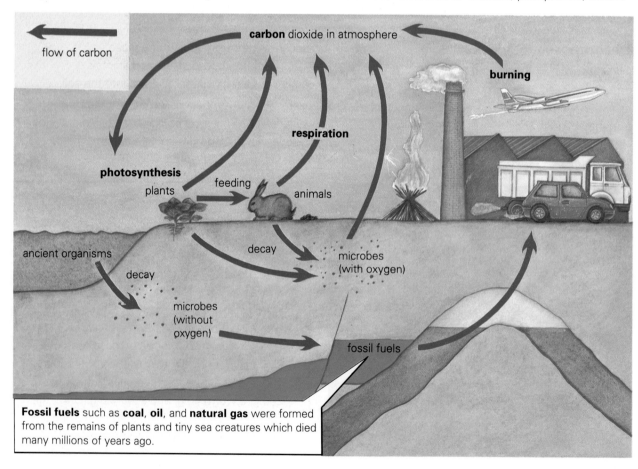

flow of carbon

carbon dioxide in atmosphere

burning

respiration

photosynthesis
plants   feeding   animals

decay

ancient organisms

decay

microbes
(without oxygen)

microbes
(with oxygen)

fossil fuels

Fossil fuels such as **coal**, **oil**, and **natural gas** were formed from the remains of plants and tiny sea creatures which died many millions of years ago.

The nitrogen cycle

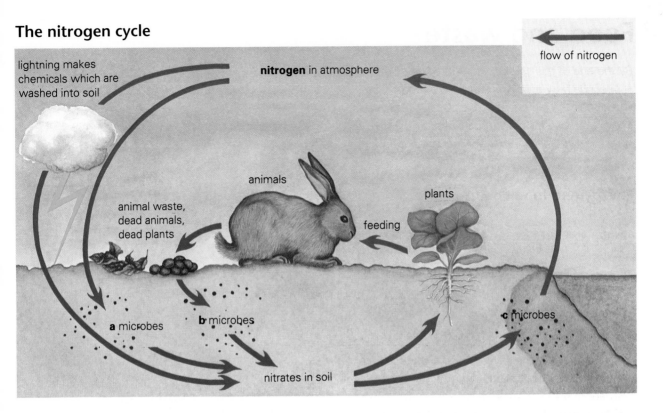

flow of nitrogen

lightning makes chemicals which are washed into soil

nitrogen in atmosphere

animals

plants

animal waste, dead animals, dead plants

feeding

a microbes

b microbes

c microbes

nitrates in soil

Living things need nitrogen to help make the proteins in their body tissues. There is plenty of nitrogen in the atmosphere, but it is of no direct use to plants or animals because it does not easily take part in chemical changes.

Plants get their nitrogen by taking in chemicals called **nitrates** from the soil. These are partly made from nitrogen. They dissolve easily and are absorbed through roots. Animals get their nitrogen by eating plants (or by eating other animals which have fed on plants).

Nitrogen is used over and over again by living things. The process is called the **nitrogen cycle**. Microbes in the soil have an important part to play:

a Some microbes use nitrogen from the air to make nitrates. They release these into the soil.

b Some microbes make nitrates from animal waste, dead animals, and dead plants.

c Some microbes in wet soil remove nitrogen from nitrates and release it into the atmosphere.

The nodules on the roots of this pea plant contain microbes which take in nitrogen and make nitrates.

---

1 *Respiration   photosynthesis   burning*
   Which of the above processes takes carbon dioxide from the atmosphere?

2 Which of the above processes put carbon dioxide into the atmosphere?

3 Describe how the carbon atoms in a lump of coal can end up as part of the body of an animal.

4 Why do living things need nitrogen?

5 How do plants get their nitrogen?

6 How do animals get their nitrogen?

7 If plants take nitrates from the soil, how are these nitrates replaced?

Food and waste

By the end of this spread, you should be able to:
- *describe how energy is lost from a food chain*
- *describe the factors affecting decay by microbes*
- *explain how sewage is processed*
- *discuss the management of food production*

Energy and food chains

> **Herbivores** are animals (such as cows and rabbits) which feed on plants.
>
> **Carnivores** are animals (such as foxes and cats) which feed on other animals.
>
> Animals (such as humans) which feed on plants *and* other animals are called **omnivores**.

Each stage of a food chain is called a **trophic level**. At the first trophic level, plants get energy from the Sun. Only about 5% of the energy at one trophic level reaches the next. A food chain rarely has more than four or five trophic levels because there is not enough energy left to support any more.

Energy is eventually lost from a food chain, but the materials needed for growth can be used over and over again (see Spreads 2.26 and 2.27). Microbes called decomposers feed on dead animals and plants, and on animal waste. They return vital elements such as nitrogen, phosphorus, and sulphur to the soil.

Decay factors

The rate at which plant or animal matter **decays** (decomposes) depends on several factors:

Temperature Most decomposer microbes thrive best in warm conditions (about 35 °C). At lower temperatures, the decay process is slower.

Water Decomposer microbes need water to live, grow, and multiply. So they require moist conditions.

Air Most decomposer microbes need oxygen. Their respiration is **aerobic** (oxygen-using) and they give off carbon dioxide gas.

Some decomposer microbes do not need oxygen. Their respiration is **anaerobic** (without oxygen) and they give off methane gas. This happens deep in a swamp or rubbish tip, where there is no air.

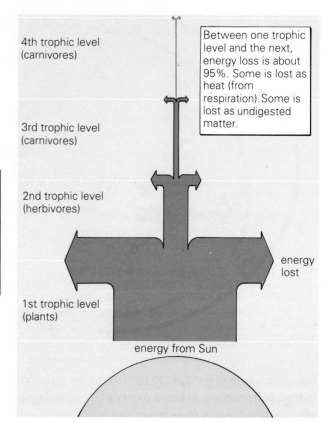

4th trophic level (carnivores)

3rd trophic level (carnivores)

2nd trophic level (herbivores)

1st trophic level (plants)

> Between one trophic level and the next, energy loss is about 95%. Some is lost as heat (from respiration). Some is lost as undigested matter.

energy lost

energy from Sun

Gardeners often put their plant clippings on a **compost heap** like the one shown above The clippings decay and make compost for the soil. The heap must be kept moist, but not too wet. And it must be turned regularly with a fork to let in the air. Warmth comes from the microbes which give off heat as they respire.

Dealing with sewage

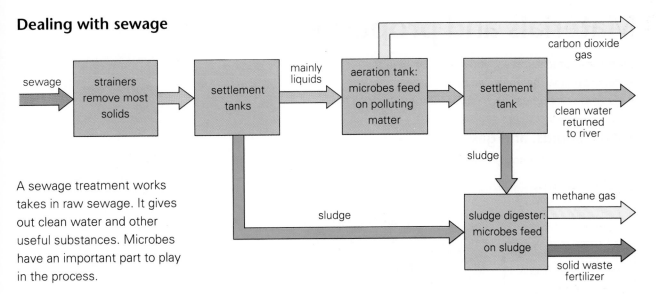

sewage → strainers remove most solids → settlement tanks → mainly liquids → aeration tank: microbes feed on polluting matter → settlement tank

carbon dioxide gas

clean water returned to river

sludge → sludge digester: microbes feed on sludge → methane gas

solid waste fertilizer

A sewage treatment works takes in raw sewage. It gives out clean water and other useful substances. Microbes have an important part to play in the process.

Food from the land...

Humans grow crops to supply themselves with food. Some crops are fed to animals, which humans then eat as meat. But this is a very inefficient way of feeding people. The land needed to produce beef for one person could produce enough wheat for twenty.

When wild plants die, they decompose, and vital elements are returned to the soil. But when crops are harvested, this natural recycling does not happen. So farmers add fertilizers to the soil to replace the elements which are missing.

Here are some of the ways in which crop yields are increased:

- adding fertilizers to the soil
- killing off competing wild plants with herbicides
- killing off pests and diseases with pesticides and fungicides
- using high-yield crop varieties produced by selective breeding (see Spread 2.17)
- digging irrigation channels or drainage channels

These measures give increased food production but they cause environmental damage (see Spread 2.22).

...and sea

Fishing must be carefully managed to preserve stocks. If too many young fish are taken from the sea, there are not enough left to breed, so the fish population falls. To prevent this happening, trawlers have to limit the size of their catches. And they must use nets which let smaller, younger fish pass through.

---

1 What is the difference between a *herbivore* and a *carnivore*? Which would you expect to find at the lower trophic level in a food chain? Why?

2 Why do food chains not normally have more than four or five trophic levels?

3 Describe *three* conditions which would encourage decomposer microbes to thrive.

4 Why are decomposer microbes useful?

5 Describe where and how microbes are used in a sewage treatment works.

6 To feed more people, why is it better to grow wheat than to raise cattle?

7 What problems would be caused if trawlers used nets with a very small mesh?

3·1 Materials and properties

By the end of this spread, you should be able to:
- *describe how materials can be classified*
- *describe properties which different materials can have*

Solids, liquids, and gases

Materials are either solid, liquid, or gas:

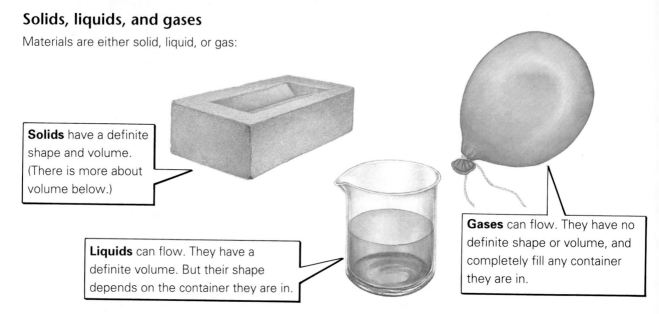

Solids have a definite shape and volume. (There is more about volume below.)

Liquids can flow. They have a definite volume. But their shape depends on the container they are in.

Gases can flow. They have no definite shape or volume, and completely fill any container they are in.

Mass, volume, and density

The amount of matter in something is called its mass. It can be measured in **kilograms (kg)**.

The amount of space something takes up is called its volume. It can be measured in **cubic metres (m³)**.

A block of steel has a much more mass in every metre cubed than a block of wood. Scientists say that steel has a greater **density** than wood.

Steel has a density of 7800 kg/m³. This means that there is 7800 kg of mass in each cubic metre. Some other density values are also shown below.

You can calculate density with this equation:

$$density = \frac{mass}{volume}$$

mass in kg
volume in m³
density in kg/m³

For example, if a block of coal has a mass of 3200 kg and a volume of 2 m³, its density is 3200 divided by 2, which is 1600 kg/m³.

Gases have mass. However, liquids and solids are usually much more dense than gases. For example, the lemonade in a bottle is about 750 times heavier than the air in an empty bottle.

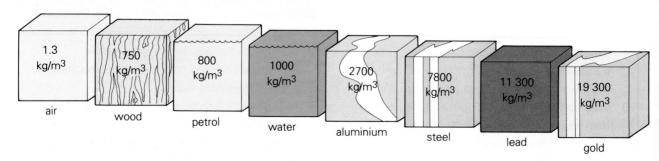

1.3 kg/m³ air
750 kg/m³ wood
800 kg/m³ petrol
1000 kg/m³ water
2700 kg/m³ aluminium
7800 kg/m³ steel
11 300 kg/m³ lead
19 300 kg/m³ gold

Densities of different materials

Looking at properties

The features of a material and how it behaves are called its *properties*. Below are some of the words for describing them:

Property	Meaning	Example
Strong	Resists the effects of forces	Steel
Brittle	Hard, but breaks easily	Glass
Malleable	Can be hammered into shape	Copper
Ductile	Can be pulled out into wires	Copper
Transparent	'See-through': lets light through	Glass
Translucent	Lets light through, but scatters it	White polythene
Flexible	Can be bent or twisted without breaking	White polythene
Conductor (heat)	Lets heat pass through easily	Copper
Conductor (electricity)	Lets electricity pass through easily	Copper
Insulator (heat)	Stops heat passing through	Expanded polystyrene
Insulator (electricity)	Stops electricity passing through	PVC

Grouping solids

Here are five important groups of materials used for making things:

Ceramics Brittle materials made by heating clay or similar materials in kilns. They can usually withstand very high temperatures.

Glasses Brittle materials, made partly from sand. They are transparent or translucent, and are good electrical insulators.

Plastics Wide range of chemically-made *(synthetic)* materials. During manufacture, while still warm, they are flexible and can be moulded. Many are also flexible when cold. They melt easily. They are good electrical insulators.

Metals Shiny solids that conduct heat and electricity. They are often malleable and ductile, and difficult to melt.

Fibres Threads made from natural or synthetic materials.

1 What are the differences between
   a) a solid and a liquid b) a liquid and a gas?

2 *Water has a density of 1000 kg/m³.*
   a) What does this tell you about the water?
   b) What would be the mass of 5 m³ of water?

3 Why would ceramics not be suitable for making springs?

4 Below, are some jobs to be done by different materials. What *properties* do you think each material should have? (You could use words on this page, or others of your own choosing.)
   a) Window in a greenhouse b) Knife
   c) Bottom of a saucepan d) Handle of a kettle
   e) Covering on an electric wire.

Moving particles

By the end of this spread, you should be able to:
- *describe the particles in a solid, liquid, and gas*
- *explain the links between particles, change of state, temperature, diffusion, and expansion*

Solids, liquids, and gases

Scientists have come up with an idea to explain how solids, liquids, and gases behave. They call this the *particle model of matter* :

Solids, liquids, and gases are made up of tiny particles. In water, for example, the particles are molecules. The particles are constantly on the move. They also attract each other. The attractions are strongest when the particles are close.

Water can be a solid, liquid or gas.

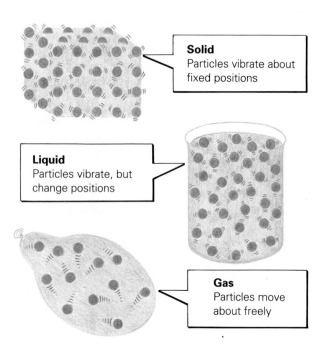

Solid
Particles vibrate about fixed positions

Liquid
Particles vibrate, but change positions

Gas
Particles move about freely

Solid The particles are held together by strong forces of attraction. The particles vibrate from side to side, but they cannot change positions.

Liquid The particles are still pulled together by forces of attraction. But strong vibrations mean that the particles have enough energy to change position and move past each other. So, the liquid can flow.

Gas The particles are spaced out, and almost free of any attractions. They move about at high speed, and quickly fill any space available.

Changing state

As something gets hotter its particles move faster.

If a very cold block of ice is heated, its particles vibrate faster. When their vibrations are strong enough, the particles can change position, so the solid becomes a liquid. In other words, the ice melts.

If water is heated, its particles vibrate faster. Some particles move fast enough to break free of the attractions holding them together. The liquid changes into a gas. In other words, the water becomes steam.

Even cold water can *evaporate* (change into gas). However, if water is hot enough, it produces bubbles of steam and evaporates rapidly. This is *boiling*.

Heat energy (see 4.12) is needed to change a solid into a liquid or a liquid into a gas. For example, if your hands are wet, they cool down as the evaporating water draws heat from them. The cooling effect of evaporation is used in the pipes of a refrigerator.

A change from solid to liquid, or liquid to gas, or back again, is called a change of *state*:

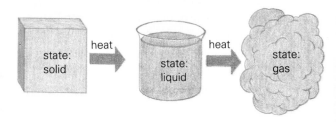

state: solid — heat → state: liquid — heat → state: gas

Temperature

When something gets hotter, and its particles move faster, scientists say that its **temperature** rises.

Everyday temperatures are normally measured on the **Celsius** scale (sometimes called the 'centigrade' scale.) Its unit of temperature is the **degree Celsius** (**°C**). The numbers on this scale were specially chosen so that ice melts at 0 °C and water boils at 100 °C.

Wandering particles

Jostled by other particles around them, some particles wander about. That is why colours spread on top of a trifle. It also why smells spread. Smells are gas particles coming from food, or perfume, or anything smelly. The wandering of particles in this way is called **diffusion**.

Expansion

If a steel bar is heated, its particles vibrate more. As a result, they push each other a little further apart and the bar gets slightly bigger. In other words, the bar **expands**. **Expansion** affects other materials, not just steel. Expansion is usually too small to notice, but it can produce very strong forces. For example, gaps are left in bridges to allow for expansion on a hot day. Without a gap, the force of the expansion might crack the structure.

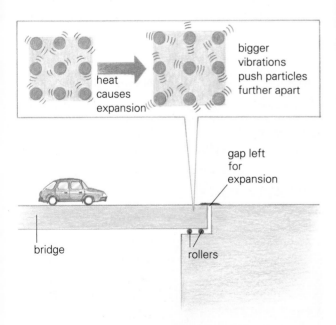

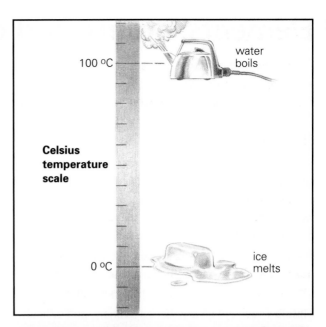

Celsius temperature scale

Diffusion on top of a trifle

1 Comparing their behaviour, what differences are there between the particles in
   a) a solid and a liquid b) a liquid and a gas?
2 What happens to the particles in something if the temperature rises?
3 On the Celsius scale, what is the temperature of
   a) melting ice b) boiling water?
4 Why does evaporation have a cooling effect?
5 How do smells spread? What is the process called?
6 Why does a bar of steel expand when heated?
7 Why is it important to leave plenty of slack when overhead wires are put up on a hot day?

Elements, atoms, and compounds

By the end of this spread, you should be able to:
- *explain what elements and compounds are*
- *describe how some metals are more reactive than others*

Elements

Everything on Earth is made from about 90 simple substances called **elements**. Elements can combine in different ways to form thousands of new substances. For example, water is a combination of the elements hydrogen and oxygen.

There are two main types of element: **metals** and **nonmetals**. Every element has its own chemical symbol. You can see some examples in the table.

Metals These are usually hard and shiny, and difficult to melt. They are good conductors of heat and electricity.

Nonmetals These are usually gases, or solids which melt easily. The solids are often brittle or powdery. Most are insulators.

Carbon has unusual properties for a nonmetal. It exists naturally in two forms: **graphite**, which is a good conductor of electricity, and **diamond**, which is the hardest substance known.

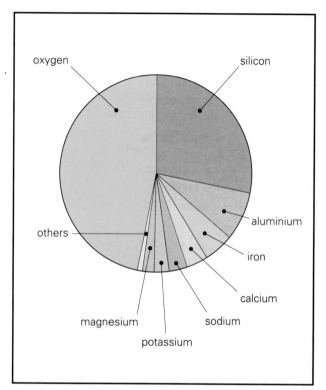

The eight most common elements in the Earth's crust (outer layer). The rocks are mainly made from oxygen and silicon.

Graphite

Diamond

Metals		Nonmetals	
Element	*Symbol*	*Element*	*Symbol*
aluminium	Al	bromine	Br
calcium	Ca	carbon	C
copper	Cu	chlorine	Cl
gold	Au	fluorine	F
iron	Fe	helium	He
lead	Pb	hydrogen	H
magnesium	Mg	iodine	I
potassium	K	nitrogen	N
silver	Ag	oxygen	O
sodium	Na	phosphorus	P
tin	Sn	silicon	Si
zinc	Zn	sulphur	S

Atoms

Elements are made up of tiny particles called **atoms**. An atom is the smallest amount of an element you can have. Atoms are far too small to see with any ordinary microscope. It would take more than a billion billion atoms to cover this full stop.

Different elements have different types of atom. Hydrogen is the lightest atom (see Spread 3.7).

Compounds

Atoms can join together to form a new substance which is quite different from the elements forming it. This new substance is called a **compound**.

Water is a compound of hydrogen and oxygen. The smallest 'bit' of water is called a **molecule** of water. It is made up of two hydrogen atoms stuck to one oxygen atom. Scientists describe it using a **chemical formula**: H_2O.

There are some examples of compounds and formulae on the right. However, not all compounds are in the form of molecules (see Spread 3.8).

Reactivity

When elements join, scientists say that they have **reacted** with each other. They have taken part in a **chemical reaction**.

Some metals react more readily than others. For example, iron can react with oxygen to form a compound called **rust**. Because iron reacts so readily, it is never found in the ground as a pure metal. Instead, it has to be extracted from a brown, rusty compound called **haematite**. On the other hand, gold is very unreactive. It is found in rocks as tiny pieces of pure metal.

Scientists have worked out a **reactivity series** for metals. You can see part of this below:

Compound	Molecule	Formula
water		H_2O
carbon dioxide		CO_2
ammonia		NH_3
methane		CH_4
sulphuric acid		H_2SO_4

1. What are the two main types of element?
2. Which of the eight most common elements in the Earth's crust are metals?
3. Which element has the lightest atoms?
4. What is the difference between an *element* and a *compound*.
5. The chemical formula for carbon dioxide is CO_2. What does this tell you about carbon dioxide?
6. Explain why gold is found in the ground as a pure metal, whereas iron has to be extracted from compounds in rocks.
7. Do you think aluminium is found in the ground as a pure metal? Explain your answer.

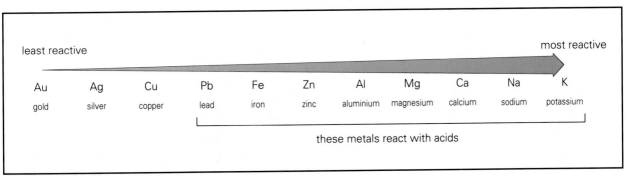

least reactive → most reactive

Au	Ag	Cu	Pb	Fe	Zn	Al	Mg	Ca	Na	K
gold	silver	copper	lead	iron	zinc	aluminium	magnesium	calcium	sodium	potassium

these metals react with acids

3·4 Mixtures and solutions

By the end of this spread, you should be able to:
- explain what solutions and alloys are
- describe ways of separating mixtures

One substance by itself is called a **pure** substance. It might be an element, such as gold, or it might be a compound, such as water. However, very few natural substances are pure. For example, rainwater contains tiny amounts of other chemicals as well. If something contains at least two separate substances, it is called a **mixture**.

Solutions

If you put sand in salt, the particles in the mixture are big enough to see. However, if you put sugar in water, the sugar breaks up into particles which are so small and spread out that you cannot see them even with a microscope. The sugar has **dissolved** in water. The result is a mixture called a **solution**:

Brass is an alloy

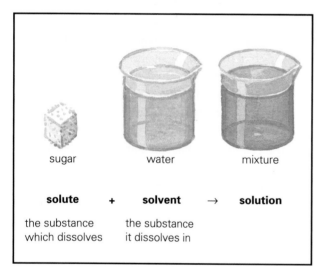

| sugar | water | mixture |

| **solute** | + | **solvent** | → | **solution** |

| the substance which dissolves | | the substance it dissolves in | | |

Scientists say that sugar is **soluble** in water.

A solution containing water is called an **aqueous solution**. However water is not the only solvent for dissolving things. Here are some other solvents:

Solvent	Dissolves...
Ethanol	Biro ink
Trichloroethane	Grease
Propanone	Nail varnish

Alloys

Metals with other substances mixed in are called **alloys**.

The instrument above is made of an alloy, brass. Brass is a mixture of copper (70%) and zinc (30%). It is harder than copper by itself. Also, unlike copper, it does not **corrode**. In other words, its surface is not spoilt by the chemical action of air or water.

Steel is an alloy of iron (99%) and carbon (1%). (Exact percentages vary depending on the type of steel). Steel is much stronger and harder than iron by itself.

---

1 What do scientists mean by a *pure* substance?
2 What do these words mean?
   soluble   solute   solvent   solution
3 What is an *alloy*?
4 Metal things are often made from alloys rather than pure metals. Why?
5 Describe how you would separate the substances in each of the following mixtures:
   a) sand and sugar b) water and mud
   c) water paints of different colours.
6 Which of the following work as filters, and what do they separate?
   tea-bag   cotton wool   bag in vacuum cleaner

Separating mixtures

Below are some methods of separating simple mixtures in the laboratory, with examples of what they might be used for:

Filtering

Example Separating sand from water.

The mixture is poured into a funnel lined with filter paper. The water passes through the paper, but the sand is stopped.

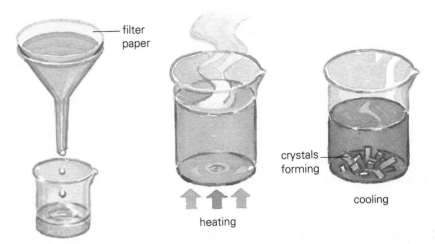

filter paper

crystals forming

cooling

heating

Dissolving

Example Separating sand from salt.

The sand and salt are mixed with water and stirred. This dissolves the salt, but not the sand. The new mixture is filtered. The salty water passes through the filter paper, but the sand is stopped.

Crystallizing

Example Separating copper(II) sulphate from water.

The solution is heated gently and some of the water evaporates. When the remaining solution is cooled, crystals of copper(II) sulphate start to form in it.

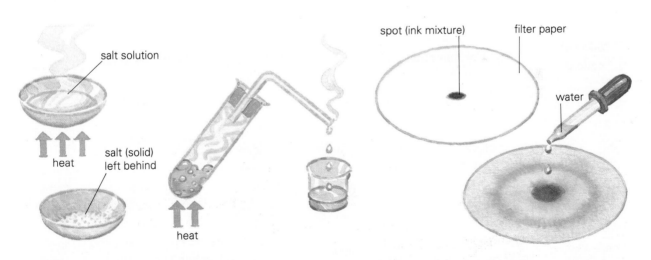

salt solution

heat

salt (solid) left behind

heat

spot (ink mixture)

filter paper

water

Evaporating

Example Separating salt from water.

The solution is heated gently until all the water has evaporated (turned to vapour). The salt is left behind as a solid.

Distilling

Example Separating water from ink.

The mixture is boiled. The vapour, which is pure water, cools as it passes down a long tube and condenses (turns liquid).

Chromatography

Example Separating inks of different colours.

A spot of ink mixture is placed at the centre of a piece of filter paper and left to dry. Water is dripped onto the spot. The ink mixture spreads through the damp paper. The different colours spread at different rates.

More mixtures

By the end of this spread, you should be able to:
* recognise various types of mixtures including solutions, suspensions, and colloids
* describe the features of composite materials

Unlike compounds, mixtures have the following features:
* Their components (ingredients) are not chemically linked and can often be separated easily.
* They keep the properties of their components.
* Their components can be in varying proportions.
* They do not have fixed melting or boiling points.

Solutions, suspensions, and colloids

Solutions, such as sugar-in-water, are mixtures consisting of tiny particles of solute spread between the molecules of a solvent. They cannot be separated by filtering. They allow light to pass through.

Suspensions, such as muddy water, are made from much larger particles shaken up in a medium (usually water). Suspensions are opaque (cloudy) and settle into separate layers.

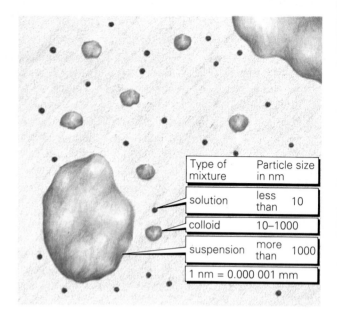

Type of mixture	Particle size in nm
solution	less than 10
colloid	10–1000
suspension	more than 1000

1 nm = 0.000 001 mm

Colloids consist of a **disperse phase** – tiny gas bubbles, liquid droplets, or solid particles – spread out in another solid, liquid, or gas – called the **dispersion medium**. These mixtures do not settle and cannot be filtered. Also, they *scatter* light. The chart below shows some common colloids.

Name of colloid	Components		Examples/Uses
aerosol	liquid droplets dispersed in...	gas	mist, fog, clouds, deodorant sprays
	tiny solid particles held in...	gas	smoke, dust clouds
sol	solid particles suspended permanently in...	liquid	paints, milk of magnesia, toothpaste
emulsion	tiny droplets of an insoluble liquid held by an emulsifier in...	liquid	mayonnaise (oil and vinegar + egg yolk emulsifier), cream, rubber latex
foam	tiny bubbles of gas trapped in...	liquid	beer froth, whipped cream, fire extinguishing foam
		solid	meringues, sponge, pumice, expanded polystyrene and polyurethane (for packaging)
gel	liquid trapped in...	solid network	jellies, agar, custard, hair gel

Composites

Sometimes, two or more materials are combined to form a composite material with the best properties of each. Here are some examples:

Concrete is a composite of rock chippings and sand, bound tightly by cement and water. When wet, it can be moulded into shape.

Reinforced concrete has steel rods through it. The concrete has great *compressive strength* (it resists squashing) but cracks when stretched. The steel adds *tensile strength* (it resists stretching).

Bone is a natural composite of tough protein fibres (collagen), giving tensile strength, set in hard calcium phosphate, giving compressive strength. Bone is nearly as strong as mild steel and much lighter.

Wood is a natural composite of cellulose fibres cemented by lignin. It can be made stronger and more flexible by glueing together several thin layers as *plywood*.

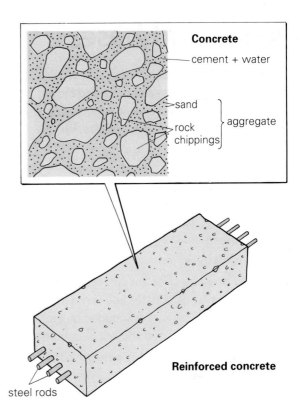

Concrete
cement + water
sand
rock chippings } aggregate

Reinforced concrete
steel rods

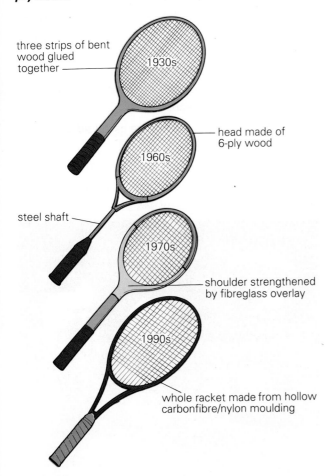

three strips of bent wood glued together — 1930s

head made of 6-ply wood — 1960s

steel shaft

1970s

shoulder strengthened by fibreglass overlay

1990s

whole racket made from hollow carbonfibre/nylon moulding

Materials used in tennis rackets

Fibreglass (glass-fibre-reinforced plastic, or GRP) is used for making canoes, baths, and vaulting poles. Its strength and flexibility come from fine strands of glass which are covered with plastic resin and heated.

Carbonfibre (carbon-fibre-reinforced plastic, or CFRP) is made from fibres of carbon set in plastic resin or nylon. Although heavier than wood, it has great tensile strength and is lighter than steel. It is easily moulded into golf clubs and tennis rackets.

1 Give *three* ways in which *mixtures* are different from *compounds*.
2 What are the main features of a) solutions b) suspensions c) colloids?
3 What is an *emulsion*? Give an example.
4 What type of colloid is a) custard b) paint c) polyurethane packaging?
5 What is meant by a *composite material*?
6 What gives reinforced concrete a) its compressive strength b) its tensile strength?
7 Give the names of two natural composites and say what they are made of.
8 What are the components and uses of a) fibreglass b) carbonfibre?

3·6 Acids and bases

By the end of this spread, you should be able to:
- *list the main properties of acids and bases*
- *use the pH scale and explain what it is for*
- *explain what is meant by neutralization*

Acids

There are acids in the laboratory. But there are natural acids in vinegar, sour fruits, and even in your stomach! Acids dissolved in lots of water are called **dilute** acids. The more **concentrated** an acid, the less water it is dissolved in.

Dissolved in water, acids are **corrosive** and eat into materials such as carbonates and some metals. Even without water, some concentrated acids are dangerously corrosive and should never be handled.

All acids contain hydrogen. In water, this becomes active and causes the acid effect. When an acid reacts with a metal, the hydrogen is given off and a new substance called a **salt** is formed. Here is a typical reaction between an acid and a metal:

$$\text{sulphuric acid} + \text{magnesium} \rightarrow \text{magnesium sulphate} + \text{hydrogen}$$

In this case, magnesium sulphate is the salt. There are many different types of salt.

Acids which release lots of hydrogen, and dissolve metals quickly, are called **strong acids**. Those which release hydrogen slowly are **weak acids**.

Some naturally-occurring acids	
	contains....
lemon juice	citric acid
vinegar	ethanoic acid (acetic acid)
tea	tannic acid
sour milk	lactic acid
grapes	tartaric acid
nettle sting	methanoic acid
stomach (juices)	hydrochloric acid

Strong acids	Weak acids
hydrochloric acid	ethanoic acid
sulphuric acid	citric acid
nitric acid	carbonic acid

Bases

Bases are the chemical 'opposites' of acids. They react strongly with acids and can **neutralize** them (cancel out the acid effect).

Bases which dissolve in water are called **alkalis**. So alkalis are soluble bases.

Alkalis can be just as corrosive as acids. Their powerful chemical action is often used in bath, sink, and oven cleaners.

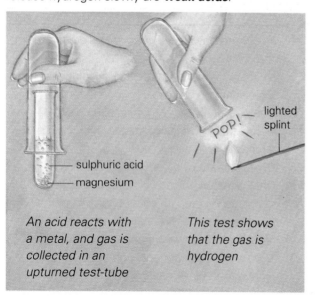

sulphuric acid
magnesium

An acid reacts with a metal, and gas is collected in an upturned test-tube

This test shows that the gas is hydrogen

POP!
lighted splint

Alkalis, including ammonia, are used in many household cleaners

Indicators and pH

There are some dyes which have a different colour depending on whether they are in an acidic or alkaline solution. Dyes like this are called **indicators**. Litmus is one example.

Acids turn litmus red.
Alkalis turn litmus blue.

Scientists use the **pH scale** to measure how strong or weak an acid or alkali is. The strongest acids have a pH of 1. The strongest alkalis have a pH of 14. Solutions with a pH of 7 are are neither acidic nor alkaline. They are **neutral**.

You can measure pH with **universal indicator**. This contains a mixture of dyes. It goes a different colour depending on the pH of the solution.

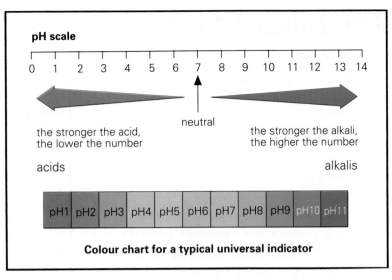

pH scale

the stronger the acid, the lower the number

neutral

the stronger the alkali, the higher the number

acids

alkalis

Colour chart for a typical universal indicator

Neutralization

If an acid reacts with a base it can form a neutral solution containing a salt. For example:

hydrochloric acid + sodium hydroxide → sodium chloride + water

In other words:

acid + base → salt + water

Neutralizing acids is called **neutralization**. Here are some everyday examples:

Sugar in your mouth produces acids which rot your teeth. Toothpaste, which is alkaline, neutralizes these acids. Acid in your stomach sometimes becomes a little too concentrated. Indigestion tablets contain an alkali, such as sodium hydrogencarbonate ('bicarb'), which helps reduce the effect.

Properties of acids (in solution)

- They have a sour taste (like vinegar)
  Note: you must never taste laboratory acids
- They turn litmus red
- They usually react with metals, producing hydrogen and a salt
- They dissolve carbonates to give salt, water, and carbon dioxide
- They have pH numbers less than 7

Properties of alkalis (in solution)

- They feel soapy
  Note: it is dangerous to touch laboratory alkalis
- They turn litmus blue
- They have pH numbers greater than 7

Strong alkalis	Weak alkali
sodium hydroxide	ammonia
potassium hydroxide	
calcium hydroxide	

1. What is the difference between a *concentrated* acid and a *dilute* acid?
2. What is the difference between a *strong* acid and a *weak* acid?
3. What element is found in all acids?
4. Someone drops some zinc into sulphuric acid and finds that a gas is given off. What gas is it? How could you tell it was this gas by experiment?
5. What is produced if an acid is added to a base?
6. Someone puts some universal indicator paper into vinegar. The pH is 3. What does this tell you about the vinegar?
7. Someone puts some universal indicator paper onto wet soap. The pH is 8. What does this tell you about the soap?
8. What would you expect the pH of pure water to be?
9. Give *two* examples of neutralization.

The periodic table

By the end of this spread, you should be able to:
* *describe the main features of the periodic table*
* *explain why different elements have different properties*

The elements differ in many ways. For example, some have a greater density than others. And some are more reactive than others.

Density is an example of a **physical property**. Reactivity is an example of a **chemical property**.

Scientists have found links between the elements, their properties, and their atoms.

Atoms, electrons, and shells

An atom's mass is mainly concentrated in a tiny **nucleus** in the centre. Around this nucleus, there are even tinier particles called **electrons**.

Each element has a different number of electrons in its atom. Hydrogen, the lightest atom, has only one electron. Uranium, one of the heaviest, has 92.

In an atom, the electrons are arranged in layers called **shells**. For example, the first shell can hold up to 2 electrons, the second up to 8, and the third up to 8. Electrons always try to fill the lowest shell they can. Some elements have full outer shells. But most have outer shells which are only partly filled. You can see some examples in the table on the opposite page.

Properties and patterns

The elements below have been arranged in order of number of electrons. Along the row, you can see that some properties tend to follow a periodic (repeating) pattern:

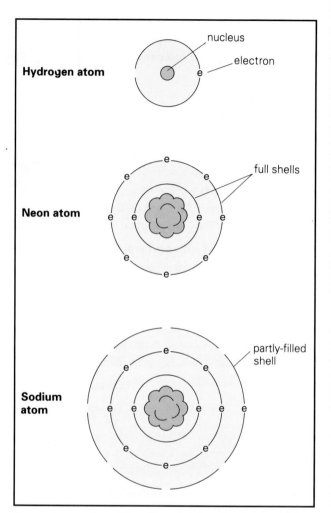

From observations like this scientists have been able to construct a chart of the elements, called the **periodic table**. There is a simple version at the top of the next page, and a full table on page 224. The elements have been arranged in several rows, called **periods**, one on top of another. As a result, elements with similar properties are in the same column.

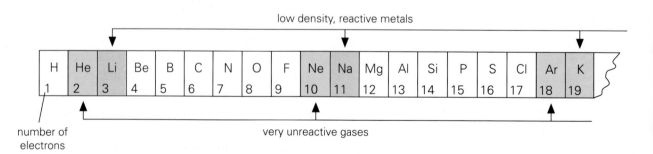

low density, reactive metals

H	He	Li	Be	B	C	N	O	F	Ne	Na	Mg	Al	Si	P	S	Cl	Ar	K
1	2	3	4	5	6	7	8	9	10	11	12	13	14	15	16	17	18	19

number of electrons

very unreactive gases

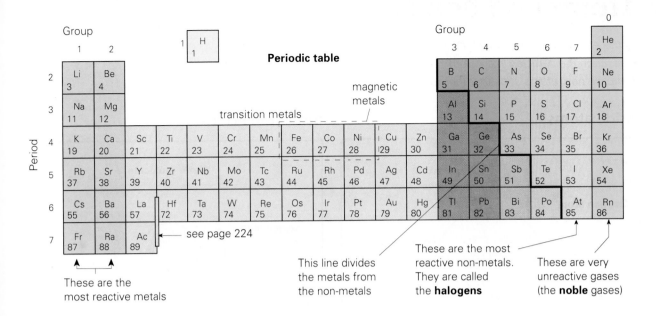

Periodic table

Group 1, 2 ... transition metals ... magnetic metals ... Group 3, 4, 5, 6, 7, 0

| | Group 1 | 2 | | | | | | | | | | | | Group 3 | 4 | 5 | 6 | 7 | 0 |

These are the most reactive metals

This line divides the metals from the non-metals

These are the most reactive non-metals. They are called **the halogens**

These are very unreactive gases (the **noble** gases)

see page 224

Some of the columns have **group** numbers. For example, the elements in Group 1 all have one electron in the outer shell and are reactive metals of low density. The elements in Group 0 all have full outer shells and are very unreactive gases.

Element	Symbol	Number of electrons				
		Shell				Total
		1	2	3	4	
hydrogen	H	1				1
helium	He	2				2 — full shell
lithium	Li	2	1			3
beryllium	Be	2	2			4
boron	B	2	3			5
carbon	C	2	4			6
nitrogen	N	2	5			7
oxygen	O	2	6			8
fluorine	F	2	7			9
neon	Ne	2	8			10 — full shell
sodium	Na	2	8	1		11
magnesium	Mg	2	8	2		12
aluminium	Al	2	8	3		13
silicon	Si	2	8	4		14
phosphorus	P	2	8	5		15
sulphur	S	2	8	6		16
chlorine	Cl	2	8	7		17
argon	Ar	2	8	8		18 — full shell
potassium	K	2	8	8	1	19

Electrons and reactions

Scientists think they can explain why elements in the same group have similar properties. It is because of their similar electron arrangements:

Electrons are the bits of atoms which take part in chemical reactions. For example, when sodium reacts with chlorine, a sodium atom's one outer electron is pulled across to fill the one space in a chlorine atom's outer shell. So, sodium and chlorine are both left with full outer shells. (See also Spread 3.8.)

A full outer shell is a very stable arrangement. Elements with full outer shells are very unreactive because the electrons tend to stay where they are. On the other hand, elements with one outer electron, or one unfilled space, are very reactive.

1 Give *three* features which are common to the elements in Group 1.
2 Give *three* features which are common to the elements in Group 0.
3 How many outer-shell electrons do the elements have in a) Group 2 b) Group 6?
4 Use the periodic table to give as much information as you can about each of these elements: *krypton (Kr) caesium (Cs) cobalt (Co)*
5 Sodium has only one more electron than neon, yet its properties are very different. Why?

Atoms and bonds

By the end of this spread, you should be able to:
- *describe the particles in an atom*
- *explain how atoms stick together to form compounds*

Inside atoms

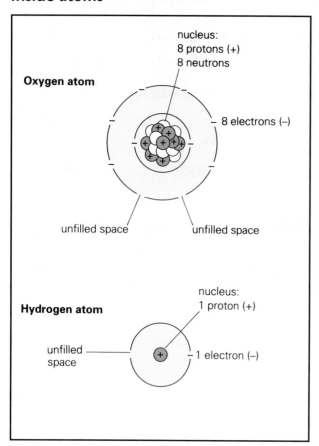

Inside molecules

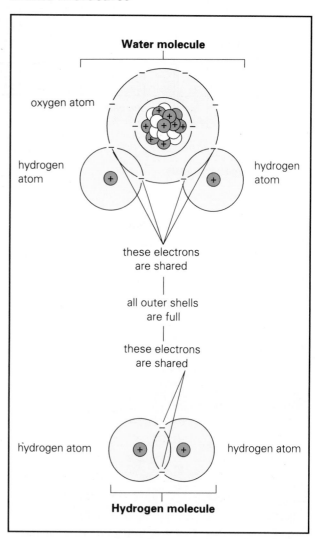

In an atom, **electrons** move around a central **nucleus**. The nucleus is itself made up of smaller particles called **protons** and **neutrons** (apart from hydrogen, which just has one proton as its nucleus).

Protons and electrons have an **electric charge**. Protons have a **positive (+)** charge. Electrons have an equal **negative (–)** charge. Neutrons are uncharged.

Atoms have the same number of electrons (–) as protons (+), so, overall, they are uncharged.

Opposite charges (+ and –) attract each other with an electric force (see also Spread 4.1). That is why electrons stay around the nucleus. Protons repel each other, but this 'pushing apart' is overcome by another force which binds the nucleus together.

Some atoms stick together in clumps called **molecules**. They do so by sharing electrons. They are held together by electric forces called **bonds**.

In a water molecule, the two hydrogen atoms share their electrons with the oxygen atom. In this way, the atoms all end up with full outer shells. Bonding by sharing electrons is called **covalent bonding.**

Some molecules have atoms of the same type. For example each molecule of hydrogen gas is made up of two hydrogen atoms.

Forces between molecules

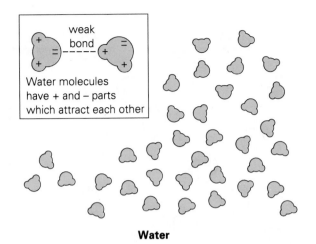

Water

Bonds hold atoms together in a molecule. Much weaker bonds pull some molecules together to form solids and liquids. For example:

In a water molecule, the bonding electrons are not equally shared between the atoms. This means that the oxygen is slightly negative (–) and the hydrogen slightly positive (+). Positive (+) parts of one molecule are attracted to negative (–) parts on others, so water molecules tend to stick to each other. However this weak bond is easily broken by heating. That is why ice melts so easily.

Ions

Some atoms stick together because electrons are transferred from one to another. For example:

In sodium chloride (common salt), each sodium atom has *lost* an electron, making it positively (+) charged. Each chlorine atom has *gained* an electron, making it negatively (–) charged. The opposite charges attract, holding the charged atoms tightly together in a lattice. The result is a crystal of sodium chloride.

Charged atoms are called ***ions***. So sodium chloride is made up of positive (+) sodium ions and negative (–) chlorine ions. This type of bonding is called ***ionic bonding***.

The bonds between ions are much stronger than those between molecules. That is why ionic compounds, such as sodium chloride, have higher melting temperatures than covalent compounds, such as water. The particles are more difficult to separate.

Dissolving

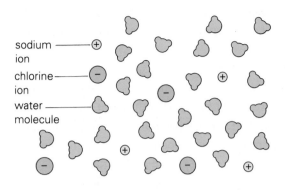

Sodium chloride dissolved in water

Ionic compounds, such as sodium chloride, dissolve in water. When sodium chloride dissolves, it splits into sodium ions (+) and chlorine ions (–), which spread between the water molecules. Water with ions in it will conduct electricity (see Spread 4.1).

---

1 Which particles in an atom have a) positive charge b) negative charge c) no charge?
2 A boron atom has 5 protons and 6 neutrons. How many electrons does it have?
3 What are *ions*?
4 What holds the atoms together in a water molecule?
5 Why does ice melt at a lower temperature than sodium chloride?
6 Describe what happens to its particles when sodium chloride dissolves in water.

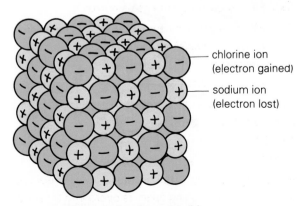

Crystal of sodium chloride

3·9 Structures of solids

By the end of this spread, you should be able to:
- *describe ionic, molecular, and metallic crystals*
- *link the properties of solids to their structures*

Ionic substances, such as sodium chloride, form **ionic crystals** – lattices in which positive and negative ions are bound tightly to each other (see Spread 3.8).

In covalent substances, the bonds holding atoms in each molecule are strong, but those *between* molecules are weak. As a result, many covalent substances are gases. However, if the temperature is low enough, the molecules may move slowly enough to bond together. That is why iodine (at room temperature) and carbon dioxide (cooled to −79 °C) both solidify as **molecular crystals**. But the weak molecule-to-molecule bonds are easily broken by heat, so these solids *sublime* (change to gas).

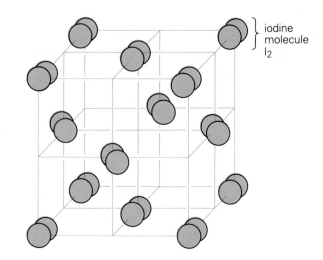

Structure of an iodine crystal. The blue lines show how the molecules are arranged. They are not bonds.

Macromolecular crystals

These are huge lattices in which millions of atoms are joined in one giant molecule (a **macromolecule**). Examples include diamond and graphite – two different forms (called **allotropes**) of carbon.

Diamond Each carbon atom forms covalent bonds with *four* others. The bonds are very strong, which is why diamond is one of the hardest substances known and has a very high melting point (3550 °C).

Graphite The carbon atoms are arranged in flat sheets in which each atom links with *three* others. Weaker forces hold these sheets loosely together in a layered structure. The layers slide over each other easily, making graphite suitable for the 'lead' in pencils and as a lubricant. The fourth outer electron of each carbon atom can move through the structure, allowing graphite to conduct electricity.

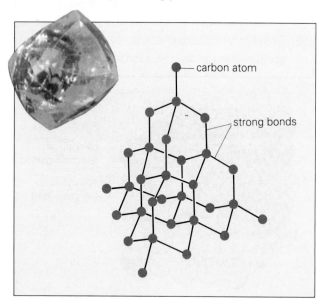

Structure of diamond

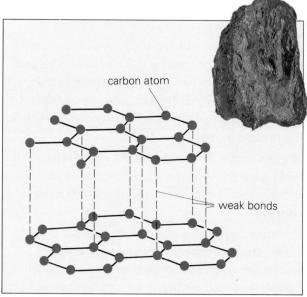

Structure of graphite

From quartz to ceramics

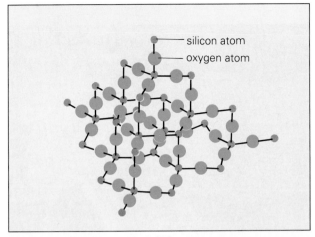

Structure of quartz (silica) SiO$_2$

Quartz (pure silica, SiO$_2$) has a diamond-like structure. It is very hard and has a high melting point. Many rocks are based on silica combined with metals.

Sand is ground-up quartz mixed with impurities.

Glass is made by strongly heating a mixture of sand, soda (sodium carbonate), and limestone (calcium carbonate) to produce a thick, sticky liquid. This gradually hardens as it cools but it does not form crystals and remains transparent. Glasses are mixtures, not compounds, so their composition can vary and they do not have fixed melting points.

Clay is based on quartz combined with aluminium and hydrogen atoms. It has a giant layered structure something like graphite. Water molecules can get between the layers and allow them to slide over each other. Wet clay is therefore pliable and slippery.

When clay is fired (heated in a kiln), the atoms form new bonds with the layers above and below. The result is a hard, brittle material called a ceramic.

---

1 What holds the particles together in
   a) ionic crystals b) molecular crystals
   c) metallic crystals?
2 Why is carbon dioxide a gas at room temperature?
3 Why is it so difficult to melt diamond?
4 Why does graphite feel slippery?
5 Glass does not have a fixed melting point. Why?
6 Why are alloys harder than pure metals?

Metallic crystals

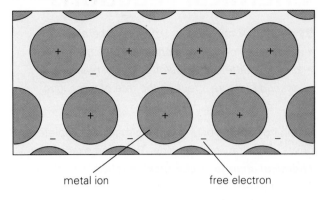

metal ion   free electron

Metals are also giant structures. The atoms are packed together closely – like oranges on display. Metals are malleable, so the bonds binding the atoms are both strong and flexible. These **metallic bonds** arise because the outer electrons become separated from their atoms. As a result, there is a lattice of positive ions surrounded by a 'sea' of free electrons. The mobile electrons bond the metal ions tightly into the lattice, making it difficult to melt. They also provide a means of conducting electricity.

Alloys

Metals bend easily because the layers of atoms in them can slide over each other. If a small amount of another metal is added to make an alloy, the atoms of the added metal are a different size. They make it more difficult for the layers to slide. That is why the alloy is harder than the pure metal.

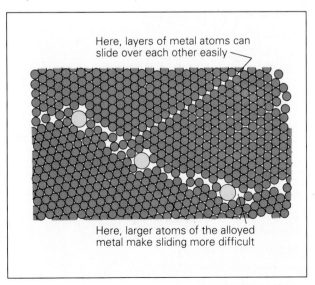

Here, layers of metal atoms can slide over each other easily

Here, larger atoms of the alloyed metal make sliding more difficult

Structure of an alloy

Chemical reactions

By the end of this spread, you should be able to:
• give the evidence for a chemical change
• describe different types of chemical reaction
• describe factors affecting the rate of a reaction

When iron and sulphur join, they make a completely new substance, iron sulphide. This is an example of a **chemical change**. A **chemical reaction** has taken place between the iron and the sulphur. Iron sulphide is the **product**. The reaction can be described using this **word equation**:

iron + sulphur → iron sulphide

Signs of chemical change

If a chemical change has taken place:

One or more new substances are formed
In the reaction above, iron is a metal, sulphur is a yellow powder, but iron sulphide is a black solid.

Energy is given out or taken in
When iron reacts with sulphur, heat is given out. Reactions which give out heat are called **exothermic** reactions. On the other hand, some reactions take in heat. They are **endothermic**.

The change is usually difficult to reverse
Several reactions are needed to change iron sulphide back into iron and sulphur.

Very rapid chemical reactions

Speed of reaction

Before substances can react, their moving particles (atoms, ions, or molecules) must meet. The speed of a reaction depends on how quickly this happens. Below are some of the factors it depends on:

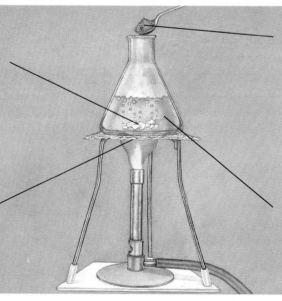

Size of bits A powdered substance reacts more quickly than one with larger bits. This is because the powder has a much bigger surface area, so more reacting particles come into contact.

Temperature A reaction goes faster if the temperature rises. This is because the reacting particles collide with each other more quickly.

Catalyst This is any chemical added which makes a reaction go faster without being used up itself. It helps other particles meet and join more quickly.

Concentration Increasing the concentration of a substance makes a reaction go faster. A higher concentration means that more particles are likely to meet and join.

Types of chemical reaction

Here are some different types of chemical reaction:

Synthesis (combination) Two substances join to make a single new substance. For example, this reaction takes place when magnesium burns:

magnesium + oxygen → magnesium oxide
  (metal)   (gas)   (grey ash)

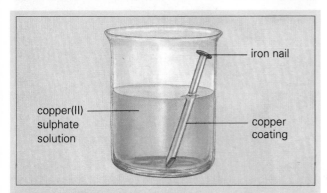

Displacement One substance pushes out another and takes its place. For example, if an iron nail is placed in copper(II) sulphate solution, some iron dissolves and displaces copper in the solution. The copper is deposited on the nail as a brown coating:

iron + copper sulphate → copper + iron sulphate

There is a displacement reaction whenever a metal reacts with an acid. The metal displaces hydrogen in the solution. (Remember: all acids contain hydrogen).

Acid-base If an acid reacts with a base, it can form a neutral solution containing a salt. (See Spread 3.6.)

Redox When hydrogen gas is passed over hot copper(II) oxide, this reaction takes place (Symbols have also been used so that you can see what is happening to the atoms):

copper(II) oxide + hydrogen → copper + water
     CuO + H_2 → Cu + H_2O

This is an example of a redox reaction:
Copper(II) oxide has *lost* oxygen: it has been **reduced**. Hydrogen has *gained* oxygen: it has been **oxidized**. **Red**uction and **ox**idation always happen together, which is why the name **redox** is used.

Precipitation When some solutions are mixed, they react and give a product which is insoluble (it doesn't dissolve). It appears as tiny, solid bits called a **precipitate**. For example:

silver nitrate	+	sodium chloride	→	silver chloride	+	sodium nitrate
(soluble)		(soluble)		(insoluble precipitate)		(soluble)

Decomposition A substance splits to form simpler substances. For example, if calcium carbonate is heated to 1100 °C, it splits to form calcium oxide and carbon dioxide:

            heat
calcium carbonate → calcium oxide + carbon dioxide
   (limestone)   (quicklime)   (gas)

---

1. Solid ice melts to become liquid water. Explain why this is not a chemical change?
2. Magnesium burning is a chemical reaction.
   a) What is the product of this reaction?
   b) Is the reaction *exothermic* or *endothermic*? Explain your answer.
3. Which would burn most quickly, a strip of magnesium or powdered magesium? Why?
4. Warm, liquid glucose, with yeast added as a catalyst, splits up to form two simpler substances: ethanol and carbon dioxide.
   a) What type of reaction is this?
   b) What is a *catalyst*?
   c) Write a word equation for the reaction.

Burning and oxides

By the end of this spread, you should be able to:
- *describe the products of burning*
- *explain what conditions are needed for burning*
- *explain what causes corrosion and food oxidation*

Combustion

Combustion is another word for burning. It happens when substances react with oxygen in the air, and gives out energy as heat and light.

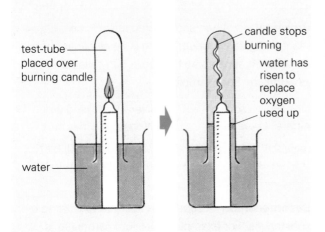

test-tube placed over burning candle

water

candle stops burning

water has risen to replace oxygen used up

This experiment shows that about 1/5 of the air is used up when something burns. That is because about 1/5 of the air is oxygen.

When an element burns, it becomes **oxidized**. The product of the reaction is an **oxide**. For example:

sulphur + oxygen → sulphur dioxide

magnesium + oxygen → magnesium oxide

Extra weight If you burn magnesium ribbon in a crucible and trap the ash, the ash weighs more than the magnesium because of the added oxygen:

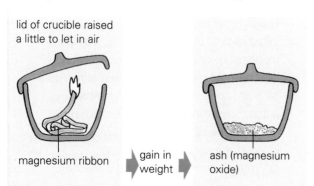

lid of crucible raised a little to let in air

magnesium ribbon

gain in weight

ash (magnesium oxide)

Burning fuels

Fuels include wood, coal, petrol, and natural gas (methane). Most are compounds of hydrogen and carbon. When they burn, the main products are carbon dioxide and water. For example:

methane + oxygen → carbon dioxide + water

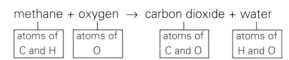

| atoms of C and H | atoms of O | atoms of C and O | atoms of H and O |

Some fuels are compounds of hydrogen, carbon, and oxygen. Ethanol (alcohol) is an example. Fuels like this also produce carbon dioxide and water when they burn.

Respiration is a kind of 'slow combustion' without any flames (see Spread 2.2). Our body cells use it to get energy from glucose (a compound of carbon, hydrogen, and oxygen):

glucose + oxygen → carbon dioxide + water

Testing for carbon dioxide Carbon dioxide turns a liquid called **lime water** milky. You can use this fact to tell that there is carbon dioxide in the air you breathe out. Just gently blow through lime water with a drinking straw and watch what happens.

Testing for oxygen Fuels which burn in air burn more fiercely in pure oxygen. You can use this fact to test for oxygen. If a smouldering wooden splint is put into a jar containing oxygen, the splint will burst into flames.

Fire!

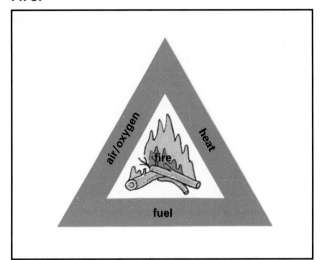

This **combustion triangle** shows the three things needed for burning. Removing any of them stops the burning. So firefighters have three ways of putting out a fire:

- **Cutting off the fuel**, for example by turning off gas at the mains.
- **Cutting off the air supply** by using fire blankets, foam, or carbon dioxide gas.
- **Getting rid of the heat**, for example, by cooling things down with water.

Note: water is not safe for some fires. It conducts electricity and can give people shocks. And it can make burning fat or oil splatter and spread.

Foods oxidizing

Things do not necessarily have to burn to react with oxygen. For example:

Some foods react with oxygen in the air. Fats such as butter and lard are like this. When they become oxidized, they taste very unpleasant. People say they are **rancid**. Keeping fats in a refrigerator slows the oxidizing process. Keeping out the air is another way of tackling the problem. For example, crisp manufacturers fill crisp bags with nitrogen to stop the fat on the crisps becoming oxidized.

Corrosion

If a metal is reactive, its surface may be attacked by air, water, or other substances around it. The effect is called **corrosion**. For example, when iron corrodes, the iron becomes oxidized, and the product is the brown, flaky substance we call **rust**. Steel, which is mainly iron, can also go rusty.

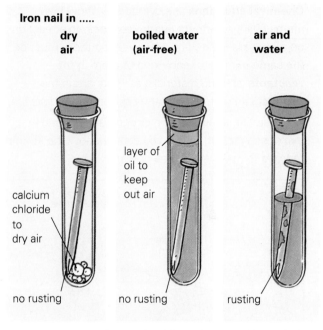

This experiment shows that air *and* water are needed for rusting. Dry air alone has no effect. Nor does water alone (if all air has been removed by boiling).

To stop iron and steel rusting, they can be coated with paint, grease, plastic, or a thin layer of non-corroding metal such as tin. This keeps out the air and water. (Stainless steel does not rust, but is far too expensive for many jobs.)

1 What *three* things are necessary for burning?
2 What is the product when an element (such as sulphur) burns?
3 What are the products when a fuel (such as methane) burns?
4 How could you tell whether a gas was
  a) carbon dioxide b) oxygen?
5 *Two* things are needed for iron or steel to rust. What are they?
6 What problems are caused by food oxidation? Describe *two* ways in which these can be prevented.

Equations, calculations, and moles

By the end of this spread, you should be able to:
- understand the meaning of chemical equations
- calculate masses and volumes of reacting substances

Chemical equations use symbols to show how atoms change partners during reactions. In a reaction, no atoms are created or destroyed, so there must be the same number of each kind of atom in the **reactants** (starting materials) as there are in the **products**. In other words, the equation must *balance*.

For example, a mixture of hydrogen and oxygen explodes when lit. Below you can see how the atoms regroup to make molecules of water.

Element/symbol		A_r	Element/symbol		A_r
hydrogen	H	1	phosphorus	P	31
helium	He	4	sulphur	S	32
carbon	C	12	chlorine	Cl	35.5
nitrogen	N	14	potassium	K	39
oxygen	O	16	calcium	Ca	40
fluorine	F	19	iron	Fe	56
sodium	Na	23	copper	Cu	64
magnesium	Mg	24	zinc	Zn	65
aluminium	Al	27	iodine	I	127
silicon	Si	28	lead	Pb	207

A_r = relative atomic mass (see page 224 for full list)

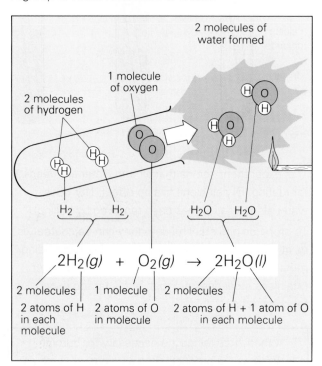

2 molecules of water formed

1 molecule of oxygen

2 molecules of hydrogen

$$2H_2(g) \ + \ O_2(g) \ \rightarrow \ 2H_2O(l)$$

2 molecules	1 molecule	2 molecules
2 atoms of H in each molecule	2 atoms of O in molecule	2 atoms of H + 1 atom of O in each molecule

The symbols in brackets give the physical state of the substances: *(s)* is solid, *(l)* is liquid, *(g)* is gas, and *(aq)* is an aqueous solution (a solution in water).

Relative atomic mass (A_r)

Atoms have such small masses that it is easier to use a mass scale on which atoms are compared with each other. The lightest atom, hydrogen, was originally chosen as 1 unit. Now, carbon-12 is used as the standard: its mass is defined as 12.000 units.

The mass of an atom on this scale is called the **relative atomic mass**. It is usually taken to be the same as the **mass number** (the total number of protons and neutrons in the nucleus of an atom). Most elements are mixtures of **isotopes** – different versions of an element, whose atoms have different numbers of neutrons (see Spread 4.34). So for an *element*, the relative atomic mass, **A_r**, is an *average* for the isotopes present.

Relative molecular mass (M_r)

The relative molecular mass (**M_r**) of a molecule is the sum of the A_rs of the atoms in the molecule. Below, you can see how to calculate M_r for carbon dioxide:

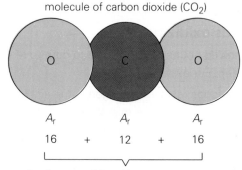

molecule of carbon dioxide (CO_2)

A_r	A_r	A_r
16	+ 12	+ 16

relative molecular mass M_r = 44

For ionic compounds, the term used is the **relative formula mass**, but the calculation is the same.

The mole

In chemical reactions, *equal amounts* of different substances means *equal numbers of particles* (such as atoms or molecules), and *not equal masses*.

If you take the A_r or M_r of any substance (for example, 12 for carbon) and write it as a mass in grams (12 g), then the mass contains 6×10^{23} particles. This amount is called one **mole**.

The number 6×10^{23} is known as the **Avogadro constant**. The mass of one mole of a substance is called the **molar mass**:

1 mole (6×10^{23}) of	Molar mass
.. atoms of helium ($A_r = 4$)	4 g
.. molecules of oxygen ($M_r = 32$)	32 g
.. molecules of carbon dioxide ($M_r = 44$)	44 g

Molar gas volume

One mole of any gas contains 6×10^{23} particles. At normal room temperature and pressure (**r.t.p.**), these always occupy the same volume, 24 dm^3 (24 litres). This **molar gas volume** is the same for all gases.

What is the mass of 48 dm^3 of methane (at r.t.p.)?

The M_r of methane (CH_4) = 12 + (1 × 4) = 16
1 mole of methane occupies 24 dm^3. Its mass is 16 g.
2 moles of methane occupy 48 dm^3. Its mass is 32 g.

Concentration of a solution

The **concentration** of a solution is the amount (in moles) of solute dissolved per dm^3 of solution.

If some dilute sulphuric acid has 196 g of pure acid in 1 dm^3 of solution, what is the concentration?

For sulphuric acid (H_2SO_4): M_r = 98
So, number of moles of $H_2SO_4 = {}^{196}/_{98} = 2$
So, concentration = 2 mole/dm^3, written 2M

Calculating from equations

The equation for a reaction is used when solving problems about masses and volumes:

What mass of calcium oxide could be produced by heating 500 g of calcium carbonate? What volume of carbon dioxide (at r.t.p.) would be given off?

The equation for this reaction is:

	calcium carbonate		calcium oxide	+	carbon dioxide
	$CaCO_3(s)$	$\rightarrow$	$CaO(s)$	+	$CO_2(g)$
Amount:	1 mole	gives	1 mole	and	1 mole
M_rs:	40 +12 + (16 × 3)		40 + 16		12 + (16 × 2)
Molar mass:	100 g	gives	56 g	and	44 g

Since 100 g of calcium carbonate is 1 mole, 500 g is 5 moles, which form 5 moles of each product.
So, mass of calcium oxide = 5 × 56 = 280 g
As 1 mole of a gas occupies 24 dm^3 at r.t.p.:
volume of carbon dioxide = 5 × 24 = 120 dm^3

Finding a formula

From the masses of substances involved in a reaction, it is possible to work out the formula of a compound:

When 8.0 g of copper(II) oxide are heated in a stream of hydrogen, the oxygen is removed, and 6.4 g of copper remain. What is the formula of copper(II) oxide?

To make copper(II) oxide, 6.4 g of copper were linked to 8.0 – 6.4 =1.6 g of oxygen. So:
The ratio of copper to oxygen is   6.4 g : 1.6 g
Dividing by the A_rs..... ${}^{6.4}/_{64}$: ${}^{1.6}/_{16}$
....changes the ratio to moles   0.1 mole : 0.1 mole
Therefore, the ratio of atoms is   1 : 1
So, formula for copper(II) oxide is Cu_1O_1, or just CuO.

---

1 $2Mg(s) + O_2(g) \rightarrow X MgO(s)$
   In this equation a) what should the number X be, and why? b) what do *(s)* and *(g)* stand for?
2 What do the symbols A_r and M_r stand for? What is the M_r for water (H_2O)?
3 What is meant by a *mole* of methane molecules? What is their a) mass b) volume at r.t.p?

4 If a solution has a *concentration of 3M*, what does this mean?
5 Methane (CH_4) burns in oxygen, forming water and carbon dioxide. Write a balanced equation for the reaction. If there is 48 dm^3 of methane at r.t.p, calculate a) the mass of water b) the volume of carbon dioxide at r.t.p.

3·13 Getting at metals

By the end of this spread, you should be able to:
- *explain why different methods are needed to extract metals from their ores*
- *explain how iron, steel, pure copper, and aluminium are produced*

Most of our metals come from rocks in the ground. A few occur naturally as elements. But most are in compounds called **ores**. Bonds which form easily are also the most difficult to break. So the more reactive a metal is, the more difficult it is to separate from its ore. (See the table on the opposite page and the information on the **reactivity series** in Spread 3.3.)

Gold is very unreactive

Iron and steel

Haematite (iron ore) is a compound of iron and oxygen. The iron can be extracted by a process called **smelting** which takes place in a **blast furnace**. Very hot limestone and coke are used to remove oxygen from the ore so that molten (melted) iron is left.

Iron from a blast furnace is called **pig iron**. It is not pure, and has a carbon content of about 4%. This makes it hard, but brittle.

To make steel, oxygen is passed through molten pig iron to 'burn off' most of the impurities, including carbon. Then controlled amounts of carbon (and other elements) are put back in. The result is the tough, springy alloy we call steel. Its carbon content is usually less than 1.5%.

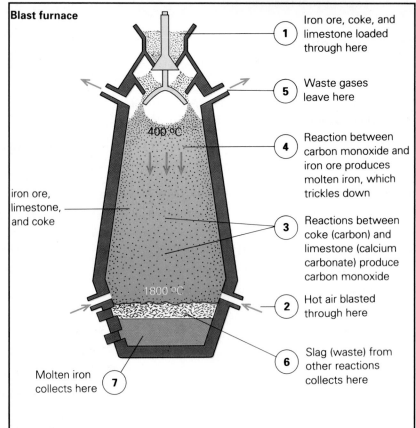

Blast furnace

1. Iron ore, coke, and limestone loaded through here
5. Waste gases leave here
4. Reaction between carbon monoxide and iron ore produces molten iron, which trickles down
3. Reactions between coke (carbon) and limestone (calcium carbonate) produce carbon monoxide
2. Hot air blasted through here
6. Slag (waste) from other reactions collects here
7. Molten iron collects here

iron ore, limestone, and coke

400 °C

1800 °C

---

1. In a blast furnace, why are the coke and limestone needed?
2. What method must be used to separate the most reactive metals from their ores?
3. During the electrolysis of copper sulphate, why does pure copper collect on the cathode?
4. How is pig iron made into steel?
5. *Gold   copper   aluminium*
   a) Which of these metals is the most reactive?
   b) Which is only found as an element? Why?
   c) Which is the most difficult to separate from its ore? Why?

Metal	Ore/how found	Reactivity of metal	Separating metal from ore
potassium (K) sodium (Na) calcium (Ca) magnesium (Mg) aluminium (Al)	silvine (KCl) rock salt (NaCl) limestone ($CaCO_3$) magnesite ($MgCO_3$) bauxite (Al_2O_3)	very reactive ↑ getting more difficult to separate from ore	electrolysis (using electricity)
zinc (Zn) iron (Fe) tin (Sn) lead (Pb)	calamine ($ZnCO_3$) haematite (Fe_2O_3) cassiterite (SnO_2) galena (PbS)		heating with carbon or carbon monoxide
copper (Cu)	chalcopyrite ($CuFeS_2$) and as an element		heating in air
silver (Ag)	argentite (Ag_2S) and as an element		
gold (Au)	as an element	unreactive	

Electrolysis and copper

Electricity can be used to decompose (split) a compound. The process is called *electrolysis*.

Impure copper can be purified by electrolysis. The diagram on the right shows how. The liquid in the tank is copper(II) sulphate solution. This is the *electrolyte*. Dipping into it are two metal *electrodes*: the *cathode* (connected to the – terminal of the battery) and the *anode* (connected to the + terminal). The lump of impure copper is the anode.

In the tank, copper(II) sulphate splits to form positive (+) copper ions and negative (–) sulphate ions. The copper ions (+) are attracted to the cathode (–), where they build up as a layer of pure copper. As this happens, copper from the impure lump dissolves in the electrolyte to replace the copper ions. In this way, copper is removed from the impure lump and pure copper collects on the cathode.

Aluminium

Aluminium can be separated from its ore (bauxite) by electrolysis. The electrolyte is hot, purified bauxite (aluminium oxide) dissolved in a molten aluminium compound called cryolite. The aluminium oxide splits into positive (+) aluminium ions and negative (–) oxide ions. The aluminium ions (+) are attracted to the cathode (–), where they become aluminium atoms. These collect at the bottom of the tank as molten aluminium.

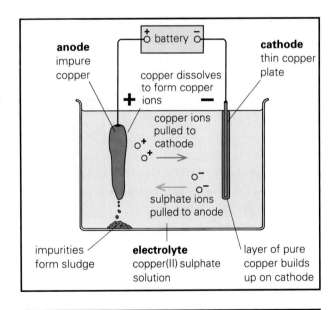

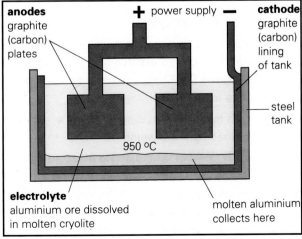

3·14 From water and rocks

By the end of this spread, you should be able to:
* *explain why salt, water, and limestone are useful, and how new materials can be made from them*

On Earth, there are many natural materials which can be processed to make other things. These are called **raw materials**. They include salt, water, and rocks.

Common salt

Common salt (sodium chloride) is very plentiful on Earth. Sea-water has salt dissolved in it (about 3%). Solid salt is also found underground, as on the right. In this form, it is known as rock salt.

Salt has many uses, and is the raw material for making many other chemicals:

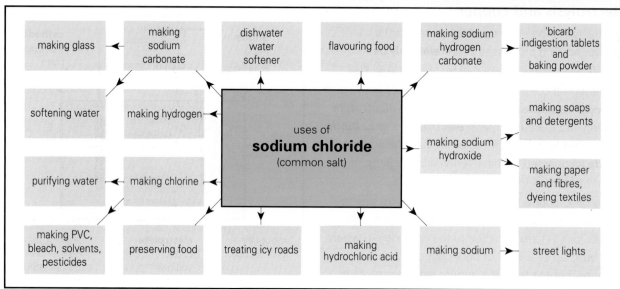

More from electrolysis

When sodium chloride dissolves in water, its ions are free to move. So it can be electrolysed. The diagram on the right shows what happens when this is done using graphite (carbon) electrodes:

Hydrogen gas bubbles off at the cathode (the hydrogen comes from the water).

Chlorine gas bubbles off at the anode (the chlorine comes from the salt). The electrolyte also contains sodium ions and hydroxide ions. In an industrial version of the process on the right, these form sodium hydroxide which can be collected.

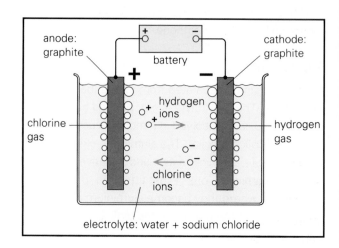

Gases from water

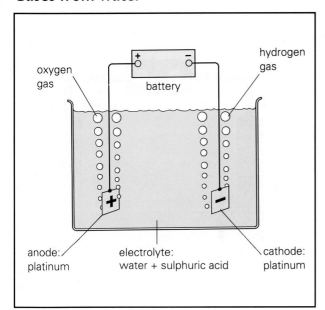

The diagram above shows the electrolysis of acidified water (water with acid in it). Platinum electrodes are being used. The effect is to split the water (H_2O) into hydrogen gas and oxygen gas:

$$\text{water} \xrightarrow[\text{electricity}]{\text{acid}} \text{hydrogen} + \text{oxygen}$$

For industry, hydrogen and oxygen are normally produced by other methods, rather than electrolysis. For details of these methods, and why the gases are useful, see Spread 3.20.

Limestone

Limestone is one of the most common rocks in Britain. It is mainly calcium carbonate, and was formed from the shells and bones of sea creatures which lived millions of years ago.

The building industry uses huge amounts of limestone:

Cement is made from limestone. It is produced by burning limestone, clay, and sand in a kiln, and then grinding the product with gypsum.

Chippings are often tiny pieces of limestone. Mixed with tar, they make Tarmac for roads. They are also used in blast furnaces and in making concrete.

Concrete is made by mixing chippings, sand, cement, and water, and leaving them to set.

Kettles, kidneys, and caves

Rainwater is slightly acid. It slowly reacts with limestone (calcium carbonate) to form calcium hydrogencarbonate, which dissolves in water. In limestone areas, the tap water contains dissolved calcium hydrogencarbonate. This makes it more difficult for soap to lather. People say that the water is **hard**.

When water is boiled, dissolved calcium hydrogen-carbonate changes back to solid calcium carbonate. This is the **scale** which builds up on the insides of kettles and water pipes.

In people's kidneys, calcium carbonate can form very attractive but painful crystals called **kidney stones**. In dripping, limestone caves, calcium carbonate forms **stalactites** and **stalagmites**.

---

1 Look at the chart on the opposite page, showing some uses of common salt:
   a) Give *three* direct uses of salt
   b) Give *three* substances made in chemical reactions which use salt.
2 If sodium chloride solution is electrolysed using graphite electrodes, hydrogen gas is produced.
   a) Where does the hydrogen come from?
   b) What other gas is produced?
   c) What is this other gas used for?
3 Give *two* reasons why limestone is important for the building industry.

3.15 Ionic equations

See also Spread 3.12 on equations and moles

By the end of this spread, you should be able to:
* *write equations for reactions involving ions*

Neutralization

Here is the equation for a reaction in which an acid is neutralized by an alkali to give salt plus water:

$$HCl\,(aq) \ + \ NaOH\,(aq) \ \rightarrow \ NaCl\,(aq) \ + \ H_2O\,(l)$$

| hydrochloric acid | sodium hydroxide (alkali) | sodium chloride (salt) | water |

The acid, alkali, and salt are ionic compounds. In water, they split up into separate ions. So it is more accurate to rewrite the equation showing the ions:

$$H^+(aq) \ + \ Cl^-(aq) \ + \ Na^+(aq) \ + \ OH^-(aq)$$
$$\rightarrow \ Na^+(aq) \ + \ Cl^-(aq) \ + \ H_2O\,(l)$$

In the reaction, the Na^+ and Cl^- ions, shown in yellow, do not change. The only change taking place is that hydrogen ions (H^+) and hydroxide ions (OH^-) join up to form water molecules. This is the same for all acids. It can be shown by an *ionic equation*:

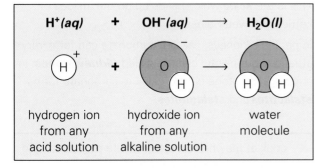

| $H^+(aq)$ | + | $OH^-(aq)$ | $\longrightarrow$ | $H_2O\,(l)$ |

| hydrogen ion from any acid solution | hydroxide ion from any alkaline solution | water molecule |

Electrolysis equations

Ionic equations are used to describe what happens during electrolysis. However, it is usual to write separate equations for the reaction at each electrode. These are called *half-reaction equations*.

During electrolysis, the battery moves electrons from the cathode to the anode round the outside circuit. So the number of electrons *released* from the negative ions to the anode must always equal the number of electrons *taken* from the cathode by the positive ions.

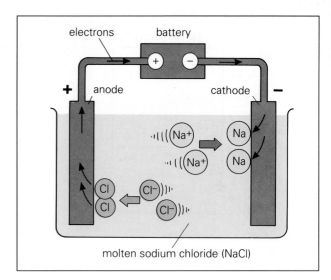

molten sodium chloride (NaCl)

Electrolysis of molten sodium chloride

When heated strongly, sodium chloride (NaCl) melts, and its ions (Na^+ and Cl^-) become free to move. Negative ions are attracted to the anode (+) and positive ions to the cathode (−), as shown above.

Anode reaction Two chloride ions (Cl^-) give up their extra electrons and become a molecule of chlorine gas.

$$2Cl^-(l) \ \rightarrow \ Cl_2(g) \ + \ 2e^- \qquad (e^-\text{ is an electron})$$

Cathode reaction Two sodium ions (Na^+) take up one electron each to become molten sodium metal.

$$2Na^+(l) \ + \ 2e^- \rightarrow 2Na\,(l)$$

These half equations show that when *two* moles of electrons flow, *two* moles of sodium atoms and *one* mole of chlorine molecules are released.

In the electrolysis of molten sodium chloride, what volume of chlorine (at r.t.p) will be formed at the same time as 92 g of sodium?

Molar mass of Na = 23 g; molar gas volume = 24 dm^3

	Sodium (Na)		Chlorine (Cl₂)
Ratio:	2 moles	:	1 mole
	2 x 23 g	:	1 x 24 dm^3
	46 g	:	24 dm^3
As 92 = 2 x 46	92 g	:	2 x 24 dm^3

So, with 92 g of sodium, there is 48 dm^3 of chlorine.

electrons   battery

anode   cathode

Electrolysis of sodium chloride solution

Concentrated solution The ions present are $Na^+(aq)$ and $Cl^-(aq)$, plus some $H^+(aq)$ and $OH^-(aq)$ ions because water always contains a tiny fraction of molecules that are split into ions.

In the **membrane cell** below, the electrodes are separated by a porous barrier which lets only water and sodium ions through. Chlorine, hydrogen, and sodium hydroxide are the products.

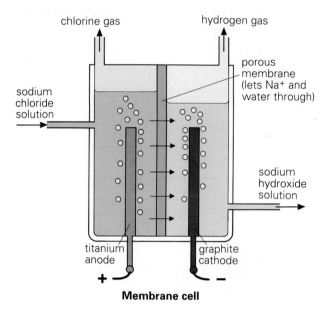

Membrane cell

Anode reaction Two chloride ions give up their electrons and are released as chlorine gas:

$$2Cl^-(aq) \rightarrow Cl_2(aq) + 2e^-$$

Cathode reaction Hydrogen ions take on electrons from a graphite cathode much more easily than do sodium ions. Hydrogen gas is given off:

$$2H^+(aq) + 2e^- \rightarrow H_2(g)$$

The solution coming from the cathode compartment contains sodium ions and hydroxide ions. These join to form solid sodium hydroxide when the water is evaporated.

Very dilute solution If both electrodes are made of platinum, oxygen is released at the anode and hydrogen at the cathode.

Anode reaction Four hydroxide ions give up their electrons and rearrange themselves into two molecules of water plus one molecule of oxygen:

$$4OH^-(aq) \rightarrow O_2(g) + 2H_2O(l) + 4e^-$$

Cathode reaction Four hydrogen ions accept electrons to become two molecules of hydrogen gas:

$$4H^+(aq) + 4e^- \rightarrow 2H_2(g)$$

So for every four molecules of water used up, two of water, two of hydrogen, and one of oxygen are made. Overall, water is split into hydrogen and oxygen (as in the electrolysis of acidified water in Spread 3.14).

Electrolysis of copper(II) sulphate solution

In copper(II) sulphate solution, the ions present are copper $Cu^{2+}(aq)$, sulphate $SO_4^{2-}(aq)$, plus some hydrogen $H^+(aq)$ and hydroxide $OH^-(aq)$ ions. In this case, each copper ion has a $2+$ charge because it has lost *two* electrons. The electrolysis of the solution is shown in Spread 3.13. There however, the copper ions are just marked with a single '+' for simplicity.

Cathode reaction A copper ion accepts two electrons and is deposited as an atom of pure copper:

$$Cu^{2+}(aq) + 2e^- \rightarrow Cu(s)$$

Anode reaction If the anode is made of copper, neither of the negative ions is affected. Instead, a copper atom passes from the metal into solution as a copper ion, leaving behind two electrons:

$$Cu(s) \rightarrow Cu^{2+}(aq) + 2e^-$$

The solution remains unchanged and pure copper passes from anode to cathode. Copper can be coated onto any conducting material which is used as the cathode. This is an example of **electroplating**.

---

1 What particles are present in solutions of
   a) hydrochloric acid b) sodium hydroxide?
2 Write the ionic equation for the neutralization of any acid by any alkaline hydroxide.
3 During electrolysis, which electrode are hydrogen ions attracted to? Why?
4 Explain what happens during *electroplating*.

5 What elements are released at the *anode* and *cathode* during the electrolysis of sodium chloride a) when molten b) in concentrated solution c) in very dilute solution?
6 During the electrolysis of copper(II) sulphate solution, what mass of copper is deposited on the cathode when one mole of electrons flows?

Table trends (1)

See also Spread 3.7 on the periodic table

By the end of this spread, you should be able to:
* *describe the differences in properties of metals and nonmetals, and some of their compounds.*

The nature of an element and the way it reacts are related to its position in the periodic table:

Down any one group, the atoms get *bigger*. They lose their outer electrons more easily to become positive ions. The elements become more **metallic**.

Across a period, the atoms get *smaller*, and their nuclei more positive. The attraction for extra electrons increases, so negative ions form more easily. The elements become more **nonmetallic**.

Element	Melting point °C	Group	Ion	Electrical conduction	Nature of oxide
sodium	98	1	Na⁺	good	basic
potassium	63	1	K⁺	good	basic
magnesium	650	2	Mg²⁺	good	basic
calcium	840	2	Ca²⁺	good	basic
iron	1540	trans	Fe²⁺	fair	basic
copper	1084	trans	Cu²⁺	good	basic
germanium	937	4	–	semi	acidic + basic
carbon (diamond)	sublimes	4	–	poor	acidic
sulphur	113	6	S²⁻	poor	acidic
chlorine	–101	7	Cl⁻	poor	acidic

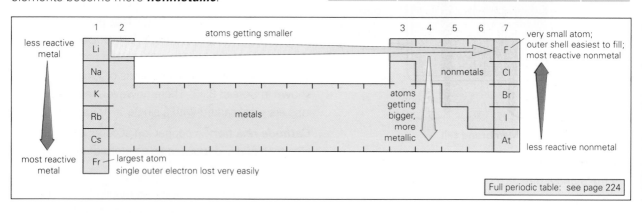

Group 1: the alkali metals

Atoms of metals in Group 1 all have a single electron in the outer shell. This electron is easily lost, so that the atom becomes a positive ion with the same electron structure as a Group 0 (noble) gas. Sodium, for example, forms ionic compounds in this way:

$$2Na(s) + Cl_2(g) \rightarrow 2Na^+Cl^-(s)$$
sodium   chlorine   sodium chloride

$$2Na(s) + O_2(g) \rightarrow (Na^+)_2O^{2-}(s)$$
sodium   oxygen   sodium oxide

$$2Na(s) + 2H_2O(l) \rightarrow 2Na^+OH^-(aq) + H_2(g)$$
sodium   water   sodium hydroxide   hydrogen

Sodium oxide and sodium hydroxide are strong alkalis (see Spread 3.6) – hence the name given to the group.

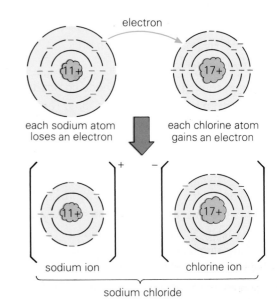

each sodium atom loses an electron

each chlorine atom gains an electron

sodium ion   chlorine ion

sodium chloride

Group 2: the alkaline-earth metals

The outer shell of a Group 2 atom has two electrons. Both must be lost for the atom to reach a stable (noble gas) structure. An ion with a 2+ charge is then formed. It is more difficult to remove two electrons than one (especially as the atom is smaller), so Group 2 metals tend not to be as reactive as those in Group 1. However, Group 2 metals also form ionic chlorides, and **basic oxides** and hydroxides. For example, magnesium burns to form magnesium oxide. This neutralizes acids, which is why it is called a basic oxide.

Group 7: the halogens

Fluorine, at the top of Group 7, is the most reactive nonmetal. It easily gains one extra electron to become a negative ion with a stable structure of 8 electrons. Chlorine, next down, also forms an ion with a 1− charge, but less easily because its atom is bigger.

Chlorine combines with oxygen or other nonmetals by sharing electrons. The covalent compounds formed are usually gases or liquids. For example, chlorine oxide is an explosive gas which dissolves in water to give chloric(I) acid. It is therefore an **acidic oxide**. You can see another example of a chlorine compound with shared electrons on the right.

Metals tend to form.....

.. positive ions, by losing electrons

.. ionic chlorides (solids with high melting points)

.. ionic oxides (solids which are bases)

Nonmetals tend to form.....

.. negative ions by gaining electrons

.. covalent chlorides (liquids with low boiling points)

.. covalent oxides (gases which react with water to give acids) such as the examples below.

Oxide		Acid formed with water	
carbon dioxide	CO_2	carbonic	H_2CO_3
nitrogen dioxide	NO_2	nitric	HNO_3
sulphur trioxide	SO_3	sulphuric	H_2SO_4
chlorine oxide	Cl_2O	chloric	$HClO$

When magnesium burns:

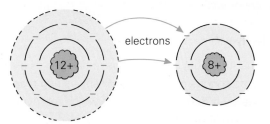

$$2Mg \quad + \quad O_2 \quad \rightarrow \quad 2Mg^{2+}O^{2-}$$
magnesium   oxygen   magnesium oxide

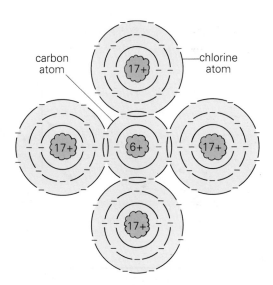

Each magnesium atom loses two electrons to become a magnesium ion: Mg^{2+}

Each oxygen atom gains two electrons to become an oxide ion: O^{2-}

Molecule of tetrachloromethane CCl_4. The chlorine and carbon have combined by sharing electrons.

---

1 Why is sodium a) less reactive than potassium b) more reactive than magnesium?

2 What type of compound is sodium oxide? How would it affect universal indicator?

3 Draw a diagram to show how a fluorine atom (9 electrons) becomes a negative ion.

4 Give *three* chemical properties of metals.

5 The elements in Group 4 change in nature from nonmetallic carbon at the top to metallic lead at the bottom. List the properties of germanium. Why do you think it is called a *metalloid*?

Table trends (2)

By the end of this spread, you should be able to:
* *describe the properties and uses of chlorine and its compounds and the transition metals and their compounds*

Chlorine

Chlorine, the most commonly used halogen, is a green, poisonous gas. When it dissolves and reacts with water, it forms a mild bleach which removes the colour from litmus paper. This bleach also kills germs, which is why chlorine is added to swimming pools like the one on the right. More uses of chlorine are shown in the chart below:

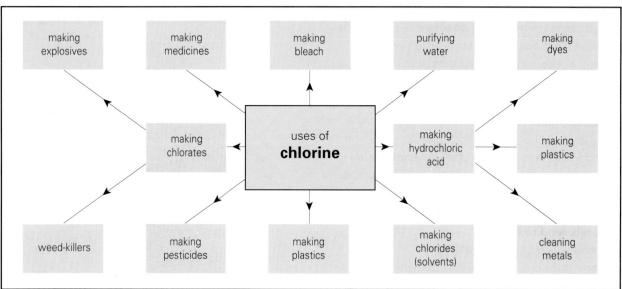

making explosives	making medicines	making bleach	purifying water	making dyes
making chlorates		**uses of chlorine**	making hydrochloric acid	making plastics
weed-killers	making pesticides	making plastics	making chlorides (solvents)	cleaning metals

From chlorine to acid

If hydrogen reacts with chlorine, the gas hydrogen chloride (HCl) is formed:

$$H_2(g) + Cl_2(g) \rightarrow 2HCl(g)$$

Hydrogen chloride is very soluble in water. It dissolves and becomes ionized to form hydrochloric acid.

Like other acids, hydrochloric acid reacts with bases, many metals, and carbonates (see also Spread 3.6). For example if hydrochloric acid is added to calcium carbonate, the reaction below takes place.

The following word equations describe what happens when any acid reacts with a base, metal, or carbonate:

acid + base	→ salt + water
acid + metal	→ salt + hydrogen
acid + carbonate	→ salt + water + carbon dioxide

When, for example, magnesium reacts with hydrochloric acid, it is the hydrogen which causes the fizzing. When calcium carbonate reacts with the acid, it is the carbon dioxide which causes the fizzing.

$$2H^+(aq) + 2Cl^-(aq) \ + \ CaCO_3(s) \ \rightarrow \ Ca^{2+}(aq) + 2Cl^-(aq) \ + \ H_2O(l) \ + \ CO_2(g)$$

| hydrochloric acid | calcium carbonate | calcium chloride | water | carbon dioxide |

The transition metals

Between Groups 2 and 3 of the period table, there is a block of metals called the **transition metals**. It includes many of the most common metals.

Although the transition metals each have a different number of electrons in their atoms, their outermost electrons are arranged in a similar way. In any one row of the block, the atoms are of a similar size.

transition metals									
these have similar properties									
Sc scandium 21	Ti titanium 22	V vanadium 23	Cr chromium 24	Mn manganese 25	Fe iron 26	Co cobalt 27	Ni nickel 28	Cu copper 29	Zn zinc 30
Y yttrium 39	Zr zirconium 40	Nb niobium 41	Mo molybdenum 42	Tc technetium 43	Ru ruthenium 44	Rh rhodium 45	Pd palladium 46	Ag silver 47	Cd cadmium 48
La lanthanum 57	Hf hafnium 72	Ta tantalum 73	W tungsten 74	Re rhenium 75	Os osmium 76	Ir iridium 77	Pt platinum 78	Au gold 79	Hg mercury 80
Ac actinium 89									

Because of these similarities, most of the metals have many properties in common:

- They have high melting points.
- They have medium-to-high densities.
- They are hard, strong, malleable, and ductile (for the meanings of these terms, see Spread 3.1)
- They can form more than one type of ion (see also Spread 3.18). For example, copper ions can be Cu^+ or Cu^{2+}.
- They can form alloys (see Spread 3.4.)
- Iron, nickel, and cobalt are strongly magnetic. Some others have weakly magnetic compounds.
- They are less reactive than the alkali metals and the alkaline-earth metals.
- They are often found in the ground as oxides or sulphides and can be separated from their ores using heat, air, and carbon (see Spread 3.13).
- Their compounds are coloured. For example, copper sulphate is blue. Coloured glasses and gemstones contain transition metal compounds.
- They and their compounds are often good catalysts. For example, iron is used as a catalyst in the manufacture of ammonia (see Spread 3.22). For more examples, see the table on the right.

---

1 What effect does chlorine have on wet litmus paper?
2 Give *three* uses of chlorine.
3 Name *three* transition metals and give one use of each.
4 Give *three* properties which most of the transition metals have in common.

Some uses of transition metals

Engineering and manufacturing	Iron (in steel) for machinery, vehicles, and structures
	Titanium for aircraft parts needing strength and lightness
	Tungsten for bulb filaments
	Chromium for plating and in stainless steel
	Manganese and nickel in special steel alloys
Building	Iron (in steel) for scaffolding and girders
Electrical	Copper for conducting cables
Chemical	Compounds for dyes and pigments
	Catalysts (see table below)

Metal/compound	Use as a catalyst
Iron	Combining nitrogen and hydrogen to make ammonia
Nickel	Combining hydrogen and vegetable oil to make margarine
Platinum, rhodium	Turning harmful car exhaust fumes into safe gases
Vanadium(V) oxide	Manufacturing sulphuric acid

Redox and reversible reactions

By the end of this spread, you should be able to:
- *recognise that oxidation is the loss of electrons*
- *understand that many reactions are reversible*

Redox reactions

The transfer of an oxygen atom from an oxidizing agent to a reducing agent is a redox reaction (see Spread 3.10).

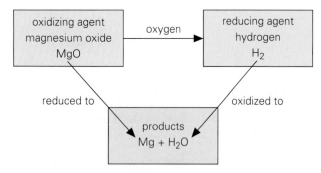

When oxygen combines with magnesium, oxidizing it to magnesium oxide, the two outer electrons of the magnesium atom are transferred to the oxygen atom. The magnesium is *oxidized* and *loses electrons;* the oxygen *gains electrons* as it is *reduced.*

In redox reactions, electrons pass from a reducing agent to an oxidizing agent.

The term redox can be applied to a large range of reactions, including many not involving oxygen:

Reaction	Electrons pass from reducing agent to oxidizing agent		
zinc dissolving in sulphuric acid	$Zn(s)$	$\xrightarrow{2e}$	$2H^+(aq)$
sodium dissolving in water	$Na(s)$	$\xrightarrow{1e}$	$H_2O(l)$
sodium combining with chlorine	$2Na(s)$	$\xrightarrow{2e}$	$Cl_2(g)$
silver plating (electrolysis)	cathode	$\xrightarrow{1e}$	$Ag^+(aq)$
iron displacing copper from copper(II) sulphate solution	$2Fe(s)$	$\xrightarrow{2e}$	$Cu^{2+}(aq)$

Some metals can form more than one type of ion. For example, copper and iron can each form two.

Ion	Name	Example of compound
Cu^+	copper(I) ion	copper(I) oxide: Cu_2O
Cu^{2+}	copper(II) ion	copper(II) oxide: CuO
Fe^{2+}	iron(II) ion	iron(II) chloride: $FeCl_2$
Fe^{3+}	iron(III) ion	iron(III) chloride: $FeCl_3$

So, the (II) in the name shows that the ion has a charge of 2+, and so on.

Here is an example of how electrons are transferred in redox reactions:

Hydrogen peroxide (H_2O_2) will oxidize acidified iron(II) sulphate solution to iron(III) sulphate. The oxygen released from the peroxide does not join on to the iron(II) sulphate. Instead, it removes one electron from each iron(II) ion to give an iron(III) ion:

$$H_2O_2(l) + 2H^+(aq) + 2Fe^{2+}(aq) \rightarrow 2Fe^{3+}(aq) + 2H_2O(l)$$

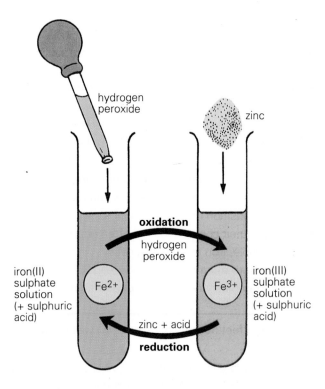

The process can be reversed by treating iron(III) sulphate with zinc and dilute sulphuric acid. The hydrogen formed gives an electron to the iron(III) ion changing it back to an iron(II) ion.

Reversible reactions

A **reversible** reaction is one in which the products can recombine to form the original substances again. It can be shown as a single equation using the symbol:

$$\rightleftharpoons$$

When calcium carbonate is heated strongly, it splits up to form calcium oxide and carbon dioxide gas:

$$CaCO_3(s) \rightarrow CaO(s) + CO_2(g)$$

If the container is sealed, as on the right, the gas cannot escape and some of it reacts with the calcium oxide, changing back to calcium carbonate:

$$CaO(s) + CO_2(g) \rightarrow CaCO_3(s)$$

A time will come when the rate of decomposition of carbonate is balanced by the rate of recombination of the products. An **equilibrium** will exist:

$$CaCO_3(s) \rightleftharpoons CaO(s) + CO_2(g)$$

If the carbon dioxide is allowed to escape, the equilibrium is upset and the reaction proceeds until all the gas has gone.

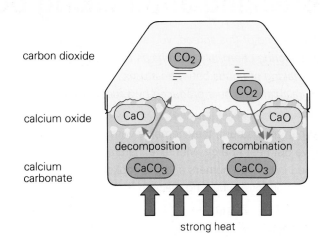

carbon dioxide

calcium oxide

calcium carbonate

decomposition   recombination

strong heat

Manufacture of ammonia

Many of the reactions by which industrial chemicals are made are reversible. But some of the valuable product splits up again and only a small percentage may remain when equilibrium is reached. The percentage remaining is called the **yield**. Producers have to find ways of getting the best possible yield without too much cost. For example:

Ammonia is manufactured by combining nitrogen with hydrogen:

$$N_2(g) + 3H_2(g) \rightleftharpoons 2NH_3(g)$$

Increasing the pressure gives a better yield because it makes it more difficult for the ammonia to split up again. But a higher pressure also means that the cost and maintenance of equipment is greater. The favoured compromise is a pressure of about 150 atmospheres. Decreasing the temperature gives a better yield because this too makes it more difficult for the ammonia to split up again. However, the process is uneconomically slow at low temperatures. The use of an iron catalyst enables a satisfactory yield to be obtained quickly at a moderate temperature (450 °C).

For more on making ammonia, see Spread 3.22.

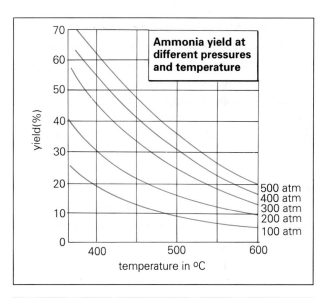

Ammonia yield at different pressures and temperature

yield(%)

temperature in °C

500 atm
400 atm
300 atm
200 atm
100 atm

1 What are *redox reactions* and *reducing agents*?
2 Which substance is oxidized in the reaction between a) zinc and sulphuric acid b) water and calcium c) chlorine and iron?
3 When iron(II) sulphate solution is oxidized a) what does it become? b) what indication is there that the change has taken place?
4 a) What is a *reversible reaction*? b) How can the decomposition of calcium carbonate be reversed? Write the equation for this.
5 When ammonia is manufactured a) what pressure and temperature are used? b) why are these conditions chosen? c) Use the graph above to estimate the yield under these conditions. d) What conditions would give a yield of 70%?

Breaking and making bonds

By the end of this spread, you should be able to:
- describe chemical reactions as the breaking and making of bonds between atoms
- calculate the heat produced by a fuel burning

Before studying this spread, see:
3.8 on bonds
3.12 on chemical equations and moles
4.12 on energy

When things burn, they combine with oxygen and give out heat energy. Methane (natural gas) is the fuel used in bunsen burners and gas cookers. The equation for the burning reaction is:

$$CH_4(g) + 2O_2(g) \rightarrow CO_2(g) + 2H_2O(l) + heat$$

methane   oxygen   carbon dioxide   water

To start the fuel burning, some heat energy must first be supplied by a match or a spark. This **activation energy** breaks down the bonds between the carbon and hydrogen atoms in the methane, and between the two atoms in the oxygen molecule, as shown below. The separated atoms are free to form new bonds between carbon and oxygen (making carbon dioxide) and between hydrogen and oxygen (making water). Much more energy is released in this process than was taken in to break down the old bonds, so the reaction gives out heat – it is **exothermic**. Many chemical changes, besides burning, are exothermic.

A covalent bond is usually shown as a line between the symbols for the atoms joined together.

A hydrogen molecule, H–H, has a **single bond** (two shared electrons).

An oxygen molecule, O=O, has a **double bond** (four shared electrons).

In a chemical reaction, the starting substances are called the **reactants**, the new substances formed are the **products**.

In other reactions, a lot of energy is needed to break down the bonds in the reactants, and only a little is given out by the making of the new bonds of the products. Such reactions take in heat from the surroundings and feel cold – they are **endothermic**.

Energy is **absorbed** when bonds are **broken**.
Energy is **released** when bonds are **formed**.

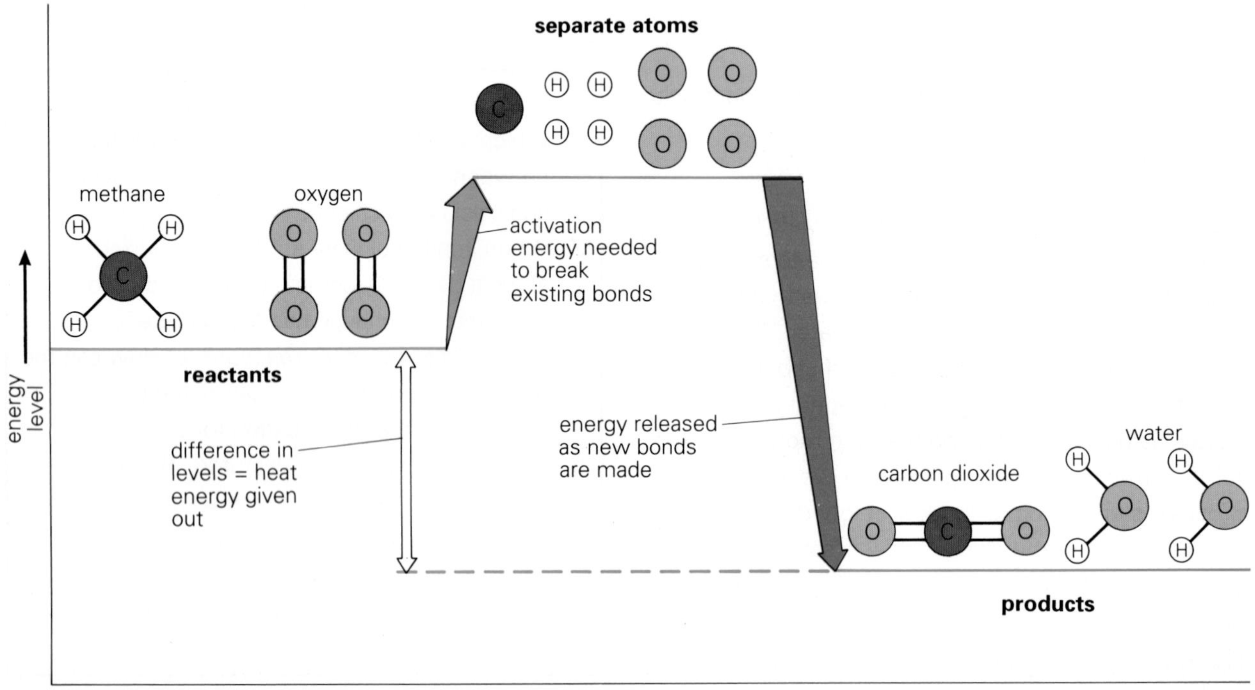

separate atoms

methane   oxygen   activation energy needed to break existing bonds

energy level

reactants

difference in levels = heat energy given out

energy released as new bonds are made

carbon dioxide

water

products

Bond energies

The amount of energy needed to break a particular bond is the same as the amount given out when the bond is made. This is the **bond energy**. It is measured in kilojoules per mole (kJ/mol). The table on the right shows some typical values.

Calculating energy changes

If you know the equation for a reaction and the structures of the substances taking part, you can use bond energies to calculate the overall heat change:

How much heat energy is given out when 24 dm³ of methane is completely burned in oxygen? (24 dm³ is the volume of 1 mole of gas.)

The chart below shows how to calculate the answer:

Bond	Bond energy in kJ/mol
C – C	347
C = C	612
C – H in methane	435
C – H in others	413
C = O	805
O – H	464
O = O	498
H – H	436

– single bond   = double bond

Bond breaking	Bond making
methane	carbon dioxide
4 C–H bonds need 4 x 435 = 1740 kJ	2 C=O bonds release 2 x 805 = 1610 kJ
oxygen	water
2 O–O bonds need 2 x 498 = 996 kJ	4 O–H bonds release 4 x 464 = 1856 kJ
Total energy absorbed = 2736 kJ	Total energy released = 3466 kJ

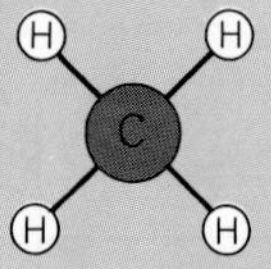

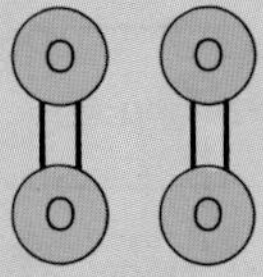

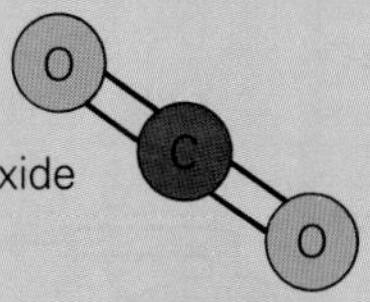

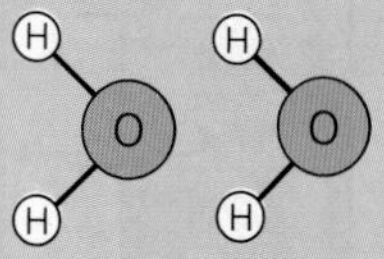

Heat given out in reaction = total energy released – total energy absorbed
$$= 3466 \text{ kJ} - 2736 \text{ kJ}$$
$$= 730 \text{ kJ}$$

---

1 Give an example of a molecule containing a double bond. What does this mean?
2 What is meant by activation energy?
3 Why is heat given out when methane burns?
4 Why are some reactions *endothermic*?
5 What is meant by *bond energy*?
6 Calculate the heat energy given out when 1 mole of propane (C_3H_8) is burnt in 5 moles of oxygen to give 3 moles of carbon dioxide and 4 moles of water. (The structure of propane is on the right.)

Structural formula of propane

From oil and air

By the end of this spread, you should be able to:
* *describe some of the substances in oil and air, and how these can be obtained and used*

Oil and air are mixtures. They contain useful substances which can be turned into new materials by chemical reactions. For example, sustances in oil are used to make plastics like those on the right.

Oil

Oil companies get their oil from the ground. They call it **crude oil**. It was formed from the remains of tiny sea animals and plants which died millions of years ago. It is a mixture of substances called **hydrocarbons**. These are compounds of hydrogen and carbon.

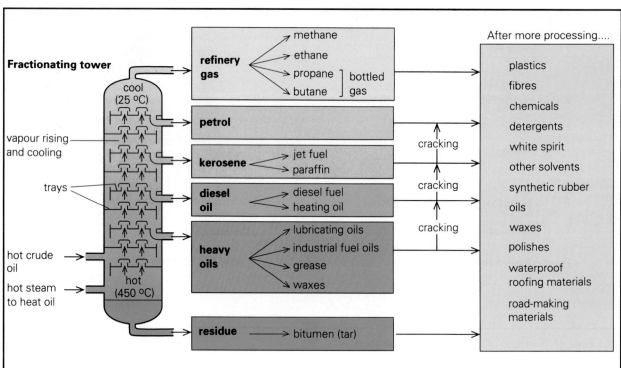

At an **oil refinery**, the different substances in crude oil are separated in a **fractionating tower**. The oil is boiled so that most rises up the tower as vapour (gas). As it rises, it cools. Different substances condense (turn liquid) at different temperatures, and are collected at different levels. The different parts of the mixture are called **fractions**. Separating fractions by boiling is called **fractional distillation**.

Heavier fractions have longer molecules than lighter fractions. Using a chemical process called **cracking**, long molecules can be broken up to make shorter ones. So, if there is too much diesel oil, it can be changed into petrol by cracking.

Short molecules can also be joined together to make longer one. This process is called **polymerization**. Plastics are made by polymerization.

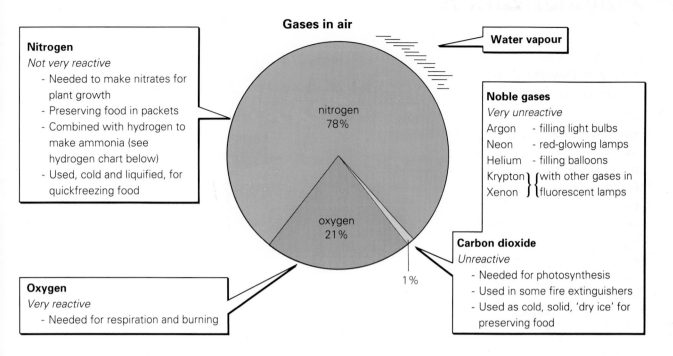

Gases in air

Nitrogen
Not very reactive
- Needed to make nitrates for plant growth
- Preserving food in packets
- Combined with hydrogen to make ammonia (see hydrogen chart below)
- Used, cold and liquified, for quickfreezing food

nitrogen 78%

oxygen 21%

1%

Water vapour

Noble gases
Very unreactive
Argon   - filling light bulbs
Neon   - red-glowing lamps
Helium   - filling balloons
Krypton ⎱ ⎰with other gases in
Xenon   ⎰ ⎱fluorescent lamps

Carbon dioxide
Unreactive
- Needed for photosynthesis
- Used in some fire extinguishers
- Used as cold, solid, 'dry ice' for preserving food

Oxygen
Very reactive
- Needed for respiration and burning

Natural gas, and hydrogen

Many heating systems and cookers use natural gas as their fuel. Natural gas was formed in a similar way to oil. Like oil, it is collected from underground. It is mainly methane, and is similar to the gas collected at the top of an oil fractionating tower.

Methane (CH_4) is industry's main source of hydrogen. The hydrogen is produced when a mixture of methane and steam is passed over catalysts. The chart below shows some of the uses of hydrogen:

Air

Air is a mixture of gases (see chart above). They are separated as follows:

First, the carbon dioxide and water vapour are removed. Next, the remaining air is cooled to –200 °C, so that it turns liquid (apart from neon and helium, which are removed). Then the liquid air is slowly warmed up. The gases boil off at different temperatures and are collected separately. This is another example of ***fractional distillation***.

Combined with nitrogen to make
ammonia
which is used to make nitric acid, fertilizers, and plastics

Combined with chlorine to make
hydrochloric acid
for metal cleaning, dyes, and drugs

Hydrogen
very reactive
- used as a fuel
- used in welding torches
- once used in balloons (hazardous because of fire risk)

Combined with carbon monoxide to make
methanol
which is used to make plastics

Combined with vegetable oil to make
margarine
and other solid fats

---

1 Why are the substances in crude oil called *hydrocarbons*?
2 Name *three* fuels extracted from crude oil.
3 What is *cracking*? Why is it done?
4 Which is the most plentiful gas in air? Give *two* uses of this gas.
5 In this spread and Spread 3.14, there are *three* different ways of producing hydrogen. What are they?
6 Name *two* gases which will make balloons float. Which is the safer? Why?
7 Look at the methods used for separating the substances in oil and in air. In what ways are the two methods similar?

3·21 Polymerization

By the end of this spread, you should be able to:

- *describe how alkenes are made from alkanes and can link to form polymers*

Hydrocarbons with large molecules have higher boiling points than those with smaller molecules (see Spread 3.20). They also burn less easily. To get a more useful fuel, a large hydrocarbon molecule can be cracked by heating with steam or a catalyst. Two smaller molecules are formed. One is still an **alkane** – a hydrocarbon with only single bonds. The other is an **alkene** – a hydrocarbon with at least one double bond in its carbon chain. This is said to be **unsaturated** because extra atoms can add on when the double bond breaks down to a single bond again. By contrast, alkanes are **saturated**.

On the right, molecules are shown using **structural formulae**.

Addition polymers

Short, unsaturated molecules (**monomers**) can join up with each other when their double bonds break open. This is called **addition polymerization**. The very long chain molecule formed is a **polymer** (commonly known as a plastic).

The chart on the right gives some examples of polymers. The diagram above it shows how the simplest alkene, ethene, is changed into polythene. The process can be represented by an equation, in which *n* is a variable number of ethene molecules (up to 4000):

$$n(H_2C{=}CH_2) \rightarrow C_{2n}H_{4n}$$

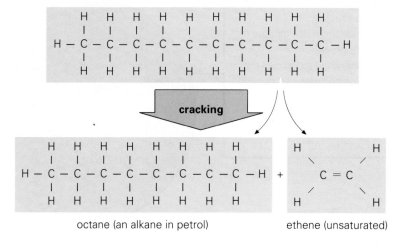

decane (an alkane)

cracking

octane (an alkane in petrol)   ethene (unsaturated)

monomer (ethene)

addition polymerization

part of a very long chain of polymer molecule: poly(ethene)

Monomer		Polymer	Uses
propene	$CH_3, H \diagdown C{=}C \diagup H, H$	polypropene	carpets, crates, rope fibre
chloroethene	$Cl, H \diagdown C{=}C \diagup H, H$	PVC	pipes, flooring, electrical insulation
cyanoethene	$CN, H \diagdown C{=}C \diagup H, H$	acrylic fibre	wool substitute
phenylethene	$C_6H_5, H \diagdown C{=}C \diagup H, H$	polystyrene	insulation, cups, plastic toys

Condensation polymers

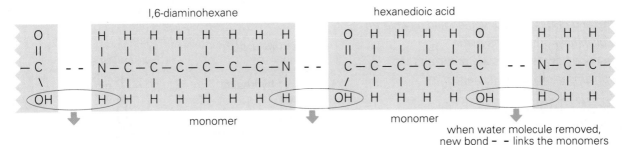

1,6-diaminohexane   hexanedioic acid

monomer   monomer

when water molecule removed, new bond – – links the monomers

Some polymers are formed when two *different* monomers link together by eliminating molecules of water. This is **condensation polymerization**, and it must happen at both ends of each monomer to produce the giant polymer molecule, as shown above.

The polymer nylon 66 can be made from 1,6-diaminohexane and hexanedioic acid. Polyester, used for clothing and videotape, is another condensation polymer.

Starch is a natural condensation polymer which plants make by joining up chains of glucose molecules. It can be changed into glucose again by putting water molecules back in. This is done by warming with dilute acid or the enzyme, amylase.

Proteins are condensation polymers too. They are made when amino acid molecules join up. Like starch formation, the process is easily reversed. In this respect, natural polymers are very different from synthetic polymers like nylon which do not break down easily.

Fibres

Nylon can be moulded into shapes such as gearwheels. In this form, the long polymer chains are intertwined something like tangled string. If nylon is melted and pulled out into fine strands, the chains are stretched parallel to each other, as on the right. These strands are twisted into fibres similar to cotton. Fibres are strong because to snap them you have to break millions of polymer chains all at once.

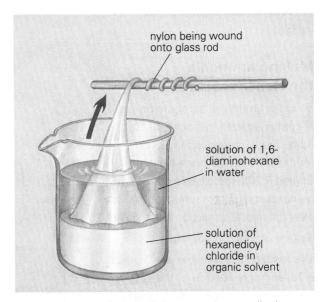

To make nylon 66 in the laboratory, hexanedioyl chloride is used instead of hexanedioic acid

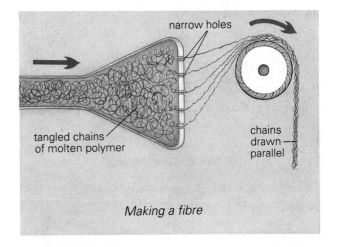

Making a fibre

---

1 What is meant by *cracking*?

2 What are *alkanes* and *alkenes*?

3 What happens to the monomers during a) addition polymerization b) condensation polymerization?

4 How is *nylon 66* made?

5 Name *two* natural polymers. In what way are they very different from synthetic polymers?

6 How are the molecules arranged in a *fibre*?

Ammonia and fertilizers

By the end of this spread, you should be able to:
- explain how ammonia is made
- describe how fertilizers are made and the problems in siting a suitable factory

Plants constantly take in nitrates from the soil. The nitrates must be replaced, either naturally or by adding fertilizers usually made from ammonia (NH_3).

Making ammonia: the Haber process

To make ammonia, nitrogen (from air) is combined with hydrogen, as on the right. The hydrogen is made from methane heated with steam (see Spread 3.20). The gases are then pumped at high pressure over hot iron catalyst, and this reaction takes place:

$N_2(g) + 3H_2(g) \rightleftharpoons 2NH_3(g)$

The reaction is reversible (see Spread 3.18) and only 10-15% of the gases become ammonia. The ammonia is removed as a liquid by cooling the mixture down. The unchanged gases are recirculated until conversion is complete.

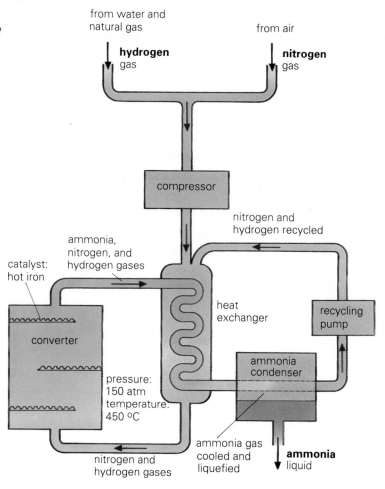

Nitric acid and Nitram

Ammonia can be combined with oxygen to make nitric acid in a series of reactions as shown below:

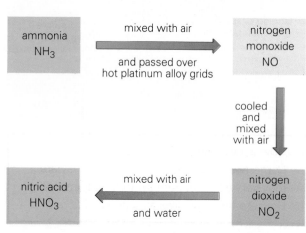

Nitric acid is used to make explosives, plastics, and drugs but much of it is converted into **Nitram** fertilizer. This is done by neutralizing nitric acid with ammonia to produce ammonium nitrate solution:

$HNO_3(aq) + NH_3(g) \rightarrow NH_4NO_3(aq)$
nitric acid   ammonia   ammonium nitrate (solution)

Evaporating the solution leaves crystals of ammonium nitrate – the Nitram fertilizer.

Nitram is often mixed with ammonium phosphate and potassium chloride to produce **NPK compound fertilizers**. These provide nitrogen, phosphorus, and potassium – the three essential elements for good plant growth.

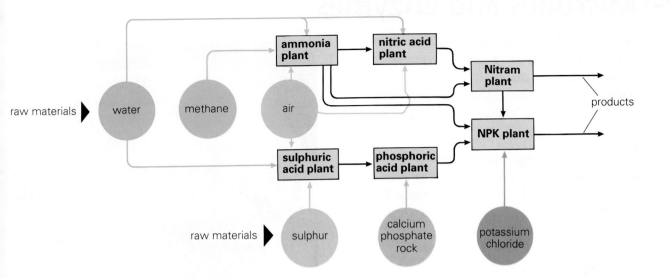

Siting a fertilizer factory

All the chemical processes for making fertilizers are normally carried out on one site. The diagram above shows how the six chemical plants are interlinked.

In choosing a site for the factory both economic and environmental costs have to be considered. To produce fertilizers competitively, the factory should be near:

- a river for a water supply
- a port for sulphur and phosphate supplies
- a natural gas (methane) supply
- a town to supply the workforce
- motorways and railways to transport the product.

The huge area of land needed for the plant will affect the environment greatly. The site should not be in:

- good farmland
- a conservation area
- a built-up area, because of the possibility of accidental leakage of dangerous chemicals.

Wherever the site is situated, emissions of polluting gases (especially nitrogen oxides) must be strictly controlled.

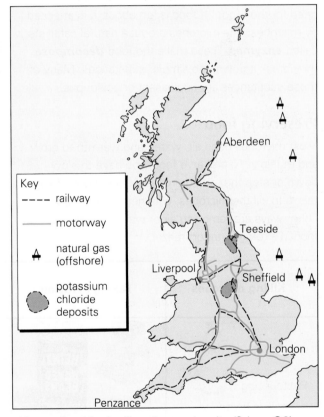

Where should a fertilizer factory be sited? (see Q6)

---

1. What gases are needed to make ammonia? How are they obtained?
2. What is the catalyst in the Haber process?
3. What is *Nitram* and how is it made?
4. Name *three* elements needed for good crop growth.

5. How many separate plants are there in a fertilizer factory? What does each one do?
6. Look at the map above. Decide where you would site a new fertilizer factory. Give the reasons for your choice.

Microbes and enzymes

By the end of this spread, you should be able to:
- *explain why food rots, and how the process can be slowed down or stopped*
- *describe how microbes and enzymes are used in the dairy, brewing, and baking industries.*

Like other living things, microbes (bacteria and fungi) use chemical reactions to make new materials. Some microbes cause food to rot and can threaten health. But without microbes, there would be no cheese, yogurt, beer, or light, airy bread.

Rotting food

Our food can supply microbes with the things they need for their food! If food is left about, it is attacked by microbes. The microbes produce natural catalysts called **enzymes**. These make the food **decompose**: they break it down into simpler substances. Many of these substances are unpleasant or poisonous.

This fruit is over two months old

Preserving food

Most microbes need air, water, and warmth to grow and multiply. To preserve food, you have to slow down or stop the rotting process. One way of doing this is to kill the microbes, with heat for example. Other ways are removing air or water, or keeping the food in a refrigerator or freezer.

Food may be safely preserved in the supermarket, but things can still go wrong in the kitchen. If meat isn't cooked properly, microbes can quickly multiply and you may end up with food poisoning. If food stays warm and uncovered, this too makes it easier for microbes to multiply.

Killing microbes	Taking away air	Taking away water (liquid)	Lowering the temperature
Pasteurizing *milk is heated to 60 °C to kill harmful microbes, then cooled quickly* Sterilizing *liquid is boiled, or chemicals are used*	Bottling Canning *foods may also be heat treated* Vacuum packing	Drying Freezing *turns water solid* Salting Sugaring Pickling *these draw out water*	Refrigerating Freezing

Dairy food

Not all microbes turn food into nasty substances. Cheese and yogurt are made by microbes, or by enzymes taken from microbes. The starter material for these foods is milk. Each enzyme works best at one particular temperature.

Cheese Milk already has microbes in it. They make it go sour and lumpy. The lumpy bits are called **curds**, and adding an enzyme called **rennin** makes them form more quickly. Curds can be changed into cheese by putting in more microbes. Different microbes can be added later to give the cheese blue 'veins', or holes (gas bubbles).

Yogurt To make yogurt, an enzyme is added to milk. It changes sugar in the milk to lactic acid. This makes the milk go thick and slightly sour.

---

1 Sometimes microbes can be *harmful*, sometimes they can be *useful*. Give *two* examples of each.
2 Give *two* reasons why freezing preserves food.
3 Why is it important to defrost a chicken thoroughly before cooking it?
4 Why is it important to cover leftovers and put them in the fridge as soon as possible?
5 How does the dairy industry use microbes?
6 What is *fermentation* and what is it used for?
7 Why are there lots of tiny holes in bread?
8 What are *enzymes* and what do they do? (For a full answer to this question you may need to look back to Spread 2.6.)

Making alcohol

Yeast cells: magnification x3500. Some of the cells are 'budding'. They are about to form new cells.

Yeast is a single-celled fungus. So yeast is made up of microbes. Yeast has several useful enzymes in it. One of these can make the alcohol in wine:

Grape juice contains lots of natural glucose (a type of sugar). An enzyme in yeast can change this into **ethanol** (often called **alcohol**):

$$\text{glucose} \xrightarrow{\text{enzyme}} \text{ethanol} + \text{carbon dioxide}$$

This process is called **fermentation**. As it takes place, the grape juice froths as carbon dioxide gas is given off. Slowly, the sugary grape juice is turned into wine with alcohol.

Beer is also made by fermentation. But the starter materials are grain and sugar, rather than grapes.

Making bread

Yeast is also used in breadmaking.

Dough is a mixture of flour, water, and yeast. The yeast causes slight fermentation, and the bubbles of carbon dioxide gas make the dough swell up. That is why most of the bread you buy is full of tiny holes.

Changes in the atmosphere

By the end of this spread, you should be able to:
- *describe how conditions in the atmosphere can change*
- *describe how the Earth's atmosphere has evolved*
- *describe some of the effects of weathering*

We live at the bottom of an ocean of air called the atmosphere. It is more than 100 km deep, but most of the air lies within 10 km of the Earth's surface. Changes in this air give us our weather.

At sea level, air pressure is about **100 000 pascals (Pa)**. On many weather maps, this would be marked as **1000 millibars (mb)**. It is equivalent to the weight of ten cars pressing on every metre squared! (For more on pressure, see Spreads 4.17 and 4.18).

Winds Air pressure varies slightly from one region to another. Air tends to flow from high pressure to low pressure. This causes winds.
Temperature differences also cause winds. Some places have more sunshine than others. Also, the land warms up more quickly than the sea. As warm air rises, cooler air flows in to take its place. This is an example of **convection** (see Spread 4.13)

Clouds Water on the Earth's surface evaporates: it turns into a gas called water vapour. This happens most quickly when the air is warm and dry.
When water vapour cools, it condenses (changes to liquid). In the air, it turns into billions of tiny water droplets called **clouds**. **Fog** and **mist** are really the same as clouds. In some clouds, the droplets are frozen as ice crystals.

Dew and frost
Water vapour condenses on cold ground or plants to form **dew**. Frozen dew is called **frost**.

Thunder and lightning
Air movements and a temperature difference can make electric charge build up in a cloud. A sudden flow of charge lights up the air as **lightning**. It heats up the air as well. The rapid expansion produces a noise called **thunder**.

Rain, snow, and hail If the tiny water droplets in a cloud stick together into larger drops, they may fall as **rain**. If it is cold, they may form larger ice crystals and fall as **snow**. Sometimes, tiny droplets freeze, and gather extra layers of ice as they are carried up and down by air currents in a cloud. Then they fall as **hail**. Rain, snow, and hail are all called **precipitation**, which means 'something falling'.

Origins of the atmosphere

The Earth was formed about 4500 million years ago, relatively soon after the Sun (see Spread 4.39). When its surface first solidified, intense volcanic activity created an atmosphere of mainly carbon dioxide gas. Today's atmosphere is largely due to the activities of living organisms. For example, the oxygen has come from plants (see Spread 2.2) and the nitrogen mostly from microbes (see Spread 2.27).

Keeping the balance

Here are two of the factors which help keep amounts of different gases in the atmosphere steady:

- Plants take in carbon dioxide and give out oxygen, animals do the opposite. (See also the carbon cycle on Spread 2.27)
- The oceans act as a huge reservoir for dissolved carbon dioxide. About half the carbon dioxide from burning fossil fuels is absorbed by the oceans.

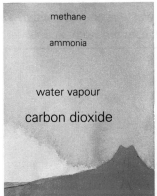
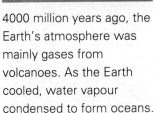
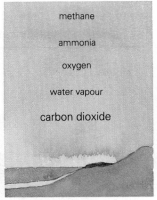
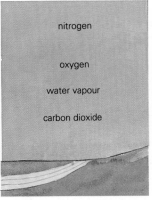
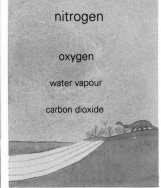

4000 million years ago, the Earth's atmosphere was mainly gases from volcanoes. As the Earth cooled, water vapour condensed to form oceans.

By 500 million years ago, early plants were giving out oxygen, some of which reacted with the methane and ammonia. In time, most of the carbon from carbon dioxide became locked up in sedimentary rocks formed from the skeletons and shells of sea creatures. And microbes were producing nitrogen.

By 200 million years ago, the Earth's atmosphere was similar to that of today. It is now mainly nitrogen (78%) and oxygen (21%).

Weathering

The surfaces of rocks, soil, and stonework can be damaged by the weather. This is called *weathering*. For example, frost will crack pieces from rock (because water expands when it freezes). And rain, which is slightly acid, will eat into stonework.

1 What are clouds? How are they formed?
2 What causes frost? How can frost cause damage?
3 What is meant by *weathering*? Give *two* examples of weathering.
4 Compared with the early atmosphere, why does the Earth's atmosphere now have a) less water vapour b) less carbon dioxide c) more oxygen?
5 How do the oceans help control carbon dioxide levels in the atmosphere?

The effects of weathering

Cycles of change

By the end of this spread, you should be able to:
- *explain how water is used over and over again*
- *describe some of the problems caused by providing a water supply*
- *explain how materials from rocks are used over and over again*

The water cycle

In one way or another, all our water comes from the sea:

Supply problems

There are many problems in supplying tap-water:
- Building reservoirs changes the landscape and affects wildlife.
- Taking too much water from undergound can change conditions on the surface. For example, it can dry out the habitats of some wildlife.
- If sewage or chemical waste is not disposed of carefully, it can contaminate the water supply.

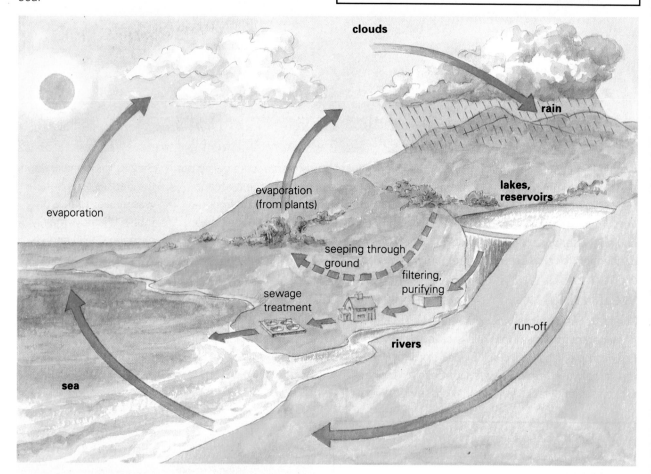

The Sun heats the sea, and water evaporates to become vapour. The vapour rises and condenses to forms clouds. These release their water as rain, often when they are blown over high ground. Rain seeps into the ground, runs into streams and rivers, and flows back into the sea. Also, plants take water from the soil and put some if back into the air as vapour. In this way, water is always being recycled. This is called the **water cycle**.

Humans also take part in the water cycle. We build reservoirs to trap water for our houses and factories. Our waste water and sewage is put back into the sea, though it is sometimes purified first.

Some water takes many thousands of years to complete the cycle. It collects in huge areas of underground, porous ('holey') rock called **aquifers**. These too are used as a source of tap-water.

The rock cycle

Materials from rocks are also used over and over again. This is called the **rock cycle**. It can take many millions of years:

Weathering
Frost, wind, moving ice, or rain loosens the surface of the rock. Chalk and limestone are attacked by the acid in rain.

Erosion
The loose surface is **eroded** (worn away). Wind, sea, rivers, rain - even people's feet - can all cause erosion.

New rock formed
In time, deposited particles are crushed by the weight of materials above, so that they bind together to form new rock.

Rock cycle

Deposition
The tiny pieces of rock get deposited (dropped) as **sediment**. For example, the sea may drop them as mud or sand.

Transport
Eroded particles of rock are carried to other places by wind, flowing water, or moving ice. Sometimes, they just fall.

Soil

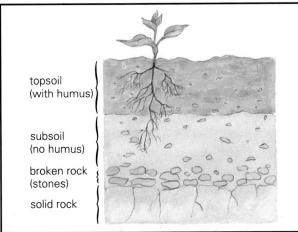

topsoil (with humus)

subsoil (no humus)

broken rock (stones)

solid rock

The effects of wind erosion

Soil is mainly formed from the rock underneath. The rock gets broken up by frost, rain, and expansion caused by the Sun's heat. The bigger fragments are **stones**. The smaller ones become the soil. Topsoil (the top layer) also contains decayed plant and animal remains. This is called **humus**. It is rich in the minerals which plants need for growth.

In some places, rivers deposit tiny rock particles as sediment. If the water retreats, this sediment becomes soil.

1 Explain how water from your tap can end up in a reservoir.
2 Cities have a huge demand for water. List the problems that this can cause.
3 What is *erosion*? What things can cause it?
4 Explain how particles worn away from one rock can end up as part of new rock.
5 Where does soil come from? How is it formed?

The Earth's rocks

By the end of this spread, you should be able to:
- *describe the main types of rock found on Earth*
- *explain how these rocks are formed*
- *describe some uses of these rocks*

The Earth was formed about 4500 million years ago from a cloud of very hot gas and dust around the Sun. Today, it is cooler, and mostly solid. But changes are still happening on its surface and beneath.

The Earth's structure

The core is mostly molten (melted) iron, though the inner core is kept solid by the great pressure there. Deep in the core, the temperature reaches 5000 °C.

The mantle is mostly solid rock made of silicates (compounds of silicon and oxygen). However, heat and pressure keep the material flexible, rather like Plasticine. Driven by heat from the core, it slowly circulates. Near the surface, any release of pressure turns it liquid. This hot, molten rock is called **magma**. Sometimes, it comes out of volcanoes as **lava**.

The crust is the thin, outer layer of the Earth. The continents are the thickest part (up to 90 km). They are mainly made of **granite**. They are like huge rafts which 'float' on the denser mantle underneath. Under the oceans, the crust is thinner (as little as 6 km). It is mainly a rock called **basalt**. In some places, the continental rafts push against each other. Here, the crust buckles and folds, forming mountain ranges.

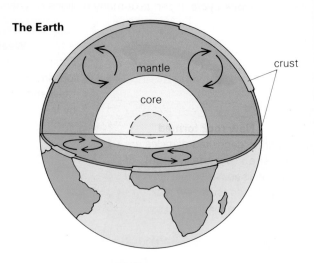

The Earth

Over millions of years, the shape of the crust slowly changes. The continental rafts move. Rocks are worn away by erosion. Pockets of magma become exposed. And rivers and seas advance and retreat.

Rocks in the crust

There are many different rocks in the Earth's crust, but they can be grouped into three main types:

Igneous rocks, such as granite and basalt, are made of tiny crystals. They are formed when molten magma cools and solidifies.

If magma cools *quickly*, the crystals are *small*. This happens when magma is exposed on the surface.

If magma cools *slowly*, the crystals have time to grow, and are *large*. This can happen to magma deep in the crust. It may take thousands of years for a large, pocket of magma to cool and solidify.

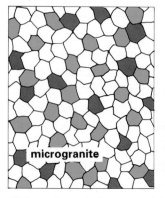

microgranite

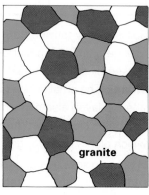

granite

This rock cooled more quickly...   *......than this*

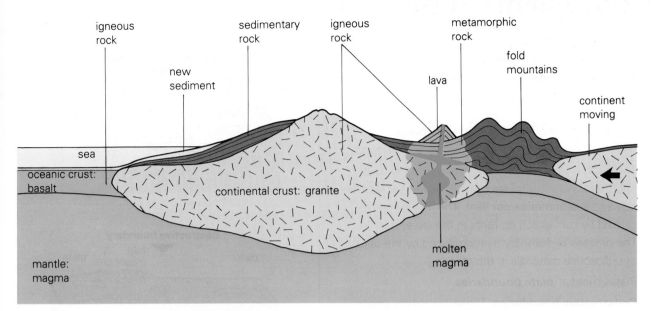

igneous rock • new sediment • sedimentary rock • igneous rock • metamorphic rock • lava • fold mountains • continent moving • sea • oceanic crust: basalt • continental crust: granite • molten magma • mantle: magma

Sedimentary rocks are formed from layers of sediment deposited by seas, rivers, wind, or moving ice. The sediments are compressed as more and more material collects above them. Then they harden, in much the same way as concrete sets. This process can take many millions of years. The layers of rock are called **strata**. You see them in sedimentary rocks such as **sandstone**, **limestone**, and **coal**.

Most sediments are particles of eroded rock. Sandstone is formed from sediments like this. However, some sediments are fragments of shells and bones from sea creatures which lived hundreds of millions of years ago. Limestone is usually formed in this way, though it can also be deposited chemically, like the scale in a kettle.

1 What is *magma*?
2 How are *igneous* rocks formed?
3 How can you tell whether an igneous rock cooled quickly or slowly when it formed?
4 How are *sedimentary* rocks formed?
5 a) Why do you think sedimentary rocks sometimes contain fossils? b) Why would you not expect to find fossils in a lump of granite?
6 What type of rock is *marble*? What was it originally, and how was it formed?
7 Some roofing tiles are made of slate. What would be the the advantages and disadvantages of using a) granite b) limestone instead?

Metamorphic rocks Deep underground, igneous and sedimentary rocks can be changed by heat or pressure or both. They become metamorphic ('changed') rock which is usually harder than the original. Examples include **marble** and **slate**:

Original rock		Metamorphic rock
limestone	$\xrightarrow{\text{heat}}$	marble
shale (mudstone)	$\xrightarrow{\text{pressure}}$	slate

Using rocks

Rocks are our source of minerals, such as diamond and gold. In fact the word 'mineral' really means anything useful that can be mined from the Earth. Here are some more uses of rocks:

Rock	Description	Examples of use
Granite	Very hard, sparkling	chippings, road stone building stone
Limestone	light colour	building/facing stone chippings in cement, concrete
Marble	light colour, hard, smooth	facing stone statues
Slate	hard, but splits into flat sheets	roofing tiles snooker tables

Movements in the Earth

By the end of this spread, you should be able to:
* *describe the theory of plate tectonics*
* *explain how seismic waves give clues about the structure of the Earth*

Scientists use the theory of **plate tectonics** to describe how the Earth's crust moves and behaves:

The Earth's crust (and upper mantle) is made up of huge sections called **plates** which move very slowly – just a few centimetres per year. The movement is caused by convection currents in the lower mantle. The process is driven by heat produced by the decay of radioactive materials in the mantle.

Plates meet at **plate boundaries**:

Constructive boundaries These are mainly under oceans. Plates move apart and get bigger as magma wells up between them to form new oceanic crust. The effect is called **sea-floor spreading** and it produces an **oceanic ridge**. Where rocks are brittle, cracks called **faults** may develop. If rock between faults drops down, a **rift valley** is formed.

Destructive boundaries Plates move together so that one is **subducted** (carried down) under the other. This causes intense heat and volcanic activity. If the sliding is not smooth, there are earthquakes.

Conservative boundaries Plates slide past each other, so their shape is 'conserved' – it does not change. Sometimes, the plates catch on each other. When they jerk free, there may be big earthquakes.

Plate boundaries are the site of many of the world's mineral deposits. The minerals are carried in by hot, high-pressure water and then deposited in cracks.

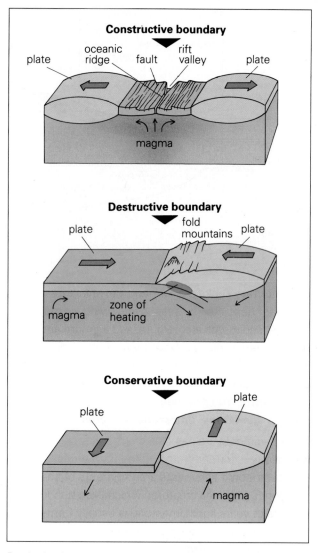

Rocks in the crust can be subducted, melt to form magma, be uplifted, and then solidify as new rock. This is another part of the **rock cycle**:

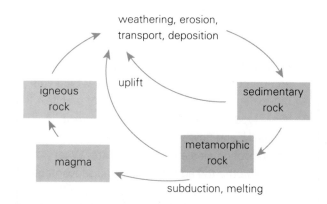

Evidence

* The radioactivity of materials trapped in rocks weakens with time. From this, scientists can work out when the rock solidified (see Spread 4.35). Results show that the crust gets older as you move away from an oceanic ridge – evidence of outward movement.
* By comparing the magnetism in rocks, scientists can work out which rocks were once close. This provides evidence that plates move.

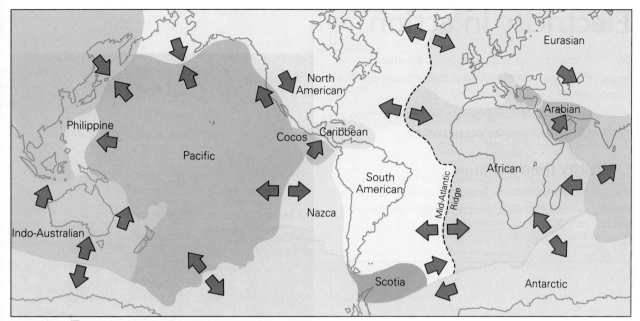

The main plates and directions of movement

Earthquakes and waves

Earthquakes are caused by sudden rock movements in the ground. When they occur, vibrations called **seismic waves** travel outwards from the **focus** (the site of the earthquake):

P-waves are 'push and pull' waves (longitudinal waves, see Spread 4.28). They can travel through solids and liquids deep in the Earth.

S-waves are 'up and down' waves (transverse waves, see Spread 4.28). They are slower than P-waves, and cannot travel through liquids such as molten rock.

L-waves produce a rolling motion. They are the most destructive, but only travel through surface rocks. They are slower than S-waves.

A **seismometer** can detect and measure seismic waves which have travelled many thousands of kilometres from their source. By analysing travel times, scientists can work out what routes the waves must have followed through the Earth. Their results give clues about the Earth's inner structure:

- As rock gets more dense, seismic waves speed up. When their speed changes, they refract (bend) rather like light waves. The curved paths of the waves and the time they take to travel suggest that the Earth has a core which is very dense.
- No S-waves travel through the core. This suggests that the outer part of the core must be liquid.

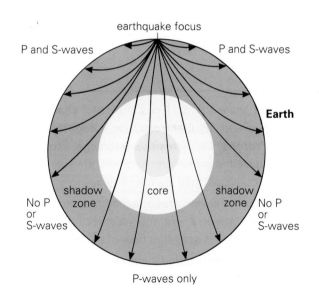

1. Why do earthquakes and volcanoes mainly occur near plate boundaries?
2. What is the difference between a *destructive boundary* and a *constructive boundary*?
3. Which will a seismometer detect first: *P-waves* or *S-waves*? Why?
4. What evidence is there that part of the Earth's core is liquid?

4·1 Electricity in action

By the end of this spread, you should be able to:
- *explain where electric charges come from, and how they affect each other*
- *explain how electric charge can be made to pass through some materials but not others*

Electricity from the atom

Electricity can make cling film stick to your hands. It can travel through wires. And it can light up the sky in a flash. But where does it come from? The answer is the atom:

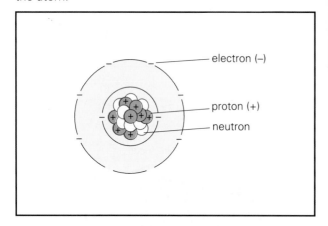

In an atom, there are two types of electric **charge** (see also Spread 3.8).**Electrons** have a **negative** *(−)* charge. **Protons** have a **positive** *(+)* charge. Atoms normally have the same number of electrons as protons, so, overall, they are uncharged.

Electrons do not always stay attached to atoms. When you switch on a light, the 'electricity' flowing through the wires is actually a flow of electrons:

A flow of electrons is called a **current**.
Put another way: a current is a flow of charge.

From conductors to insulators

Conductors are materials which let electrons flow through. In a conductor, some electrons are not very tightly held to their atoms. This means that they are free to move through the material.

Air and water can conduct, but only if they contain *ions* (see Spread 3.8). Ions are charged. In gases and liquids, they are free to move. So they can carry charge from one place to another.

Insulators are materials which do not let electrons flow through. Their electrons are held tightly to atoms, and are not free to move.

Semiconductors are 'inbetween' materials. They are insulators when cold, but conductors when warm. They are used in microchips (See Spread 4.4)

Conductors		Semiconductors	Insulators	
Good	*Poor*			
metals,	human body	silicon	plastics	glass
especially	water	germanium	e.g.	rubber
silver	air		PVC	
copper			polystyrene	
aluminium			Perspex	
carbon				

Static electricity

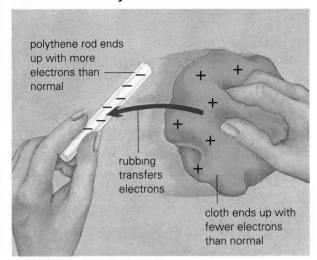

polythene rod ends up with more electrons than normal

rubbing transfers electrons

cloth ends up with fewer electrons than normal

Insulators can become charged when rubbed. People say that they have 'static electricity' on them.

If you rub a polythene rod with a cloth, the polythene pulls electrons from the cloth. The polythene ends up negatively (–) charged, and the cloth positively (+) charged.

If you rub Perspex with a cloth, the effect is opposite: the cloth pulls electrons from the Perspex.

The rubbing action doesn't make electric charge. It just separates charges already there. It works with insulators because, once the charges are separated, they tend to stay where they are.

Forces between charges If charged rods are held close, there are forces between them:

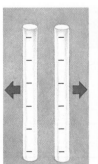 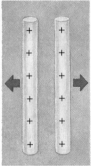 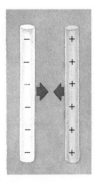

Like charges repel. Unlike charges attract.

A charge will also attract something uncharged. That is why dust is attracted to the charged screen of a TV. Being uncharged, the dust has equal amounts of + and –, so it feels attraction and repulsion. But the attracted charges are pulled slightly nearer the screen, so the force on them is stronger.

Battery and circuit

A **battery** can make electrons move. But there must be a conducting material between its two **terminals**. Then, a chemical reaction inside the battery will push electrons out of the negative (–) terminal and round to the positive (+) terminal.

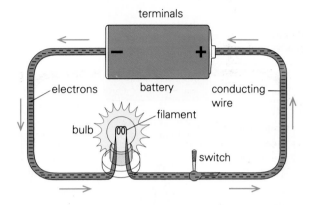

terminals

electrons   battery   conducting wire

bulb   filament

switch

The battery above is being used to light up a bulb. The conducting path through the bulb, wires, switch, and battery is called a **circuit**. As the electrons pass through the bulb, they make a **filament** (thin wire) heat up so that it glows.

There must be a *complete* circuit for the current to flow. If the circuit is broken, the flow of electrons stops, and the bulb goes out. Turning the switch OFF breaks the circuit by separating two contacts.

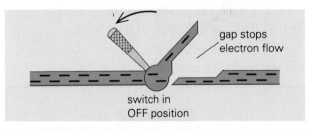

gap stops electron flow

switch in OFF position

1 Which materials are the best conductors?
2 What type of charge is there on an electron?
3 Explain why you think electrons are pushed out of the negative (–) terminal of a battery and not the positive (+).
4 If you rub Perspex with a cloth, electrons are transferred from the Perspex to the cloth. What type of charge does this leave a) on the Perspex b) on the cloth?
5 A circuit contains a bulb, battery, and switch. Explain why the bulb stops working if you turn off the switch.

Batteries and bulbs

By the end of this spread, you should be able to:
* *explain how current and voltage are measured*
* *describe the differences between series and parallel circuits*

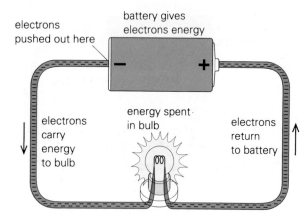

In the circuit above, the battery is *giving* the electrons energy as it pushes them out. The electrons are *spending* this energy when they flow through the bulb. The energy is given off as heat and light. (For more on energy, see Spread 4.12).

Current

Current is measured in **amperes (A)**. The higher the current, the greater the flow of electrons.

Current is measured with an **ammeter**, connected into the circuit like this:

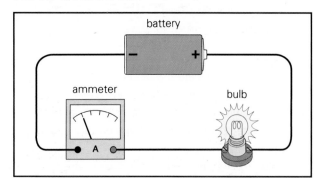

The ammeter can be connected anywhere in this circuit because the current is the same all the way round. Putting in the ammeter doesn't affect the flow of electricity.

Small currents are sometimes measured in **milliamperes (mA)**. 1000 mA = 1 A

Voltage

Batteries have a **voltage** marked on the side. It is measured in **volts (V)**. The higher the voltage, the more energy each electron is given - so the more energy it has to spend as it flows round the circuit.

The voltage of a battery can be measured by connecting a voltmeter across the terminals:

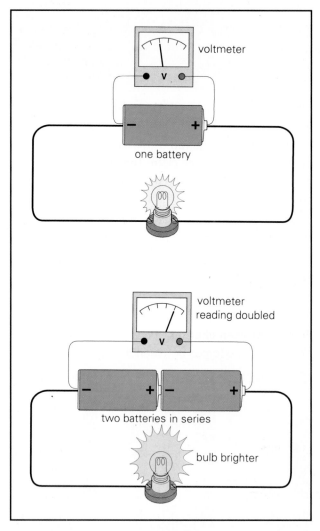

If *two* batteries are connected in **series** (in a line), the total voltage is twice what it was before. Also, the bulb glows more brightly because a higher current is pushed through it:

* The more batteries are connected in series, the higher the voltage.
* The higher the voltage across a bulb, the higher the current flowing though.

Series and parallel

Here are two different ways of adding an extra bulb to the previous circuit:

Bulbs in series The bulbs glow dimly. It is more difficult for the the electrons to pass through two bulbs than one, so there is less current than before.

Adding more bulbs makes them even dimmer. And if *one* bulb is removed, the circuit is broken. So *all* the bulbs go out.

Bulbs in parallel The bulbs glow brightly, because each is getting the full battery voltage. However, together, two bright bulbs take more current than a single bright bulb, so the battery will not last as long.

If one bulb is removed, there is still a complete circuit through the other bulb, so it keeps glowing brightly.

Circuit symbols

It can take a long time to draw pictures of circuits! That is why scientists and electricians prefer to use **symbols**.

On the right, you can see the parallel bulb circuit, drawn using symbols.

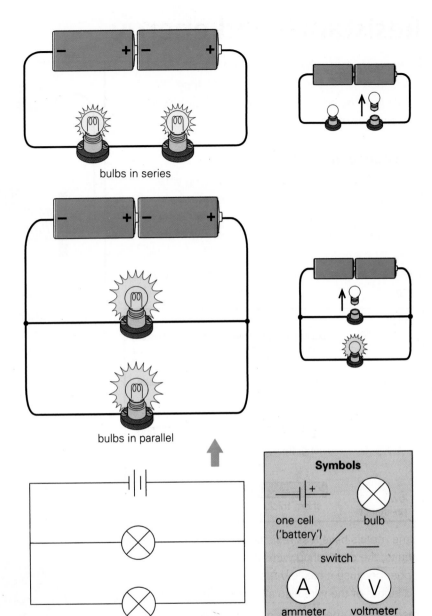

bulbs in series

bulbs in parallel

Symbols

one cell ('battery')   bulb

switch

A ammeter   V voltmeter

1   In the circuit on the right, what type of meter is X? What reading would you expect to see on it?
2   What type of meter is Y?
3   Redraw the circuit, so that it has two batteries instead of one, and Y is across both. What difference would you expect to see in a) the brightness of the bulb b) the reading on X c) the reading on Y?
4   If an extra bulb is added to your new circuit in *series*, how will this affect a) the brightness b) the current?
5   What are the advantages of connecting the extra bulb in *parallel*?

reading
2.0

Resistance and energy

By the end of this spread, you should be able to:
* *describe some of the effects of resistance*
* *calculate the cost of running different electrical appliances at home*

Resistance and resistors

Bulbs do not conduct as well as connecting wire. Scientists say that they have more **resistance** to electricity. Energy has to be spent overcoming this resistance. The bulb gives off this energy as heat and light.

The more resistance there is in a circuit, the lower the current.

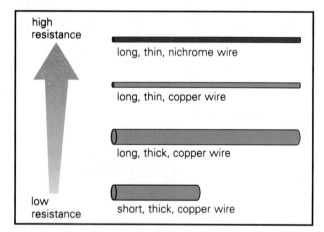

high resistance

long, thin, nichrome wire

long, thin, copper wire

long, thick, copper wire

low resistance

short, thick, copper wire

Some metals have less resistance then others. In circuits, the connecting wires are usually made of copper because it has low resistance. The thickness and length of the wire also affects the resistance.

Resistors are specially designed to provide resistance. They are used in electronics circuits so that the right amount of current is fed to different components (parts) to make them work properly.

resistors

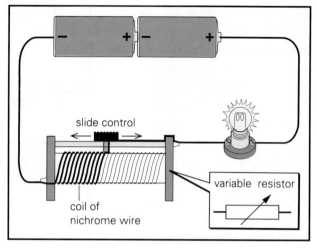

slide control

coil of nichrome wire

variable resistor

Above, a **variable resistor** is being used to control the brightness of a bulb. The variable resistor contains a long coil of thin nichrome wire. Sliding the control to the right puts more resistance into the circuit, so the bulb gets dimmer.

Heat from resistance

Whenever current flows through a resistance, heat is given off. This idea is used in the filament of a light bulb. It is also used in the **heating elements** in **appliances** such as kettles, irons, and toasters. The elements normally contain lengths of nichrome wire.

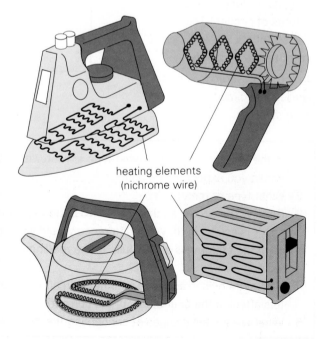

heating elements
(nichrome wire)

Paying for energy

Most appliances get their energy from the **mains**. This energy has to be paid for.

Appliances usually have a **power** marked on them, in **watts (W)** or in **kilowatts (kW)**. There are some examples on the right. The higher the power, the quicker the appliance takes energy from the mains. (For more on energy and power, see 4.12 and 4.24).

The energy supplied depends on the power of the appliance *and* on how long it is switched on for. Electricity Boards measure energy in **kilowatt hours (kW h)**, also called **units**. For example:

If 1 kW is switched on for 1 hour, then 1 kW h of energy is supplied.

If 2 kW is switched on for 3 hour, then 6 kW h of energy is supplied.

These results can be worked out with an equation:

energy	=	power	×	time
in kW h		in watts		in hours

Electricity Boards charge for each kW h (unit). On the right, you can see how to calculate the cost of running an appliance.

If the power is given in watts, you must change this into kilowatts before using the equation.
1 kW = 1000 W. So, for example, 100 W = 0.1 kW.

Reading the meter

Every house has an 'electricity meter'. Really, it is an energy meter. Below, you can see how the meter reading in one house changed over a 24-hour period. To work out how many units (kW h) were supplied, you take one number from the other.

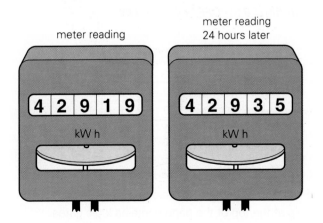

meter reading

meter reading 24 hours later

4 2 9 1 9   4 2 9 3 5

kW h   kW h

Typical powers			
in kW		**in W**	
kettle	2.4	vacuum cleaner	600
fan heater	2	electric drill	500
hairdrier	2	food mixer	500
hotplate	1.5	colour TV	120
iron	1	table lamp	60
toaster	1	stereo	60
1 kW = 1000 W			

Using a 3 kW heater for 4 hours

Energy = power × time
= 3 kW × 4 h
= 12 kW h

The Electricity Board charges 10p per kW h (unit). So,
cost = 12 × 10p
= 120p
= £1.20

1 Why is thick copper better than thin for connecting wire? Why would you not use nichrome for connecting wire?

2 What is nichrome wire used for? Why?

3 In the circuit at the top of the opposite page, what will happen to the bulb if the variable resistor control is moved to the *left*? Why?

The table on this page gives the powers of some appliances. Assume that energy costs 10p per unit:

4 How much energy (in kW h) is needed to run the toaster for 2 hours? What will it cost?

5 What is the cost of running a) the fan heater for 4 hours b) the food mixer for 2 hours?

6 Use the meter readings on the left to work out the cost of the energy supplied.

4·4 Switches and gates

By the end of this spread, you should be able to:
- *explain what sensors are, and how they can be used to control electronic switches*
- *explain how logic gates can be used*

You turn ordinary switches on and off with your fingers. However, ***electronic switches*** are turned on and off by tiny electric currents. Electronic switches are normally in ***microchips*** like the one on the right. A single 'chip' contains several switches.

Sensors

The current which controls an electronic switch comes from a ***sensor***. Sensors detect heat, light, sound, pressure from your finger, or some other ***stimulus*** from the outside world.

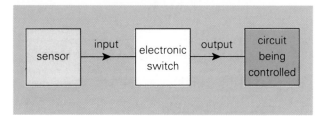

This ***flow diagram*** shows what happens. The electronic switch gets an ***input*** (a tiny current) from the sensor. As a result, it produces an ***output*** (it is either ON or OFF).

Here are some jobs for electronic switches:

Type of sensor	Use of electronic switch
Light sensor *light-dependent resistor*	Turning on light which comes on automatically when dark
Heat sensor *thermistor*	Turning on alarm bell in fire alarm
Pressure sensor	Touch switch on video
Smoke sensor	Turning on bleeper in smoke detector

**microchip
(containing logic gates)**

Electronic switches can only handle tiny currents. So they cannot directly switch on powerful things, like electric motors and alarm bells. To get round this problem, a ***relay*** is used (see the next spread, 4.7). The electronic switch turns on the relay, and this switches on the more powerful circuit.

Logic gates

Switches can be grouped together to make ***logic gates***. Here is a simple logic gate, a box containing two switches in series:

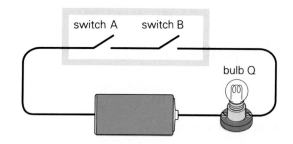

With this gate:
If A *and* B are ON, the bulb is ON,
but if either A or B is OFF, the bulb is OFF.

You can use a ***truth table*** to show the results of all the switch settings. The table uses two ***logic numbers***: *0* for *OFF*, and *1* for *ON* :

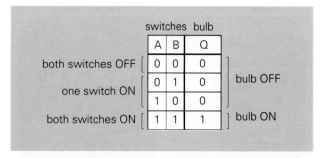

	switches		bulb	
	A	B	Q	
both switches OFF	0	0	0	
one switch ON	0	1	0	bulb OFF
	1	0	0	
both switches ON	1	1	1	bulb ON

Electronic switches are used in most logic gates. The chip at the top of the page contains logic gates.

Here are three types of logic gate:

AND gate

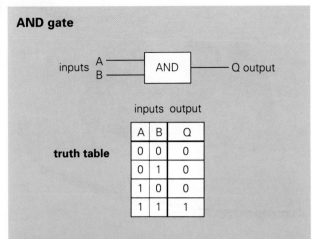

inputs A B — AND — Q output

truth table

inputs		output
A	B	Q
0	0	0
0	1	0
1	0	0
1	1	1

The output is only ON if both inputs are on.
In other words, Q is ON if A *AND* B are ON.

OR gate

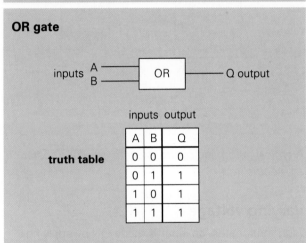

inputs A B — OR — Q output

truth table

inputs		output
A	B	Q
0	0	0
0	1	1
1	0	1
1	1	1

The output is ON if either input is ON.
In other words, Q is ON if A *OR* B is ON.

NOT gate

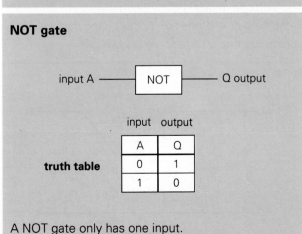

input A — NOT — Q output

truth table

input	output
A	Q
0	1
1	0

A NOT gate only has one input.
The output is ON if the input is OFF, and vice versa.
In other words, Q is ON if A is *NOT* ON.

Using sensors and gates

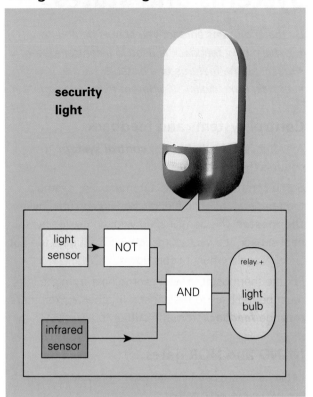

security
light

This security light uses sensors and logic gates. If it is
dark, and someone approaches, the light switches on
automatically.

The *light sensor* detects whether it is light or dark.
The *infrared sensor* detects body heat.

The gates are connected so that:
• the bulb is OFF if the light sensor is ON (in other
  words, if it is daytime).
• the bulb is ON if the light sensor is OFF *and* the
  infrared sensor is ON (in other words, if it is dark,
  and someone is approaching).

The NOT gate 'reverses' the effect of the light sensor.
Without it, the light would only work in the daytime!

1 If you have two ordinary switches in series,
   what type of logic gate do they make?
2 With an OR gate, what input settings are
   needed so that the output is OFF.
3 What effect does a NOT gate have?
4 What type of gate would you use in
   a) a safe which will only open if two buttons are
   pressed at once? b) a door which can be
   opened by either of two buttons?

Systems and states

By the end of this spread, you should be able to:
- *explain how feedback is used in a control system*
- *describe the features of a bistable*
- *explain how 'digital' is different from 'analogue'*

Control systems and feedback

A switch is a simple form of **control system**. It controls the operation of a circuit.

Some control systems are automatic. For example, the temperature of an electric iron is regulated by a **thermostat**. This contains a switch controlled by a heat sensor. It switches the iron OFF if it gets too hot, and ON again when it cools down.

For the thermostat to work, some heat from the iron must be fed back to the sensor. In other words, there must be **feedback** from the output to the input.

NAND and NOR gates

Logic gates are used in many control systems. Here are two more logic gates:

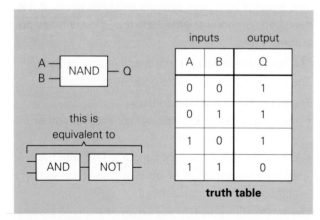

inputs		output
A	B	Q
0	0	1
0	1	1
1	0	1
1	1	0

truth table

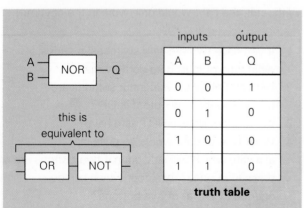

inputs		output
A	B	Q
0	0	1
0	1	0
1	0	0
1	1	0

truth table

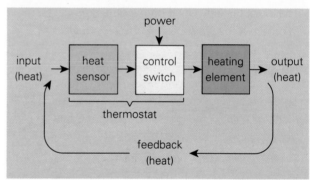

A typical automatic control system: the thermostat on an electric iron

Varying voltage

With most gates, an input is made ON by applying a small positive voltage (such as +5 V). However, in some electronic circuits, a variable voltage is needed. The **voltage divider** below can deliver from 0 to 9 V depending on the position of the sliding contact. The volume control on a radio works like this.

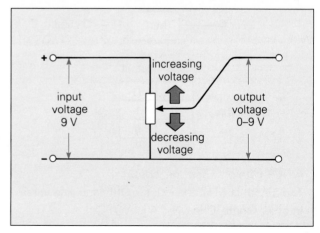

A bistable

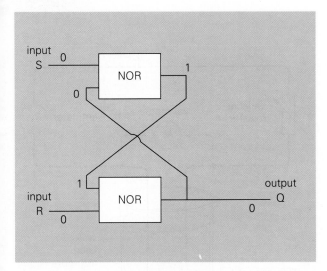

The arrangement above is called a **bistable**. Two NOR gates have been cross-coupled so that the output of each is fed back to one input on the other. This arrangement has a special feature – with both inputs OFF (0), there are *two* possible output states:

- *either* the output is OFF (0) as shown above.
- *or* the output is ON (1).

The bistable can be made to flip from one state to the other. For example if, above, the top input is made ON (1), the bistable flips to the other output state. One brief pulse is enough to make the change. The bistable 'remembers' its new output state. This feature makes bistables very useful in computers, where data is stored in **binary code** as a series of 0s and 1s.

With the bistable above:

- The only way of turning the output ON is to apply a positive pulse to S (the *set* input).
- The only way of turning the output OFF is to apply a positive pulse to R (the *reset* input).

A bistable can have *two* outputs – one from each gate. With just one in use, as above, it is called a **latch**.

Analogue and digital

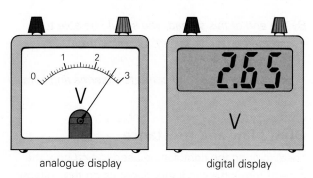

analogue display   digital display

The meters above have different types of display. One has a pointer which can move continuously up a scale. It has an **analogue** display. The other shows its reading as a number. It has a **digital** display. Digital readings are more easily handled by computers.

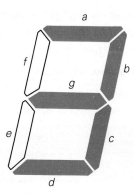

This is how a digital display shows the number '3'. The segments are ON (red) or OFF as follows:

a	b	c	d	e	f	g
ON	ON	ON	ON	OFF	OFF	ON

This sequence can be stored using bistables.

Light-emitting diodes (LEDs) glow when a tiny current passes through. They are often used as the segments in digital displays.

---

1 Explain how feedback is used to stop an electric iron getting too hot or too cold.

2 In the diagram on the left, what would you expect the voltage output to be if the sliding contact is a) at the top of the resistor b) half-way down?

3 Redraw the diagram of the bistable above to show the system in its other possible output state (both inputs should again be zero).

4 Someone claims that a bistable has a 'memory'. What do you think they mean by this?

5 In a digital display like the one above, what values of *a* to *g* are needed for the number '5'?

6 The output, P, of a NOR gate is connected to the input of a NOT gate of output Q. Write a truth table showing possible values of P and Q. What type of gate is the combination equivalent to?

Circuit calculations

By the end of this spread, you should be able to:
- *use the equations linking voltage, current, resistance, and power*
- *calculate voltages and currents in series and parallel circuits*

Ohm's law and resistance

The circuit on the right can be used to find how the current through a conductor depends on the voltage across it. The conductor in this case is a coil of nichrome wire, kept at a steady temperature. The table shows some typical results. Note that:
- If voltage doubles, current doubles, and so on.
- Voltage divided by current always has the same value (3 in this example).

Mathematically, these mean that the **current is directly proportional to the voltage** (provided the temperature does not change).

This is called **Ohm's law**. All metals obey Ohm's law.

The value of voltage/current for a conductor is called its **resistance**. It is measured in **ohms (Ω)**.

$$resistance = \frac{voltage}{current}$$

resistance in Ω
voltage in V
current in A

A **resistor** (e.g. metal wire) has a resistance which increases slightly when the temperature rises.
A **thermistor** (see 4.4) has a high resistance when cold but a low resistance when hot.
A **light dependent resistor** (see 4.4) has a high resistance in the dark but a low resistance in the light.
A **diode** (see 4.11) has an extremely high resistance in one direction but a low resistance in the other.

Useful equations

$$R = \frac{V}{I} \qquad I = \frac{V}{R} \qquad V = IR$$

R = resistance
V = voltage
I = current

Above, the resistance equation has been written using letter symbols and also rearranged in two ways.

If, say, you want to find the voltage that makes a current of 2 A flow through a 3 Ω resistor, use the last equation: $V = IR = 2 \times 3$. So the voltage is 6 V.

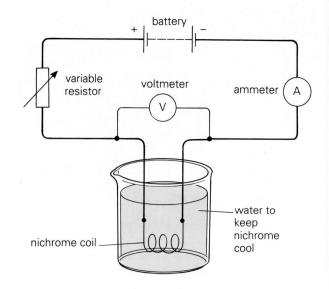

Voltage in V	Current in A	Resistance = $\frac{voltage}{current}$ in Ω
3.0	1.0	3.0
6.0	2.0	3.0
9.0	3.0	3.0
12.0	4.0	3.0

Calculating power

When a battery pushes a current through a resistor, energy is spent. This is given off as heat. The energy spent per second is called the **power** (see 4.24), and measured in **watts (W)**. It can be calculated like this:

$$power = voltage \times current$$

in W   in V   in A

If, say, a resistor has 12 V across it and a current of 2 A through it, the power = 12 x 2, which is 24 W.

The power equation can be written in symbols, and combined with $R = V/I$ to give two other versions:

$$P = VI \qquad P = I^2R \qquad P = \frac{V^2}{R}$$

P = power in W
V = voltage in V
I = current in A

Use whichever is most convenient. For example, if you know the current and resistance, but not the voltage, then use $P = I^2R$ to calculate the power.

Resistors in series

If two resistances, R_1 and R_2 are in series:

Combined resistance $R = R_1 + R_2$

In the circuit on the right, the combined resistance is 9 Ω. Knowing this, you can calculate the current in the circuit. The battery puts 18 V across a combined resistance of 9 Ω. So, current = V/R = 18/9 = 2 A.

In a circuit like this:

• Each resistor has the same current through it (because the same electrons flow through each).
• The voltages across the two resistors add up to equal the battery voltage (because the resistors share the energy from the battery).

You can calculate the voltage across each resistor. The 3 Ω resistor has a current of 2 A through it, so the voltage across it = IR = 2 × 3, which is 6 V. Similarly, the voltage across the 6 Ω resistor is 12 V.

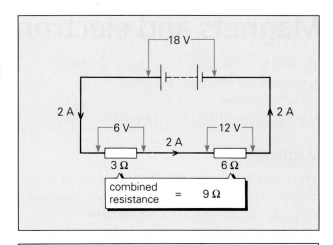

The current arrows show the direction from the + terminal of the battery round to the −. This is called the **conventional direction.** It is the direction you would expect positive charge to move. Electrons have negative charge, so they flow the other way.

Resistors in parallel

The circuit on the right contains two resistors in parallel. In a circuit like this:

• Each resistor gets the full battery voltage.
• The currents through the two resistors add up to equal the current from the battery (because the resistors share the electrons from the battery).

You can calculate the current in each part of the circuit. The 3 Ω resistor has 18 V across it, so its current = V/R = 18/3, which is 6 A. Similarly, the current through the 6 Ω resistor is 3 A. So the total current from the battery is 6 A + 3 A, which is 9 A. As the resistors take 9 A from an 18 V battery, their combined resistance must be 2 Ω. So:

If two resistances, R_1 and R_2 are in parallel:

Combined resistance $R = \dfrac{R_1 \times R_2}{R_1 + R_2}$

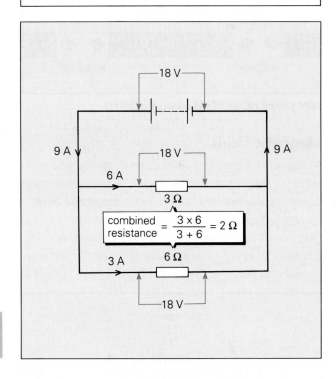

---

1 What is the current through a 4 Ω resistor if the voltage across it is a) 8 V b) 12 V c) 2 V?

2 When a 6 V battery is connected across a resistor, the current is 2 A. Calculate a) the resistance b) the power output c) the power output if the current doubles (there is no resistance change).

3 A 24 V battery is connected to resistors of 6 Ω and 12 Ω in series. Calculate a) the combined resistance b) the current in the circuit.

4 If the resistors in question 3 are in parallel, calculate a) the current though each b) the current through the battery c) the combined resistance.

Magnets and electromagnets

By the end of this spread, you should be able to:
- describe the effects of magnets and electromagnets
- explain some of the uses of electromagnets

Magnets

A few metals are **magnetic**. They are attracted to magnets and can be magnetized. The main magnetic metals are iron and steel (but not stainless steel).

The force from a magnet seems to come from two points near the ends. These are called the **north pole (N)** and the **south pole (S)** of the magnet.

When the poles of a magnet are brought close, you can feel a force between them:

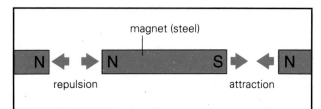

Like poles repel. Unlike poles attract.

Magnetic fields

A magnet will push or pull on other magnets, and attract unmagnetized pieces of iron and steel nearby. Scientists say that the magnet has a **magnetic field** around it. You can use a **compass**, to see the direction of the forces from this field. (A compass is a tiny magnet which is free to turn on a spindle and line up with the field.)

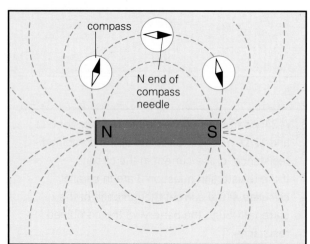

Electromagnets

If a current flows through a wire, there is a magnetic field around the wire. All currents produce a magnetic field. The effect is used in an **electromagnet**.

The electromagnet below produces a field rather like the one around a bar magnet. Without the iron **core**, it would still produce a field, but the iron makes the field much stronger. The field is even stronger if
- the current is increased
- there are more turns on the coil

The iron core becomes magnetized when the electromagnet is switched on. It *loses* its magnetism when the electromagnet is switched off. However, a steel core would *keep* its magnetism. This idea is used to make magnets.

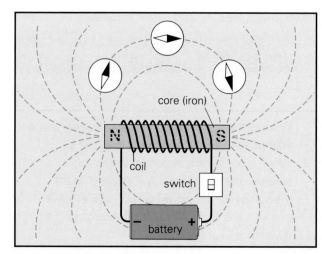

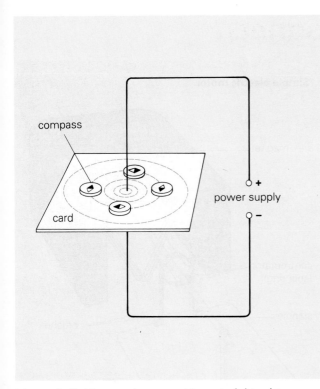

Magnetic field around a current in a straight wire.

Using electromagnets

These devices make use of electromagnets:

Relay This is a switch operated by an electromagnet. With a relay, it is possible to use a tiny switch with thin wires to turn on the current in a much more powerful circuit - for example, a mains circuit with a big electric motor in it.

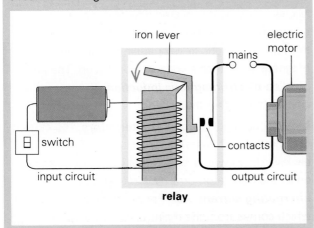

How it works If you switch on the current in the input circuit, the electromagnet pulls on an iron lever. This closes two contacts in the output circuit.

Loudspeaker This has a cone, usually made of paper, which makes the air in front of it vibrate. When these vibrations reach your ears, you hear them as sound (see also Spread 4.26).

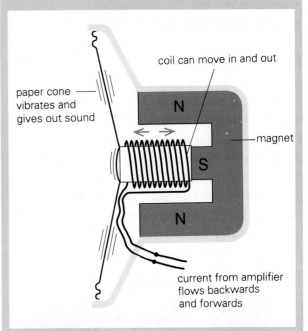

How it works The cone is attached to a coil which is in the field of a magnet. The **amplifier** in your radio or stereo gives out a current which flows backwards, forwards, backwards, forwards..... and so on, through the coil. The coil pushes and pulls on the magnet. This makes the coil move in and out, so the cone vibrates.

1 How can you show that there is a magnetic field around a magnet?
2 What changes would you make to an electromagnet to give it a stronger pull?
3 Describe how you could magnetize a steel nail.
4 Describe the magnetic field pattern around the current through a long, straight wire.
5 Explain why, with a relay, it only takes a small current to switch on an electric motor, even though the motor takes a big current.
6 Explain why a loudspeaker uses current which goes backwards, forwards, backwards, forwards ... and so on.

Turning and changing

By the end of this spread, you should be able to:
- explain how a simple electric motor works
- explain how electricity is generated
- explain what transformers can be used for

Electric motors

A current produces a magnetic field, so it feels the force of a magnet. In an electric motor, this force is used to produce a turning effect.

The diagram on the right shows a simple electric motor. The motor has a coil which can spin between the poles of a magnet. The coil is supplied with current through two contacts called **brushes**.

The current makes the coil become an electromagnet. Its poles feel forces from the poles either side. The coil flips round until *unlike* poles are facing.....

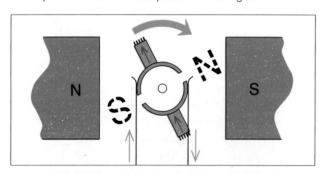

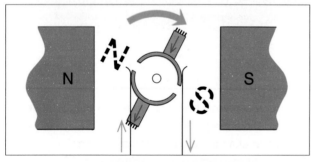

.....but as the coil passes through the vertical, the **commutator**, reverses the current. This reverses the poles of the coil. Now, *like* poles are facing each other, and repelling. So the coil flips round another half-turn until *unlike* poles are facing. Then the commutator reverses the current again....... and so on. In this way, the motor keeps turning.

Practical motors often use electromagnets rather than ordinary magnets. Also, for smoother running, they usually have several coils set at different angles.

Simple electric motor

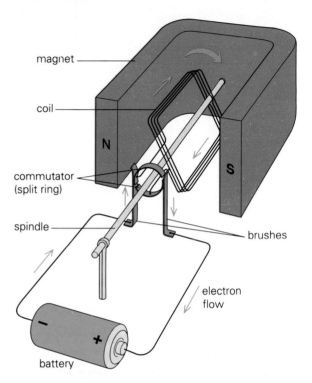

Generators, AC, and DC

If you take a simple electric motor, remove the battery, replace it with a meter, and spin the coil, the motor *produces* a current. It has become a **generator**.

Michael Faraday discovered how to generate electricity, in 1831. He found that whenever wires cut through a magnetic field, or are in a changing magnetic field, then a voltage is produced. The effect is called **electromagnetic induction**. The faster the change, the higher the voltage.

Most modern generators are **alternators**. The current they produce *alternates* in direction: it flows backwards, forwards, backwards, forwards ....and so on as the generator turns. Current like this is called **alternating current (AC)**. For example, the electricity which comes from the mains is AC. It flows backwards and forwards 50 times every second. In some equipment, this causes a slight hum.

The current from a battery always flows in the same direction. It is called **direct current (DC)**.

Simple alternator

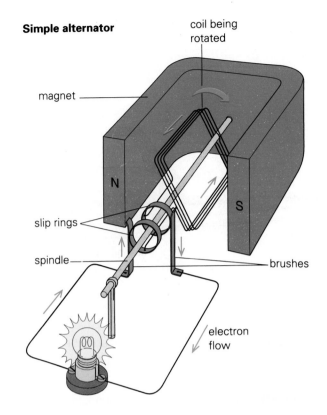

In the alternator above, the brushes rub against two metal *slip rings*. As the coil faces first one way and then the other, the current generated in the coil flows backwards and then forwards. This makes alternating current flow through the bulb.

Mains electricity comes from huge alternators in power stations (see Spreads 4.14 and 4.15). The alternators have fixed coils round the outside with rotating electromagnets in the middle.

Alternator in a power station

Transformers

Transformers can change the voltage of an alternating current. For example, they can be used to reduce the 230 volts mains voltage to the 9 volts or so needed for the electronic circuits in radios, cassette players, and video games.

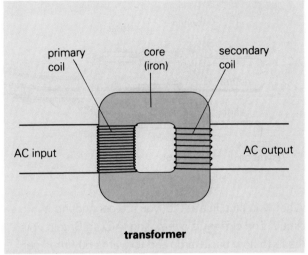

transformer

Transformers make use of Faraday's discovery that a changing magnetic field can generate a voltage. The *primary coil* is as an electromagnet. Connected to an AC supply, it produces an alternating magnetic field. This generates AC in the *secondary coil*.

For the right output voltage, the coils have to be carefully chosen. For example, if the number of secondary turns is half the number of primary turns, then the output voltage is half the input voltage.

A transformer alone is not enough to power low-voltage electronic circuits. Extra components are needed to change the transformer's AC output into the DC needed by the circuits.

---

1   In an electric motor, what job is done by
    a) the brushes b) the commutator?
2   Suggest *three* ways in which you could make an electric motor give a stronger turning effect.
3   What is the difference between *alternating current* and *direct current*? Which type comes from a) a battery b) the mains c) an alternator?
4   In a simple alternator a) how is the current generated? b) what are the slip rings for?
5   What are transformers used for? Which type of current do they use, *AC* or *DC*?

Mains electricity

By the end of this spread, you should be able to:
- *describe the features of the mains electricity supply, including those which make it safe*

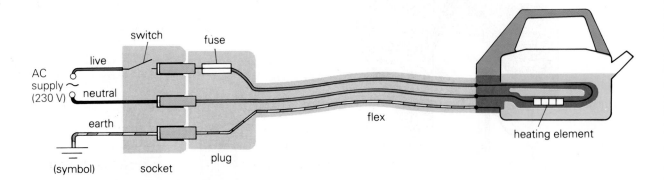

When you plug in a kettle, you are connecting it into a circuit. The current is alternating (AC). In Britain, it is made to flow backwards and forwards 50 times per second. In this case, the **mains frequency** is 50 Hz. Mains voltage in Britain is 230 V.

The live wire goes alternately – and + as electrons are pushed and pulled round the circuit.

The neutral wire is kept at zero voltage by the Electricity Board.

The switch is fitted in the live wire. This is to make sure that none of the wire in the flex is live when the switch is off.

The fuse is a piece of thin wire which overheats and melts if too much current flows through. Like the switch, it is placed in the live wire.

The earth wire is a safety wire. It connects the metal body of the kettle to a conductor which is kept at zero voltage. If, say, the live wire comes loose and touches the metal body, a current flows to earth, blows the fuse, and breaks the circuit. This means that the kettle is then safe to touch.

Appliances with an insulating plastic case do not usually have an earth wire. As their flex is also insulated, they are **double insulated**.

Three-pin plug

In the UK, appliances such as kettles are connected to the mains using a three-pin plug. For safety, this must be wired up correctly. It is also important that a fuse of the correct value is fitted.

Plugs are normally fitted with 3 A or 13 A fuses. The value tells you the current needed to 'blow' the fuse.

If a kettle takes a current of 10 A, its plug should be fitted with a 13 A fuse. The fuse should always be more than the actual current, but as close to it as possible. For example a TV taking 0.5 A will work perfectly well with a 13 A fuse. But if a fault develops, the circuits could overheat and catch fire without blowing the fuse.

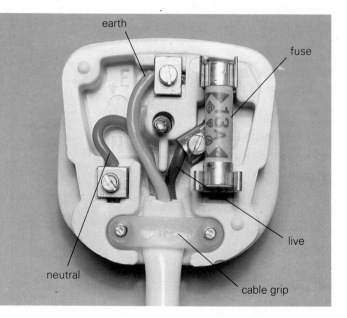

RCCB

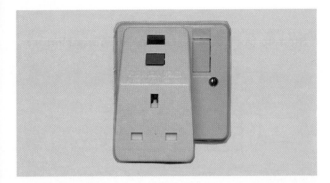

This 'power breaker' plug is a **residual current circuit breaker** (**RCCB**). It compares the currents in the live and neutral wires. They should be the same. If they are different, then current must be flowing to earth – perhaps through someone touching a faulty wire. The RCCB senses the difference and switches off the power before any harm can be done.

Two-way switches

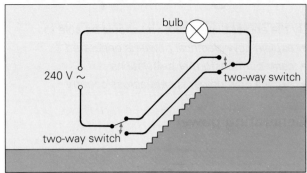

In most houses, you can turn the landing light on or off using upstairs or downstairs switches. These have two contacts instead of one. They are **two-way switches**. In the diagram, if both switches are up or down, then a current flows through the bulb. But if one is up and the other is down, the circuit is broken. Each switch reverses the effect of the other.

Circuits round the house

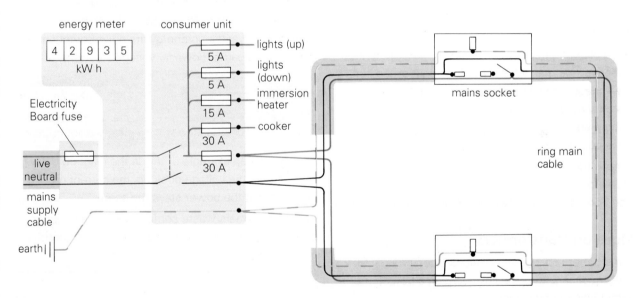

In a house, the Electricity Board's cable branches into several parallel circuits. These carry power to the lights, cooker, immersion heater, and mains sockets. Each circuit passes through a fuse or circuit breaker (RCCB) in the **consumer unit** ('fuse box'). Above, the mains sockets are connected to a **ring main**. This is a cable which begins and ends at the consumer unit. The advantage is that thinner cable can be used as there are two conducting routes to each socket.

1 In mains circuits a) in which wire is the switch fitted, and why? b) why do metal appliances need an earth wire? c) what is the advantage of connecting the sockets to a ring main?
2 A vacuum cleaner has a power of 460 W.
   a) What current does it take from the mains?
   b) What fuse should its plug have, 3 A or 13 A?
   c) Why would you *not* fit a 13 A fuse to a 60 W lamp?

Passing on the power

By the end of this spread, you should be able to:
* explain how electrical power is generated
* carry out transformer calculations
* explain how power is sent across country

Generating power

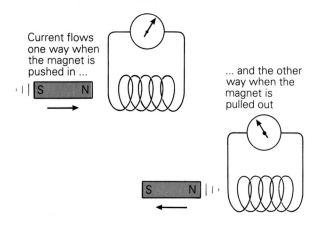

Current flows one way when the magnet is pushed in ...

... and the other way when the magnet is pulled out

In the experiment above, a small voltage is generated whenever the magnet is moved in or out of the coil. The voltage is increased if:
* a stronger magnet is used
* the magnet is moved faster
* the coil has more turns

Moving the magnet in and out generates AC. The alternators in power stations use a similar principle (see Spread 4.8), but they have magnets which rotate.

More on transformers

Transformers change AC voltages (see Spread 4.8). This equation shows the link between a transformer's output and input voltages:

$$\frac{V_2}{V_1} = \frac{n_2}{n_1}$$

V_2 = output voltage
V_1 = input voltage
n_2 = output turns
n_1 = input turns

Applying this to the transformer on the right:

$$\frac{24}{12} = \frac{1000}{500}$$

This transformer increases voltage. It is a **step-up** transformer. Some transformers are **step-down**.

Step-up transformer	Step-down transformer
Symbol:	Symbol:
Turns on output coil more than turns on input coil	Turns on output coil less than turns on input coil
Output voltage more than input voltage	Output voltage less than input voltage

Transformer power

Power is the energy supplied per second. It is measured in **watts (W)** (see Spread 4.6). If a transformer wastes no energy, its power output and input are the same. Power = voltage x current. So:

$$V_2 \times I_2 = V_1 \times I_1$$

(power output)   (power input)

V_2 = output voltage
V_1 = input voltage
I_2 = output current
I_1 = input current

You can see an example of this in the diagram below. Note that as the voltage goes *up*, the current must go *down* so that the power stays the same.

Real transformers waste some power. Their copper coils have resistance. Also, the changing magnetic field generates currents in the iron core.

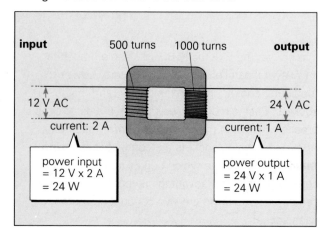

input   500 turns   1000 turns   output

12 V AC   24 V AC

current: 2 A   current: 1 A

power input
= 12 V x 2 A
= 24 W

power output
= 24 V x 1 A
= 24 W

Power across country

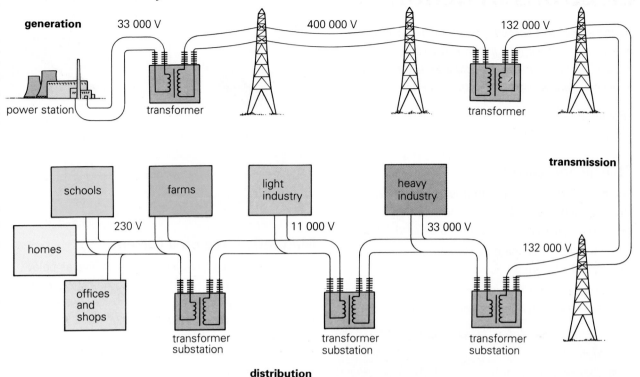

generation

33 000 V   400 000 V   132 000 V

power station   transformer   transformer

transmission

schools   farms   light industry   heavy industry

homes   230 V   11 000 V   33 000 V   132 000 V

offices and shops

transformer substation   transformer substation   transformer substation

distribution

Power stations pass their power to a national distribution network called the **Grid**. If one region needs more electricity it can come from power stations in other regions. Power is normally sent across country by overhead cables. Transformers step up the voltage before the power is passed to the cables. At the far end, more transformers step down the voltage before the power reaches consumers.

On the left, you can see why the voltage is stepped up before transmission. *Increasing* the voltage *reduces* the current, so that thinner, lighter, and cheaper cables can be used to carry the same amount of power.

In areas of outstanding natural beauty like the one on the right, the transmission cables are put underground. But this is very expensive.

1 In an alternator, a magnet is rotated inside a coil. Give *three* ways of increasing the output voltage.

2 A transformer has 2000 turns on its input coil and 200 turns on its output coil. It is being used to light a bulb, and is taking a current of 0.2 A from the 230 V mains. No power is being wasted:
   a) Is the transformer *step-up* or *step-down*?

Calculate the b) output voltage c) input power d) output power e) output current.

3 Why is mains power transmitted across country at high voltages?

4 100 kW of power is to be sent along a transmission cable. What is the current in the cable if the power is sent at a) 1 kV b) 100 kV?

145

Electrons in action

By the end of this spread, you should be able to:
- *explain how charge, current, and voltage are linked*
- *describe how a magnetic field affects a current*
- *describe some uses of electron beams*

For information about charge flow during electrolysis, see Spreads 3.13–3.15.

Charge and current

Charge is measured in **coulombs** (C). 1 C is the amount of charge on 6 million million million electrons! However the coulomb is defined like this:

I coulomb (C) is the charge which passes when a current of 1 ampere (A) flows for I second (s).

So, if a current of 3 A flows for 2 s, a charge of 6 C passes. There is an equation for working this out:

$$Q = I \times t$$

Q = charge in C
I = current in A
t = time in s

Energy, charge, and voltage

Energy is measured in **joules** (**J**) (see Spread 4.12). There is a link between energy and voltage:

If the battery voltage is 12 V, then 12 J of energy are given to each coulomb of charge pushed out.

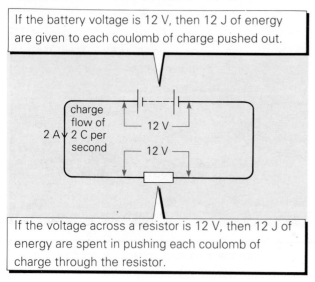

charge flow of 2 C per second

2 A

12 V

12 V

If the voltage across a resistor is 12 V, then 12 J of energy are spent in pushing each coulomb of charge through the resistor.

Capacitors and diodes

These are used in electronic circuits. **Capacitors** store small amounts of charge. They allow AC to pass through but block DC. **Diodes** let current through in one direction but not the other.

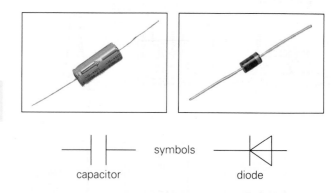

symbols

capacitor   diode

Magnetic force on a current

If a current passes through a magnetic field as below, there is a force on it. The force becomes stronger if
- the current is increased
- a stronger magnet is used.

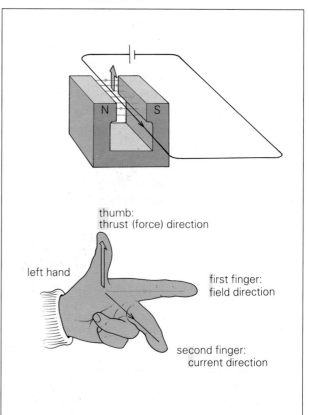

thumb:
thrust (force) direction

left hand

first finger:
field direction

second finger:
current direction

The direction of the force is given by **Fleming's left hand** rule as shown above. When using the rule:
- The current direction is the *conventional* direction (see Spread 4.6).
- The field direction is from the N to S pole.

The oscilloscope (CRO)

With a 'cathode ray' **oscilloscope (CRO)**, you can study sound waves and AC voltages. In a CRO, a beam of electrons is used to produce a trace on a screen.

The electrons come from an **electron gun** containing an oxide-coated metal plate. This is heated by a filament. The heat drives electrons from the plate. The effect is called **thermionic emission**.

The electrons (–) are accelerated towards the tube screen by a high voltage (about 1000 V) between the **cathode (–)** and **anode (+)**.

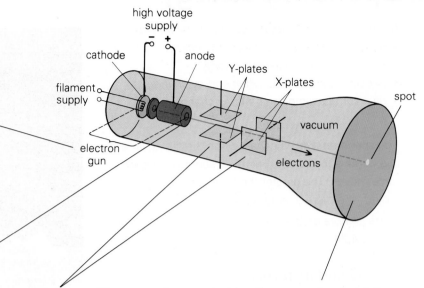

The **Y-plates** and **X-plates** are used to move the electron beam up and down and side to side. To do this, different voltages are put across each set of plates so that the electrons are repelled by the – plate and attracted towards the +. Scientists say that the beam is being bent by an **electric field**.

The screen is coated with a **fluorescent** material: it glows when the electrons hit it. As a result, you see a bright spot on the screen.

TVs also use moving electron beams to make the screen glow. However, the beams are bent by electromagnets.

X-rays

If fast-moving electrons lose speed very quickly, they give off X-rays (see Spread 4.31). This effect is used in an **X-ray tube**.

A very high voltage (10 000 V or more) is used to accelerate electrons along the tube. The electrons hit a metal target, giving off X-rays as they do so. A higher voltage means faster electrons, and shorter wavelength X-rays which are more penetrating.

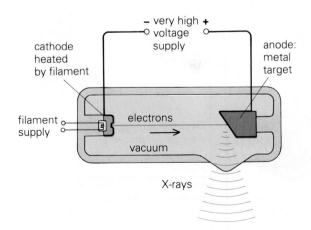

1 If a 6 V battery delivers 4 A for 3 seconds
   a) how much charge leaves the battery?
   b) how much energy is given to this charge?
2 If, in a CRO, the top Y-plate is negative (–) and the bottom one is positive (+), which way will the electron beam bend? Why?
3 In an X-ray tube, what is the effect of using a higher voltage?
4 If the electromagnet below is switched on, which way will the electron beam bend? (The direction of electron flow is opposite to the conventional direction.)

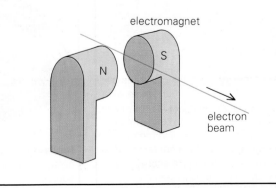

Spending energy

By the end of this spread, you should be able to:
* describe some different forms of energy
* name a unit for measuring energy
* explain what happens when energy changes form
* give some examples of energy changing form

You spend **energy** when you climb the stairs, lift a bag, or hit a tennis ball. Energy is spent whenever a force moves. The greater the force, and the further it moves, the more energy is spent.

There is more on the link between force and energy in Spread 4.24.

Energy and its forms

Energy has several different forms:

Kinetic energy means 'movement energy'. A moving thing has energy because it can make forces move when it hits something else.

Potential energy means 'stored energy'. Lift something up, and you give it potential energy. The energy is stored until you drop it. Stretch a spring, and you give it potential energy.

Chemical energy This is really another type of stored energy. Foods, fuels, and batteries have chemical energy. The energy is released by chemical reactions.

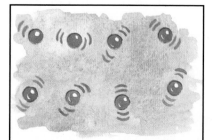

Heat energy Everything is made of particles (such as atoms). These are constantly on the move, so they have energy. The higher the temperature, the faster they move, and the more energy they have. If a hot thing cools down, its particles lose energy. The energy given out is called heat.

Radiant energy Light and sound carry energy as they radiate from their source.

Electrical energy Electrons have electrical energy when they are pushed out from the terminal of a battery.

Nuclear energy is stored in the nucleus of the atom. It is released by nuclear reactions.

Energy is measured in **joules (J)**.

On the right, you can see some examples of different amounts of energy. Large amounts are sometimes measured in **kilojoules (kJ)**. 1 kJ = 1000 J.

Energy chains

Just like money, energy doesn't vanish when you spend it. It just goes somewhere else! Below is an example of how energy can change from one form to another. Scientists call it an **energy chain**:

In every energy chain, the *total amount* of energy stays the same. Scientists express this idea in the **law of conservation of energy**:

Energy can change into different forms, but it cannot be made or destroyed.

Typical energy values	
Potential energy:	
stretched rubber band	1 J
you, on top of a step-ladder	500 J
Kinetic energy:	
kicked football	50 J
small car at 70 mph	500 000 J
Heat energy:	
hot cup of tea	150 000 J
Chemical energy:	
torch battery	10 000 J
chocolate biscuit	300 000 J
litre of petrol	35 000 000 J

In any chain, some energy is always wasted as heat. For example, you give off heat when you exercise, which is why you sweat! However, the *total* amount of energy (including the heat) stays the same.

1. Give an example of something which has a) kinetic energy b) chemical energy c) potential energy.
2. A fire gives out 10 kJ of energy. What is this in joules?
3. What type of energy is supplied to a car engine? What happens to this energy?
4. Describe the energy changes which take place when you apply the brakes on a moving cycle.
5. Describe the energy changes which take place when you throw a ball up into the air.
6. Scientists say that energy can 'never be destroyed'. Explain what they mean.

Energy changers

Here are some energy changers in action:

Energy input	Energy changer	Energy output
electrical energy →	heating element	→ heat energy
sound energy →	microphone	→ electrical energy
electrical energy →	loudspeaker	→ sound energy
kinetic energy →	brakes	→ heat energy

Heat on the move

By the end of this spread, you should be able to:
* describe three ways in which heat can travel
* explain how different materials can be used to cut down the movement of heat

Everything is made of particles (such as atoms) which are constantly on the move. If something hot cools down, its particles lose energy. The energy given out is called **heat**. It can travel in three ways:

Conduction

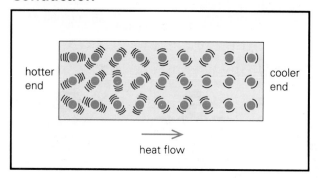

heat flow

If one end of a bar is heated, its particles vibrate faster. In time, their extra movement is passed on to particles right along the bar. Scientists say that heat is travelling by **conduction**.

Metals are the best conductors of heat. This is because their atoms have some 'loose' electrons which can quickly carry energy from one part of the metal to another. These same electrons also make metals good conductors of electricity.

Poor conductors of heat are called **insulators**.

Good conductors	Insulators (poor conductors)	
metals	glass	
especially:	water	
silver	plastic	wool
copper	wood	fibrewool
aluminium	materials with air trapped in them	plastic foam
		fur
	air	feathers

Air is a poor conductor of heat. Feathers, fibrewool, plastic foam, wool, and fur are all good insulators because they contain tiny pockets of trapped air.

Convection

If air is heated, it expands, and floats upwards. Cooler, denser air moves in to take its place. The result is a circulating flow called a **convection current**. Convection can occur in other gases as well as air. And it can occur in liquids, such as water.

Most rooms are heated by convection:

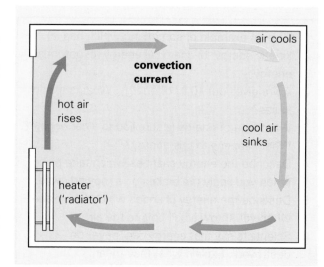

air cools

convection current

hot air rises

cool air sinks

heater ('radiator')

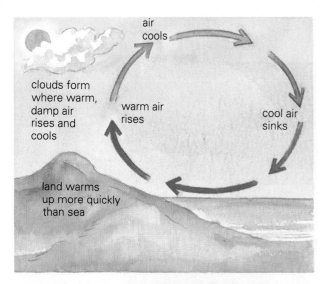

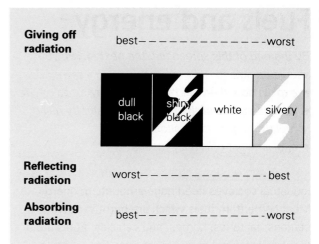

Convection has a part to play in the weather. You can see an example above. During the day, the land warms up more quickly than the sea. This sets up a convection current so that breezes blow in from the sea. Where warm, damp air rises and cools, clouds may form (see Spread 3.24).

Radiation

There is empty space between us and the Sun. But we still get heat from the Sun. The energy travels as tiny waves of **electromagnetic radiation** (see Spread 4.31). These can travel through empty space.

If you absorb any of the Sun's radiation, it heats you up. That is why it is sometimes called **heat radiation**. Often, people just call it 'radiation', though there are other types of radiation as well.

Everything gives off some heat radiation. The hotter it is, the more it radiates.

---

1 Why can the Sun's heat not reach us by conduction or convection? How does the Sun's heat reach us?
2 How can a heater warm a room by convection?
3 Explain why a) insulating materials often contain trapped air b) houses in hot countries are often painted white c) kettles are usually silvery or white.
4 What features does a Thermos flask have to stop heat losses by a) conduction b) convection c) radiation? Why is a flask good at keeping drinks cold as well as hot?

Black surfaces are the best at giving off radiation. They are also the best at absorbing it.

Silvery or white surfaces are good at reflecting radiation - which means that they are poor at absorbing it. In hot, sunny countries, buildings are often painted white so that they absorb as little of the Sun's radiation as possible.

Silvery or white surfaces are also poor at giving off radiation. Kettles are usually made silvery or white so that they lose heat slowly.

The Thermos flask

A Thermos flask can keep drinks hot (or cold) for hours. It has several features which reduce the amount of heat flowing out (or in):

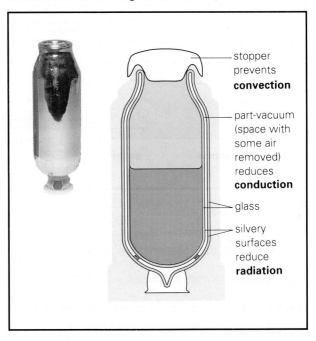

Fuels and energy

By the end of this spread and the next (4.15), you should be able to:

- explain how the world gets its energy
- describe some of the problems caused by using fuels, and give some alternatives
- explain what efficiency means

Industrial societies need huge amounts of energy. Most come from fuels which are burnt in power stations, factories, homes, and vehicles. Fuels are a very concentrated source of energy. For example, there is enough energy in a teaspoonful of petrol to move a large car more than 50 metres. Our fuel, food, is also a very concentrated source of energy.

Most of the world's energy originally came from the Sun. To find out how, see the next spread, 4.15.

Turbine

Power stations

Mains electricity comes from generators in power stations. In many power stations, the generators are turned by **turbines**, blown round by the force of high pressure steam (see below). For other ways of turning generators, see the next spread.

Engines

Engines get their energy from burning fuel. For example, in a car engine, a mixture of fuel and air is exploded. This provides the force which turns the engine. When an engine is running fast, there can be more than 25 explosions per second in each cylinder.

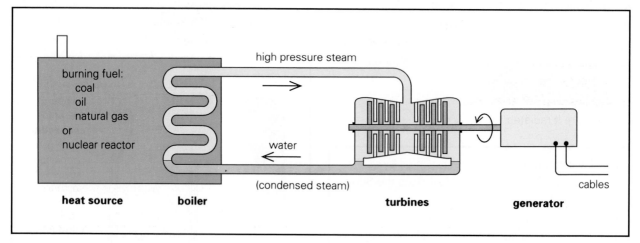

Burning fuels

Fuels use up oxygen when they burn. With most fuels (including food), this reaction takes place:

fuel + oxygen → carbon dioxide + water

There may be other products as well. For example burning coal produces some sulphur dioxide.

Using fuels brings many problems. For example:

- Carbon dioxide gas adds to global warming.
- Sulphur dioxide causes acid rain.
- Transporting fuels can cause pollution: for example, there may be a leak from an oil tanker.
- Supplies of most fuels will eventually run out.

Renewable or non-renewable?

Coal, oil, and natural gas are called *fossil fuels* (see the next spread). They took many millions of years to form. Once used up, they cannot be replaced. They are *non-renewable*.

Some fuels are *renewable*. For example, if wood is burnt, it can be replaced by growing more trees.

You can see some examples of renewable and non-renewable energy sources below. For more details on each one, see the next spread.

Non-renewable energy sources	Renewable energy sources

fossil fuels:
    coal
    oil
    natural gas
nuclear fuel:
    uranium-235
	hydroelectric energy
	tidal energy
	wave energy
	wind energy
	solar energy
	geothermal energy
	biofuels (fuels from plant
	    and animal matter)

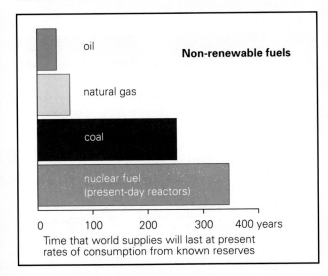

Non-renewable fuels

oil

natural gas

coal

nuclear fuel (present-day reactors)

0   100   200   300   400 years

Time that world supplies will last at present rates of consumption from known reserves

Efficiency

When fuels burn, much of their energy is wasted as heat. In a typical power station for example, for every 100 joules of energy in the fuel, only 35 joules ends up as electrical energy. The power station has an *efficiency* of 35%.

You can use this equation to work out efficiency:

$$\text{efficiency} = \frac{\text{energy output}}{\text{energy input}} \times 100\%$$

Here are some typical efficiency values:

For every **100 J** of Input energy		Output energy	Efficiency
petrol engine		25 J	25%
diesel engine		35 J	35%
fuel-burning power station		35 J	35%
human engine		15 J	15%

Low efficiency is not because of poor design. When an engine is working, some energy *has* to be wasted. Burning fuel gives particles extra energy. But some of this becomes so spread out that it cannot be used to produce motion. Instead, it is lost as heat.

In some power stations, wasted heat is used to supply the local district with hot water. This is just one way of being less wasteful with fuel so that the world's reserves last longer.

To answer the following, you may need information from Spread 4.15

1   Some fuels are *non-renewable*. What does this mean? Give *two* examples.

2   Describe *two* problems which can be caused by gases from burning fuels.

3   Give *two* ways of generating electricity in which no fuel is burnt and the energy is renewable.

4   The energy in petrol originally came from the Sun. Explain how it got into the petrol.

5   A petrol engine has an efficiency of 25%. Explain what this means.

6   Why it is important for engines and power stations to have the highest possible efficiency?

How the world gets its energy

Solar panels

These absorb energy radiated from the Sun and use it to heat water.

Solar cells

These use the energy in sunlight to produce small amounts of electricity.

The Sun

The Sun radiates energy because of nuclear reactions deep inside it. Its output is equivalent to 400 million billion billion electric fire elements. Just a tiny fraction reaches the Earth.

Energy in food

We get energy from the food we eat. The food may be from plants, or from animals which fed on plants.

Energy in plants

Plants take in energy from sunlight falling on their leaves. They use it to turn water and carbon dioxide from the air into new growth. Animals eat plants to get the energy stored in them.

Biofuels from plants

Wood is still an important fuel in many countries. When wood is burnt, it releases energy which the tree once took in from the Sun. In some countries, sugar cane is grown and fermented to make alcohol, which can be used as a fuel instead of petrol.

Fossil fuels

Coal, oil, and natural gas are called fossil fuels. They were formed from the remains of plants and tiny sea creatures which lived many millions of years ago. Industrial societies rely on fossil fuels for most of their energy. Many power stations burn fossil fuels.

Biofuels from waste

Rotting animal and plant waste can give off methane gas (the same as natural gas). This can be used as a fuel. Marshes, rubbish tips, and sewage treatment works are all sources of methane. Some waste can also be used directly as fuel by burning it.

Batteries

Some batteries (e.g. car batteries) have to be given energy by charging them with electricity. Others are manufactured from chemicals which already store energy. But energy is needed to produce the chemicals in the first place.

Fuels from oil

Many fuels can be extracted from oil (crude). These include: petrol, diesel fuel, jet fuel, paraffin, central heating oil, bottled gas.

The Moon

The gravitational pull of the Moon (and to a lesser extent, the Sun) creates gentle bulges in the Earth's oceans. As the Earth rotates, different places have high and low tides as they pass in and out of the bulges.

Tidal energy

In a tidal energy scheme, an estuary is dammed to form an artificial lake. Incoming tides fills the lake; outgoing tides empty it. The flow of water in and out of the lake turns generators.

The atom

Some atoms have huge amounts of nuclear energy, stored in their nuclei (centres). Radioactive materials have unstable atoms which release energy slowly. Nuclear reactors can release energy much more quickly.

Geothermal energy

Deep underground, the rocks are hotter than they are on the surface. The heat comes from radioactive materials naturally present in the rocks. It can be used to make steam for heating buildings or driving generators.

Nuclear power

In a reactor, nuclear reactions release energy from nuclei of uranium atoms. This produces heat which is used to make steam for driving generators.

Weather systems

These are driven by heat radiated from the Sun. Hot air rising above the equator causes belts of wind around the Earth. Heat and winds lift water vapour from the oceans and bring rain and snow.

Wave energy

Waves are caused by the wind (and partly by tides). Waves cause a rapid up-and-down movement on the surface of the sea. This movement can be used to drive generators.

Hydroelectric energy

An artificial lake forms behind a dam. Water rushing down from this lake is used to turn generators. The lake is kept full by river water which once fell as rain or snow.

Wind energy

For centuries, people have been using the power of the wind to move ships, pump water, and grind corn. Today, huge wind turbines are used to turn electrical generators.

Energy issues

By the end of this spread, you should be able to:

- calculate changes in internal energy
- explain how energy becomes less useful
- compare different types of power station and the environmental problems they cause

Internal energy

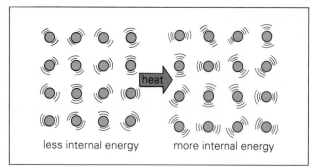

less internal energy   more internal energy

All materials are made of particles (such as atoms). These are pulled by other particles and are constantly on the move. Scientists say that materials have **internal energy**. If, say, some cold water absorbs heat, then its particles move faster, its internal energy goes up, and its temperature rises.

It takes 4200 joules of heat to raise the temperature of 1 kg of water by 1 °C. Scientists say that water has a **specific heat capacity** of 4200 J/(kg °C).

Here are some specific heat capacity values:

steel:	concrete:	aluminium:	water:
500 J/(kg °C)	800 J/(kg °C)	900 J/(kg °C)	4200 J/(kg °C)

You can calculate the heat needed to raise the temperature of a material with this equation:

heat input =	mass ×	specific heat capacity	×	temperature rise
in J	in kg	in J/(kg °C)		in °C

For example, to heat 2 kg of water by 3 °C:

heat input = 2 × 4200 × 3 = 25 200 J

More energy calculations

Equations for calculating potential energy and kinetic energy are given in Spread 4.25

Energy spreading

In most large power stations, heat is released from burning fuel or from a nuclear reactor. Although some of the energy turns the generators, more than a half of it becomes too spread out to be useful, and must be wasted as heat.

Whenever energy spreads, it becomes more difficult to change into other, useful forms. For example, heat from a hot flame could be used to make steam for a turbine. If the same heat were spread through a huge tankful of water, it would warm the water by only a few degrees. This warm water would not be useful as an energy source for a turbine.

---

1 What is meant by *internal energy*?
2 Concrete has a *specific heat capacity of 800 J/(kg °C)*. What does this mean?
3 A bath holds 100 kg of water. a) How much heat is needed to warm the water from 20 °C to 50 °C? b) How long will it take to warm the water using a 3 kW heater? (1 kW = 1000 J/s)
4 Look at the table of data at the top of the next page. a) Which power station has the greatest efficiency? b) Which cost most to build? c) If station C were 100% efficient, what would its power output be? d) Why is this not possible?

Power stations compared

Power station 🡒 (1MW = 1 000 000 W)	A Coal	B Combined cycle gas	C Nuclear	D Wind farm	E Large tidal
Power output in MW	1800	600	1200	20	6000
Efficiency (fuel energy → electrical energy) *The following are on a scale 0–5*	35%	45%	25%	–	–
Build cost per MW output	2	1	5	3	4
Fuel cost per kW h output	5	4	2	0	0
Atmospheric pollution per KWh output	5	3	<1	0	0

> ***Combined cycle gas turbine power stations*** use natural gas as fuel for a jet engine. The shaft of the engine turns one generator. Heat from the exhaust makes steam to drive another generator.

> ***Nuclear power stations*** produce highly dangerous radioactive waste (see 4.35). Decommissioning (closing down) costs for old stations are almost as much as build costs.

> ***Wind farms*** can contain 50 or so aerogenerators. They make more noise than other power stations and need an area of several km^2.

Disturbing the atmosphere

Fuel-burning power stations give off huge amounts of carbon dioxide gas. Plants take in carbon dioxide as part of their life process, but more carbon dioxide is being added to the atmosphere than is being removed.

Carbon dioxide acts like the glass in a greenhouse. It traps the Sun's heat. As a result, the Earth is slowly warming up. Scientists call this the **greenhouse effect** (see also Spread 2.25). The warming is only slight, but it may have a major effect on world climates.

Burning fuels can pollute the air in other ways. For example, many coal-burning power stations emit sulphur dioxide gas which causes **acid rain.**

Fusion future

If hydrogen nuclei collide at high enough speed, they fuse (join) to form helium nuclei. This process is called ***nucear fusion*** and it can release huge amounts of energy. It is the process which powers the Sun (see Spread 4.39).

One day, fusion reactors may be used in power stations. The hydrogen they need can be extracted from seawater. They will produce some radiation, but almost no radioactive waste or polluting gases. However, the reactors will be very difficult to design and build because they will have to heat gas to 100 million °C and keep it hot, compressed, and trapped so that fusion is maintained.

e) Why do two of the stations have a zero rating for fuel costs and atmospheric pollution? f) How do these two stations affect the environment?

5 Compared with fuel-burning power stations
a) what advantages do nuclear power stations have? b) what disadvantages do they have?

6 Look at the charts on the right. a) Which region has the largest oil reserves? b) What other fuel does this region have plentiful reserves of?
c) Which region has the largest natural gas reserves? d) Which regions do you think might be big importers of oil?

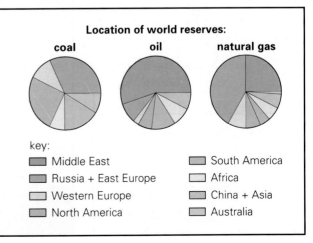

Location of world reserves:

coal　　oil　　natural gas

key:
- Middle East
- Russia + East Europe
- Western Europe
- North America
- South America
- Africa
- China + Asia
- Australia

4·17 Forces and pressure

By the end of this spread, you should be able to:
* *describe some effects of forces*
* *explain what pressure is and how to calculate it*

Forces in action

A force is a push or pull. It is measured in **newtons (N)**.

On Earth, everything has **weight**, the downward force of gravity. Like other forces, weight is measured in newtons.

On Earth, a 1 kg mass has a weight of about 10 newtons. The force can be measured using a **newtonmeter**. This has a spring inside. The greater the force, the more the spring stretches and the further the pointer moves along the scale:

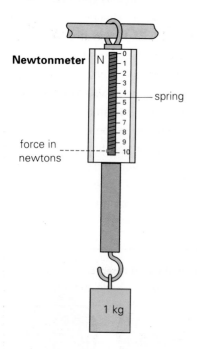

Newtonmeter

spring

force in newtons

1 kg

Forces can make things
* speed up
* slow down
* change shape
* turn
* move in a different direction

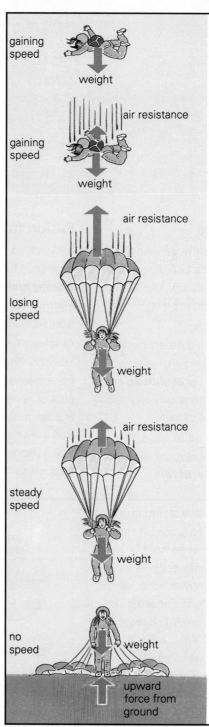

gaining speed

weight

gaining speed

air resistance

weight

air resistance

losing speed

weight

air resistance

steady speed

weight

no speed

weight

upward force from ground

A skydiver jumps from a helicopter. Weight is the only force acting on her. It makes her **accelerate** (gain speed).

As she gains speed, the force of **air resistance** gets stronger and stronger.

When she opens her parachute, there is a sudden increase in air resistance. So she loses speed until....

the air resistance equals her weight. Now, the two forces are in balance. The **resultant** force on the skydiver is zero, and her speed is steady.

The skydiver stands on the ground. The ground is slightly compressed by her feet. It provides an upward force equal to her weight. This force stops her sinking into the ground.

Pressure

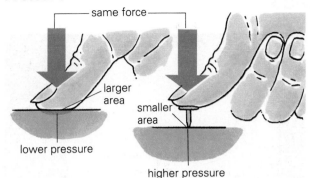

same force

larger area

smaller area

lower pressure

higher pressure

You can't push your thumb into wood. But you can push a drawing pin in using the same force. This is because the force is concentrated on a much smaller area. Scientists say that the **pressure** is higher.

Pressure is measured in **newtons per square metre (N/m^2)**, also called **pascals (Pa)**. It can be calculated with this equation:

pressure = $\dfrac{\text{force}}{\text{area}}$	force in N area in m^2 pressure in Pa

For example:

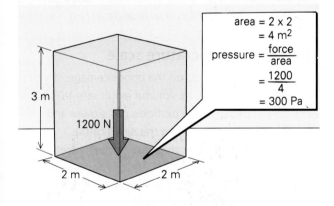

3 m

1200 N

2 m 2 m

area = 2 x 2
= 4 m^2

pressure = $\dfrac{\text{force}}{\text{area}}$

$= \dfrac{1200}{4}$

= 300 Pa

---

1 Sara has a mass of 50 kg. What is her weight?
2 Sara is using a parachute. She is descending at steady speed. Draw a diagram to show the forces on her. What is the resultant force?
3 Use your ideas about pressure to explain why
   a) it is easier to walk on soft sand if you have flat shoes rather than shoes with small heels.
   b) water is able to keep a boat afloat.
4 Redraw the diagram above to show the block resting on its side. Calculate the pressure under the block when it is resting on its side.

Liquid pressure

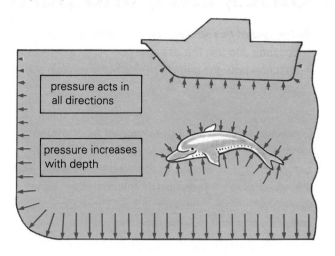

pressure acts in all directions

pressure increases with depth

The deeper you go into water, the greater the pressure becomes. This pressure pushes in all directions.

It is the pressure from water which keeps a boat afloat. Water pressing on the hull produces an upward push called an **upthrust**. This is strong enough to support the weight of the boat.

Car brakes use liquid pressure. When the brake pedal is pressed, a piston puts pressure on trapped brake fluid. The pressure is transmitted, through fluid in the pipes, to the wheels. There, the pressure pushes on pistons. These move the brake pads.

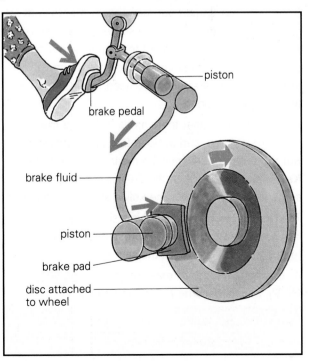

piston

brake pedal

brake fluid

piston

brake pad

disc attached to wheel

Gases, laws, and particles

By the end of this spread, you should be able to:
- describe and use the gas laws
- describe how the particle model helps explain the gas laws

Gases are squashy. So a gas does not necessarily expand when heated. If the container can resist the expansion, the volume will not change. However, there will be more **pressure** on the container. When dealing with gases, there are always *three* factors to consider: pressure, volume, and temperature.

Gas pressure

In a gas, the particles move around at high speed. As they collide with the sides of the container, they produce a force. This is the force which keeps balloons and tyres inflated. The more concentrated the force, the greater the pressure.

Pressure can be measured in pascals. However, a larger unit, the **kilopascal (kPa)** is often more convenient.

1 kPa = 1000 Pa.

The gas laws

Scientists have carried out many experiments with gases in containers. There are some typical results on the opposite page. In each of the experiments shown, one of the factors pressure *(P)*, volume *(V)*, or temperature *(T)* has been kept fixed, while the other two have been varied.

The results show that there are laws linking the pressure, volume, and temperature of a trapped gas. But the temperature *must* be measured using the **Kelvin scale** rather than the Celsius scale. There is some information about the Kelvin scale on the right.

The results can be combined in a single gas law. The law is especially useful if the pressure, volume, and temperature all change at the same time:

If conditions for a fixed mass of gas change so that P_1, V_1, and T_1 become P_2, V_2, and T_2, then:

$$\frac{P_1 \times V_1}{T_1} = \frac{P_2 \times V_2}{T_2}$$

In a balloon, P, V, and T can all change.

The Kelvin temperature scale

According to the results on the opposite page, if you keep on cooling a gas, its volume eventually falls to zero. This is because the particles get slower and slower until they stop hitting the sides of the container and causing a pressure. The temperature at which this happens is –273 °C. It is called **absolute zero**. It is the lowest possible temperature because the particles cannot go any slower.

The Kelvin temperature scale uses absolute zero as its zero. Its 'degree', is the **kelvin (K)**. This chart shows the link between Kelvin and Celsius temperatures:

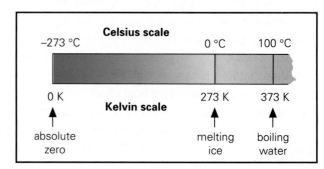

How P changes with T

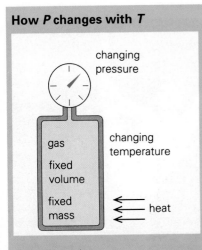

Typical results:

Temperature in K	200	400	600	800
Pressure in kPa	100	200	300	400

From these results:
- P doubles if T doubles.... and so on
- P/T has the same value each time: in this case, 0.5.

Put another way:

For a fixed mass of gas, P is proportional to T, provided V is fixed.

This is called the **pressure law**.

How V changes with T

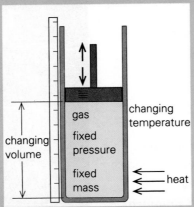

Typical results:

Temperature in K	200	400	600	800
Volume in cm³	150	300	450	600

From these results:
- V doubles if T doubles.... and so on
- V/T has the same value each time: in this case, 0.75.

Put another way:

For a fixed mass of gas, V is proportional to T, provided P is fixed.

This is called the **volume law**.

How P changes with V

Typical results:

Volume in cm³	50	40	25	20
Pressure in kPa	200	250	400	500

From these results:
- P doubles if V halves.... and so on
- P x V has the same value each time: in this case, 10 000.

Put another way:

For a fixed mass of gas, P is proportional 1/V, provided T is fixed.

This is called **Boyle's law**.

Explaining the laws

Here are some examples of how the particle model can help explain the gas laws:

Temperature rises, volume fixed
The particles move faster. They collide with the sides of the container at a higher speed, so the **pressure rises**.

Temperature rises, pressure fixed
The gas is free to expand. The particles move faster, but are more spaced out. The **volume rises**.

Volume rises, temperature fixed
The particles keep the same speed. However, they are more spaced out, so the collisons with the sides of the container are less concentrated. The **pressure falls**.

1 Change these temperatures into kelvin:
   a) 0 °C b) 100 °C c) 27 °C d) -73 °C
2 Use the results above to plot a graph of
   a) P against T b) V against T c) P against V
   d) P against 1/V. Before you do the last one, you will have to work out values of 1/V on a calculator. When you have plotted the graphs, describe in words what each one shows.
3 Using ideas about particles, explain why the pressure rises if a) you squash a balloon b) a gas canister is left too close to a fire.
4 A balloon contains 6 m³ of helium. As it rises through the atmosphere, the pressure falls from 100 kPa to 50 kPa, but the temperature stays the same. What is the new volume of the balloon?

Turning forces

By the end of this spread, you should be able to:
- calculate the turning effect of a force
- explain why some things balance
- explain what makes things stable

Moments in balance

Moments

Below, someone is using a spanner to turn a bolt. With a longer spanner, they could use the same force to produce an even greater turning effect.

The strength of a turning effect is called a **moment**. It can be calculated with this equation:

moment =	force ×	distance from turning point
in Nm	in N	in m

(The distance is the *shortest* distance from the turning point to the line of the force.)

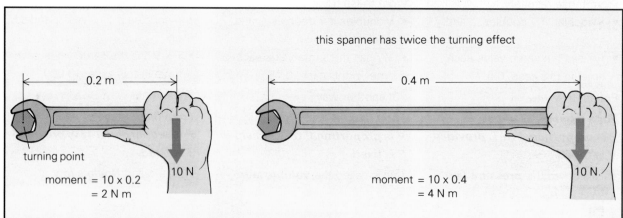

this spanner has twice the turning effect

0.2 m

turning point

moment = 10 x 0.2
        = 2 N m

10 N

0.4 m

moment = 10 x 0.4
        = 4 N m

10 N

Moments in balance

On the right, a plank has been balanced on a log. Different weights have been placed on both sides of the plank. They have been arranged so that the plank still balances.

The weight on the left has a turning effect to the left. The weight on the right has a turning effect to the right.

The two turning effects are equal. That is why the plank balances.

In other words, if something balances:

moment	=	moment
turning to the left		turning to the right

This is an example of the **law of moments**.

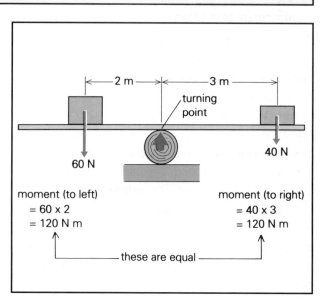

2 m

3 m

turning point

60 N

40 N

moment (to left)
= 60 x 2
= 120 N m

moment (to right)
= 40 x 3
= 120 N m

these are equal

Centre of mass

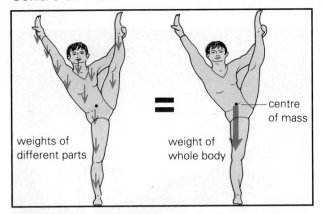

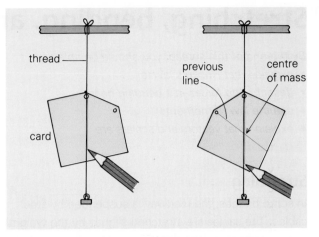

Balancing on a beam is difficult. The secret lies in how you position your weight. All parts of the body have weight. Together, they act like a single force pulling at just one point. This point is called your **centre of mass** (or **centre of gravity**). To balance on a beam, you have to keep your centre of mass over the beam.

If you suspend a piece of card from some thread, it always hangs with its centre of mass in line with the thread. You can use this idea to find the centre of mass. Suspend the card from one corner and draw a vertical line on it. Do the same using another corner. Then see where the two lines cross.

Stability

If something is in a **stable** position, it will not topple over.

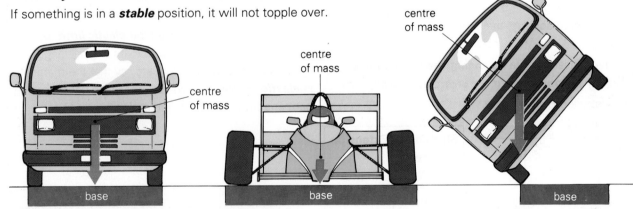

This van is in a stable position. If it starts to tip, its weight will pull it back again. As long as its centre of mass stays over its base, it will not topple.

This racing car is even more stable than the van. It has a lower centre of mass and a wider base. It has to be tipped much further before it starts to topple.

The van is now in an unstable position. Its centre of mass has just passed beyond the edge of its base. So its weight will pull it over.

The model crane on the right has a movable counterbalance.

1. Why does the crane need a counterbalance?
2. Why must the counterbalance be movable?
3. What is the moment of the 100 N force (about O)?
4. To balance the crane, what moment must the 400 N force have?
5. How far from O should the counterbalance be placed?
6. What is the maximum load the crane should lift?
7. Give *two* ways of making the design of the crane more stable.

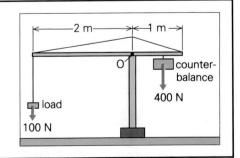

Stretching, bending, and balancing

By the end of this spread, you should be able to:
- *explain what Hooke's law is*
- *describe the forces in a bending beam*
- *use the law of moments*
- *explain what vectors and scalars are*

Stretching

In some bridges, the roadway is suspended by steel cables. The cables are stretched slightly by the weight of the roadway, so the designer must make sure that they are strong enough to take the load.

The diagram, table, and graph below show the effect of a stretching force on a long, thin, steel cable. As the force increases, so does the **extension** (the length by which the cable stretches).

Up to point X on the graph:
- Each extra 100 N of force produces the same extra extension (1 mm in this case).
- If the force doubles, the extension doubles, and so on.

Mathematically, these mean that **the extension is directly proportional to the stretching force**.

This is called **Hooke's law**.

Steel and other metals obey Hooke's law, but rubber and many plastics do not. (With these materials, the graph would be a curve, not a straight line.)

Point E on the graph is called the **elastic limit**. Up to this point, the cable will return to its original length if the force is removed. Scientists say that the material is **elastic**. However beyond E, the cable becomes permanently stretched – and at Y, it breaks.

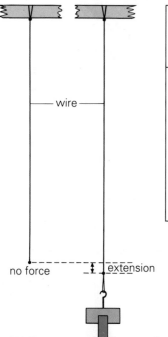

Stretching force in N	Extension in mm
0	0
100	1.0
200	2.0
300	3.0
400	4.0
500	5.6
600	–

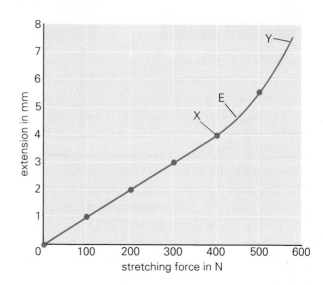

Bending beams

The diagram on the right shows a simple beam bridge. The beam is being bent by the weight of the lorry. During bending, the bottom of the beam is stretched, while the top is compressed.

Steel is good at resisting stretching and compressing. Concrete is good at resisting compressing, but it breaks easily when stretched. That is why concrete beams are reinforced with steel rods (see 3.5).

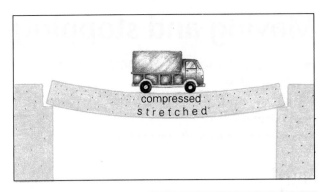

compressed
stretched

More moments

The plank on the right is balancing on a log. In this case, there are *two* forces on one side of the plank. However, as the plank is balanced, the turning effect to the left and right must be equal. Whenever something balances, the law of moments says that:

total moment to left = total moment to right

In the diagram on the right, the log has to support a total weight of 10 + 8 + 3 = 21 N. To do this, it must provide an upward force of 21 N.

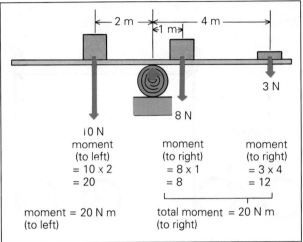

10 N
moment (to left)
= 10 × 2
= 20

8 N
moment (to right)
= 8 × 1
= 8

3 N
moment (to right)
= 3 × 4
= 12

moment = 20 N m (to left)

total moment = 20 N m (to right)

Vectors and scalars

Force has a direction as well as a 'size'. It is a **vector**.

Quantities like volume and density, which have no direction, are called **scalars**.

When dealing with vectors, you have to allow for their direction. In each diagram below, two 4 N forces are acting. Their **resultant** (combined) force is 8 N in one case but zero in the other. The resultant depends on the direction of the forces as well as their size.

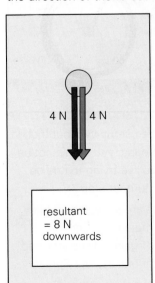

4 N   4 N

resultant
= 8 N
downwards

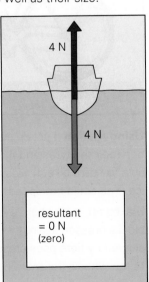

4 N

4 N

resultant
= 0 N
(zero)

You will need graph paper for question 1

Stretching force in N	0	1	2	3	4	5
Length in mm	40	49	58	67	79	99

1   When a spring was stretched, the readings above were taken. a) Make a table and draw a graph of *extension* against *force* b) How can you tell if the spring obeys Hooke's law? c) If the spring obeys this law, up to what point does it do so? d) What force produces an extension of 21 mm?

2   In the diagram below a) what is the total moment of the 3 N and 2 N forces about point O? b) what force, *X*, is needed to keep the plank balanced? c) how big is force *R*?

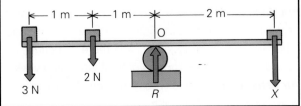

1 m   1 m   2 m

O

3 N   2 N   R   X

Moving and stopping

By the end of this spread, you should be able to:
- *calculate speed*
- *describe how friction is sometimes a nuisance and sometimes useful*
- *explain how speed affects road safety*

Speed

Here is a simple method of measuring speed. You could use it to work out the speed of a cyclist:

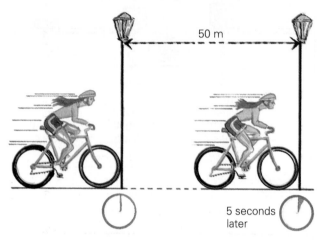

50 m

5 seconds later

Measure the distance between two points on a road, say two lamp posts. Measure the time taken to travel between these points. Then use this equation:

average speed	=	distance travelled / time taken	distance in m time in s speed in m/s

If the cyclist travels 50 metres in 5 seconds, her average speed is 50/5, which is 10 metres per second. This is written 10 m/s for short.

On most journeys, the speed changes, so the actual speed isn't always the same as the average speed. To find an actual speed, you have to find the distance travelled in the shortest time you can measure.

Friction

Friction is the force that tries to stop materials sliding past each other. There is friction between your hands when you rub them together. And there is friction between your shoes and the ground when you walk.
Air resistance is also a type of friction. It slows you down when you ride a bike.

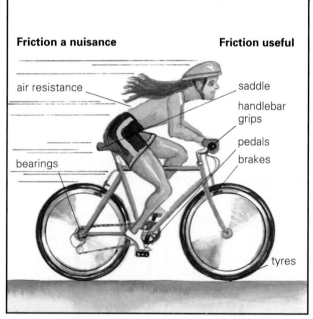

Friction a nuisance — air resistance, bearings

Friction useful — saddle, handlebar grips, pedals, brakes, tyres

Using friction Friction can be useful. Without friction between the tyres and the ground, you would not be able to ride a bike. It would be like trying to ride on ice. You could not speed up, turn, or stop.

Brakes rely on friction. Cycles are slowed by rubber blocks pressed against the wheel rims. Cars are slowed by fibre pads pressed against discs attached to the wheels (for more on car brakes, see Spread 4.17).

Problems with friction Friction can also be a nuisance. Moving things are slowed by friction. Friction also produces heat. In machinery, grease and oil reduce friction so that moving parts do not overheat and seize up. Ball bearings and roller bearings reduce friction. Their rolling action means that a wheel does not have to rub against its shaft.

Speed and safety

In an emergency, the driver of a car may have to react quickly and apply the brakes.

The car's ***stopping distance*** depends on two things:

- The ***thinking distance***. This is how far the car travels before the brakes are applied, while the driver is still reacting.
- The ***braking distance***. This is how far the car then travels, after the brakes have been applied.

It takes an average driver about 0.6 seconds to react, and press the brake pedal. This is the driver's ***reaction time***. During this time, the car does not slow down. And the higher its speed, the further it travels.

This is how to work out the thinking distance for a car travelling at 20 m/s (45 mph). The driver's reaction time is 0.6 seconds:

$$\text{speed} = \frac{\text{distance}}{\text{time}}$$

So, distance = speed × time

$$= \ 20 \ \ \times \ \ 0.6 \ \ = 12 \text{ metres}$$

So, the thinking distance is 12 metres

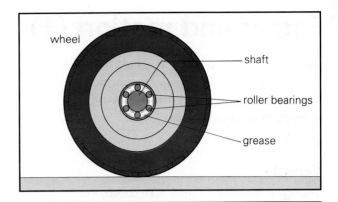

1 Mandy cycles 100 metres in 10 seconds. What is her average speed?

2 Look at the photograph on the opposite page. What features can you see for reducing friction?

3 For a car, where is friction a) *useful* b) a *nuisance*? Give *two* examples of each.

4 In the chart below, what is the thinking distance a) at 25 m/s b) at 30 m/s? Why does the thinking distance go up, even though the driver's reaction time stay the same?

5 Alcohol slows people's reactions. If a driver has a reaction time of 2 seconds a) what will his thinking distance be at 56 mph (25 m/s)? b) what will his stopping distance be? (You will need information from the chart to answer this.)

The chart shows the stopping distances for cars at different speeds. The figures are for a dry road. If the road is wet or icy, or the driver's reactions are slow, the stopping distances will be even greater.

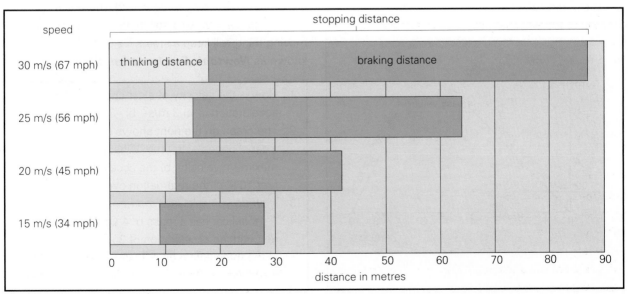

Forces and motion (1)

By the end of this spread, you should be able to:
- carry out calculations involving velocity, acceleration, force, mass, and momentum
- describe three laws of motion

Velocity

Velocity is measured in m/s. Like speed, it tells you how fast something is moving. But it also tells you the direction of travel. It is a **vector** (see Spread 4.20).

One way of showing the direction is to use a + or −. For example:

+10 m/s   (velocity of 10 m/s to the right)
−10 m/s   (velocity of 10 m/s to the left)

Note: the '+' sign is not always shown.

Acceleration

The velocity of the car, above right, is going up by 2 m/s *every second*. The car has an **acceleration** of 2 m/s^2. Acceleration can be calculated like this:

acceleration = $\dfrac{\text{gain in velocity}}{\text{time taken}}$	acceleration in m/s^2 velocity in m/s time in s

Like velocity, acceleration is a vector.

When a car slows down, it *loses* velocity. If it is loses, say, 4 m/s every second, it has a **deceleration** (also called a **retardation**) of 4 m/s^2. Mathematically, this is an *acceleration* of −4 m/s^2.

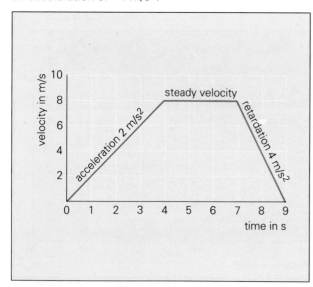

acceleration 2 m/s^2

Time	Velocity
0 s	0 m/s
1 s	2 m/s
2 s	4 m/s
3 s	6 m/s
4 s	8 m/s

Force, mass, and acceleration

The more mass something has, the more it resists acceleration. Force, mass, and acceleration are linked by this equation:

$F = m \times a$	F = force in newton (N) m = mass in kg a = acceleration in m/s^2

For example:
A 1 N force is needed to accelerate 1 kg at 1 m/s^2. (This is how the newton is defined.)
A 6 N force is needed to accelerate 2 kg at 3 m/s^2.

The equation linking force, mass, and acceleration, is sometimes called **Newton's second law of motion**.

If there is *no* resultant force ($F = 0$), there is *no* acceleration ($a = 0$), so a still thing will stay still and a moving thing will keep a steady velocity. This is known as **Newton's first law of motion**.

1 How is the velocity of a car changing if its acceleration is a) 3 m/s^2 b) −3 m/s^2?
2 The graph on the right shows how the velocity of a car changes with time. What is a) the maximum velocity b) the acceleration over the first 10 s c) the retardation over the last 20 s?
3 How do you calculate *momentum*?
4 A model car has a mass of 4 kg. It starts from rest with an acceleration of 3 m/s^2. What is a) the force acting on it b) its velocity after 5 seconds c) its momentum after 5 seconds?

Action and reaction

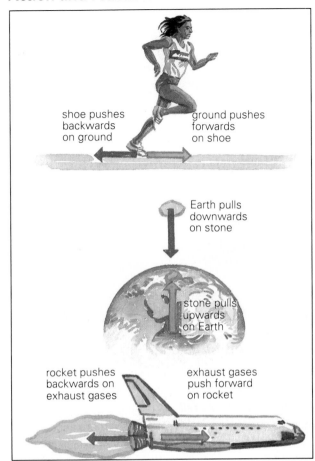

shoe pushes backwards on ground

ground pushes forwards on shoe

Earth pulls downwards on stone

stone pulls upwards on Earth

rocket pushes backwards on exhaust gases

exhaust gases push forward on rocket

Forces are pushes or pulls between *two* things. So forces always exist in pairs. One force acts on one thing. Its equal but opposite partner acts on the other. This idea is known as **Newton's third law of motion**. You can see three examples above.

The forces in each pair are known as the **action** and the **reaction**. But it does not matter which you call which. One cannot exist without the other.

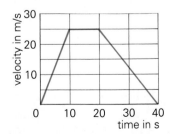

5   Use your result from part c of question 4 to work out the force on the model car. Does this agree with your answer to part a?

Momentum

If a massive truck is travelling very fast, people say that it has lots of **momentum**. Momentum is calculated with this equation:

$$momentum = m \times v$$

m = mass in kg
v = velocity in m/s
momentum in kg m/s

For example if a model car of mass 2 kg has a velocity of 3 m/s, its momentum = $2 \times 3 = 6$ kg m/s

Like velocity, momentum is a vector, so a + or – is often used to show its direction.
For example:
if car moves to right: momentum = +6 kg m/s
if car moves to left: momentum = −6 kg m/s

Force and momentum

There is a link between force and momentum:

$$force = \frac{gain\ in\ momentum}{time\ taken}$$

For example, if a 2 kg model car accelerates from zero to 6 m/s in 2 seconds:

gain in momentum = $m \times v = 2 \times 6 = 12$ kg m/s

$$force = \frac{gain\ in\ momentum}{time\ taken} = \frac{12}{2} = 6\ N$$

You could also solve this problem using $F = m \times a$. The car's velocity goes up by 6 m/s in 2 s, so its acceleration is 3 m/s^2. Its mass is 2 kg, so:
force needed = $m \times a = 2 \times 3 = 6$ N.

Forces and motion (2)

By the end of this spread, you should be able to:
- *use the law of conservation of momentum*
- *describe how gravity affects motion*
- *explain how circular motion is produced*

Conserving momentum

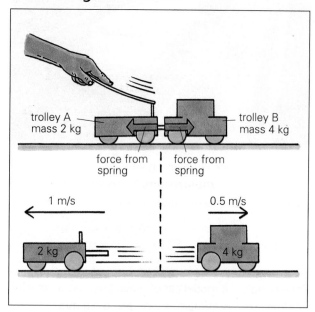

To begin with, the trolleys above are at rest. Then a spring is released between them so that they shoot off in opposite directions. The trolley with the lower mass reaches the higher velocity.

With the figures in the diagram, you can work out the momentum changes taking place (Remember: momentum = mass × velocity. It is also a vector, so you use a + or – to show motion to the right or left):

Before spring is released
total momentum of trolleys = 0

After spring is released
momentum of trolley B = 4 × (+0.5) = +2 kg m/s
momentum of trolley A = 2 × (−1)   = −2 kg m/s
So, total momentum of trolleys   = 2 + (−2) = 0

So the total momentum *after* the spring is released is exactly the same as it was *before*. This is an example of the *law of conservation of momentum*:

Things may push or pull on each other but, if there is no outside force, their total momentum stays the same.

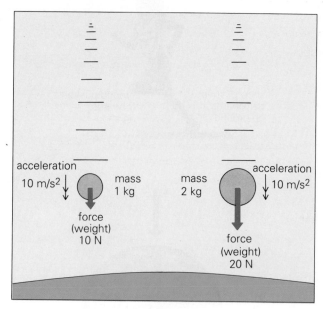

Acceleration of free fall (*g*)

With no air resistance, things falling near the Earth have an acceleration of 10 m/s². This is the *acceleration of free fall*, **g**. It is the same for *all* masses, light or heavy. (9.8 m/s² is a more accurate value, but 10 m/s² can be used in most calculations.)

Air resistance tends to affect light things more than heavy ones. But without it, a falling feather would speed up just as quickly as a falling rock. Above, you can see how falling things speed up near the Earth.

The force of gravity on something is called its **weight**. You can use $F = m \times a$ to work it out:

If 1 kg acclerates at 10 m/s², the force must be 10 N
If 2 kg acclerates at 10 m/s², the force must be 20 N

Note that, on Earth, things weigh 10 N for each kg of mass (see 4.17). The Earth's **gravitational field strength** is 10 N/kg. So you can think of *g* either as an acceleration (10 m/s²) or as a force per kg (10 N/kg).

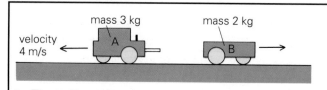

1   The trolleys above were at rest until they pushed each other apart. What is a) the momentum of A b) the momentum of B c) the velocity of B?

Downwards and sideways

On the right, one ball is dropped, while another is thrown sideways at the same time. There is no air resistance. The positions of the balls are shown at regular time intervals (every 0.1 s).

- Both balls hit the ground together. They have the same downward acceleration *(g)*.
- As it falls, the second ball moves sideways over the ground at a steady speed.

Results like this show that, if something is falling freely, its vertical and horizontal movements are quite independent of each other.

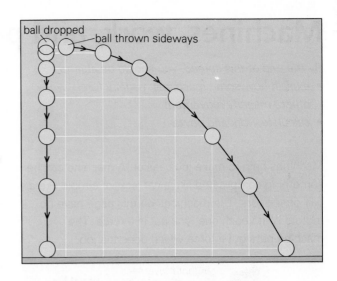

Into orbit

In the 'thought experiment' on the right, an astronaut is standing on a tower, high above the atmosphere. She can throw a ball at the speed of a rocket!

Ball A is thrown horizontally. It accelerates downwards. It also moves sideways at a steady speed.

Ball B is thrown horizontally, but much faster. Once again, the ball is falling. But this time, its sideways speed is so fast that the curve of the fall matches the curve of the Earth. The ball is in **orbit**.

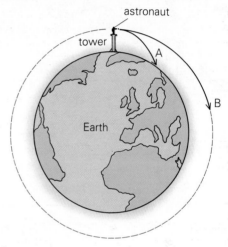

Moving in circles

The bottom diagram on the right shows another example of circular motion: a ball being whirled round on the end of a piece of string. An inward force, called a **centripetal force**, is needed to make the ball move in a circle. Without it, the ball would travel in a straight line. For a satellite orbiting the Earth, gravity provides the centripetal force.

When whirling a ball in a circle, you may say that you feel a 'centrifugal force'. But there is no outward force on the ball. If the string breaks, the ball moves off at a tangent. It isn't flung outwards.

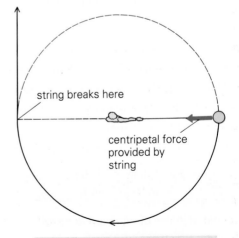

ball moves
in straight line
after string breaks

string breaks here

centripetal force
provided by
string

More centripetal force is required if:
- the mass of the ball is more
- the speed of the ball is more
- the radius of the circle is less

2 A 5 kg stone is dropped near the ground. What is
   a) its weight b) its acceleration? c) Why would a
   10 kg stone have the same acceleration?

3 If the 5 kg stone in question 2 were to be thrown
   sideways at the same time, what would its
   acceleration be?

4 What is *centripetal force*? Give an example.

4·24 Machines, work, and power

By the end of this spread, you should be able to:
- explain how some machines magnify force, while others magnify movement
- calculate work and power

Machines help to make jobs easier. A machine can be something complicated like a car jack, or simple like a pair of scissors. The machines on this page have no motors. With each one, you put in a force. The machine puts out a force which does the job.

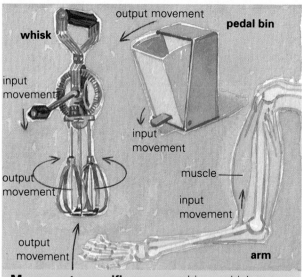

Movement magnifiers are machines which put out more movement than you put in. However, the output force is less than the input force.

Force magnifiers are machines which put out more force than you put in. However, the output movement is less than the input movement.

Work

Scientists say that **work** is done whenever a force moves. Like energy, work is measured in **joules (J)**.

One joule of work is done when a force of 1 newton (N) moves a distance of 1 metre (m).

To calculate work, you can use this equation:

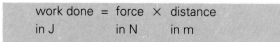

work done = force × distance
in J   in N   in m

For example, 6 joules of work are done when a force of 3 N moves a distance of 2 m.

There is a link between work and energy:
If, say, 6 joules of work are done, then 6 joules of energy are spent.

Inputs and outputs

The lever below is a force magnifier. The output force is *twice* the input force, but only moves *half* the distance. So the work output equals the work input:

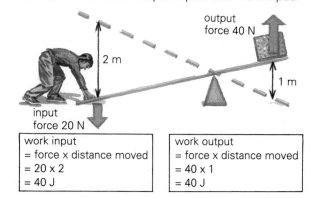

work input	work output
= force x distance moved	= force x distance moved
= 20 x 2	= 40 x 1
= 40 J	= 40 J

In the last example, the energy output is equal to the energy input. This means that the lever wastes no energy, so its **efficiency** is 100% (see Spread 4.14 for more on efficiency).

Most machines waste energy because of friction in their moving parts. So their efficiency is less than 100%. This means that the energy output is *less* than the energy input. Note: the energy output can *never* be *more* than the energy input because that would break the law of conservation of energy (see Spread 4.12).

Power

If one engine has more ***power*** than another, it can do work at a faster rate.

Power is measured in ***watts (W)***.

A power of 1 watt means that work is being done at the rate of 1 joule per second. Put another way, energy is being spent at the rate of 1 joule per second. So 1 W = 1 J/s.

A larger unit of power is the ***kilowatt (kW)***.
1 kW = 1000 W. So a motor with a power output of 1 kW can do work at the rate of 1000 joules per second.

You can use these equations to calculate power:

$$\text{power} = \frac{\text{work done}}{\text{time taken}} \quad \text{or} \quad \text{power} = \frac{\text{energy spent}}{\text{time taken}}$$

1 Give *three* examples of household machines which are force magnifiers.
2 Phil claims to have invented a machine which is both a force magnifier *and* a movement magnifier. Why would you not believe him?
3 If you use a force of 20 N to move a wheelbarrow 5 metres, how much work (in joules) do you do?
4 If, in question 3, it takes you 10 seconds to move the wheelbarrow, what is your power output?
5 If you lift a mass of 20 kg through a height of 4 metres in 8 seconds, what is your power output?

Typical power outputs

human engine
400 W

washing machine motor
250 W

small car engine
45 000 W

Land Rover engine
70 000 W

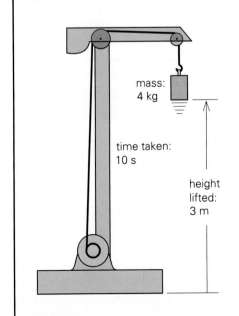

mass: 4 kg

time taken: 10 s

height lifted: 3 m

The model crane on the left can lift a mass of 4 kg through a height of 3 metres in 10 seconds. This is how you would calculate its power output:

- Calculate the force being moved. (This is the weight being lifted. On Earth, it is 10 N for each kg of mass.)

  force (weight) = 4 × 10
  = 40 N

- Use *work = force x distance* to calculate the work output.

  work output = 40 × 3
  = 120 J

- Use *power* = $\frac{\text{work done}}{\text{time taken}}$ to calculate the power output.

  power output = $\frac{120}{10}$
  = 12 W

More pressure and energy

By the end of this spread, you should be able to:
- *do calculations on hydraulic machines*
- *do calculations involving gravitational potential energy and kinetic energy*

Hydraulic machines

These are machines in which liquids are used to transmit forces. Examples include the digger on the right and the braking system on Spread 4.17. Machines like this rely on two features of liquids:

- Liquids cannot be squashed. They are virtually incompressible.
- If a trapped liquid is put under pressure, the pressure is transmitted throughout the liquid.

The diagram below shows a simple hydraulic jack. When you press on the narrow piston, the pressure is transmitted by the oil to the wide piston. It produces an output force which is larger than the input force.

Follow the sequence of circled numbers, 1-4, on the diagram below. They show you how to use the link between pressure, force, and area to calculate the output force.

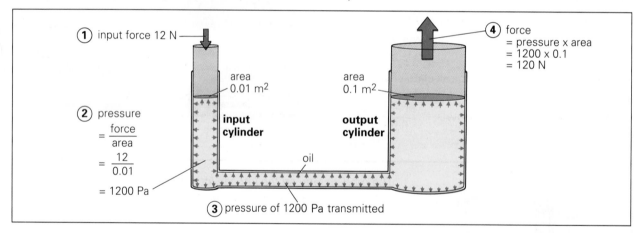

① input force 12 N

② pressure
$$= \frac{\text{force}}{\text{area}}$$
$$= \frac{12}{0.01}$$
$$= 1200 \text{ Pa}$$

area 0.01 m² · **input cylinder**

oil

area 0.1 m² · **output cylinder**

③ pressure of 1200 Pa transmitted

④ force
= pressure x area
= 1200 x 0.1
= 120 N

Gravitational potential energy (PE)

On the right, someone has lifted a stone above the ground. The equation *work = force × distance moved* has been used to calculate the work done.

The stone has gained **gravitational potential energy (PE)** equal to the work done in lifting it. So:

PE	=	weight	×	height lifted
in J		in N		in m

or, in symbols

PE = *mgh*	*m* = mass in kg	
	g = 10 N/kg	
	h = height in m	

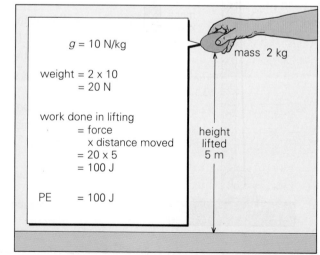

g = 10 N/kg

mass 2 kg

weight = 2 x 10
       = 20 N

work done in lifting
= force
  x distance moved
= 20 x 5
= 100 J

height lifted 5 m

PE = 100 J

Kinetic energy (KE)

Moving things have kinetic energy (KE). Scientists have worked out an equation for calculating it:

$$KE = \tfrac{1}{2}mv^2$$

KE = kinetic energy in J
m = mass in kg
v = velocity in m/s

On the right, you can see how to use this equation.

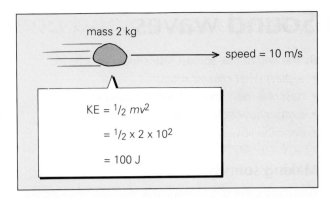

Energy problem

The stone on the right has a mass 2 kg. It is held 5 metres above the ground and then dropped. What is its speed when it hits the ground? (Assume that g is 10 N/kg and no energy is lost because of friction.)

You can solve this problem as follows:

When the stone is 5 m above the ground:

PE = mgh = 2 × 10 × 5 = 100 J

When the stone is just about to hit the ground, all its PE has been changed into KE. So, its KE is 100 J.

So $\tfrac{1}{2}mv^2 = 100$

But $m = 2$

So $\tfrac{1}{2} \times 2 \times v^2 = 100$

So $v = 10$

The stone hits the ground at a speed of 10 m/s.

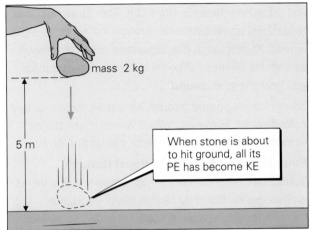

When stone is about to hit ground, all its PE has become KE

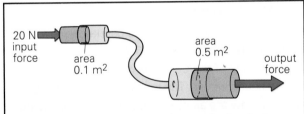

1 In the hydraulic system above a) what is the pressure of the oil? b) what is the output force? c) if the diameter of the output cylinder were greater, how would this affect the output force?

2 A rock of mass 3 kg is 20 m above the ground. What is a) its potential energy b) its potential energy when it has fallen half way to the ground c) its kinetic energy when it has fallen half way to the ground d) its kinetic energy just before it hits the ground e) its velocity just before it hits the ground f) its velocity, if it had slid to the ground down a smooth slope instead of falling? (In this question, assume that there is no air resistance)

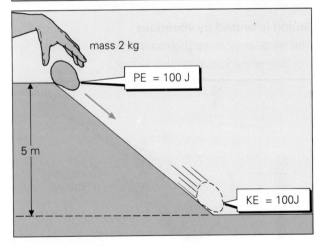

Scalar energy

The stone above starts in the same position as the stone in the previous problem. But instead of falling, it slides down an icy slope. There is no friction.

Just as before, the stone starts with 100 J of PE, which changes into 100 J of KE. So its final speed is exactly the same whether it slides down the slope or falls straight to the ground. When dealing with energy, the direction of travel does not matter. This is because energy is a scalar (see Spread 4.20).

4.26 Sound waves

By the end of this spread, you should be able to:

- explain what causes sound
- describe how sound travels as waves
- explain how echoes are produced
- describe how sounds can be absorbed

Making sounds

When the cone of a loudspeaker vibrates, it stretches and squashes the air in front of it. The 'stretches' and 'squashes' travel outwards through the air as invisible waves. (In diagrams, the 'squashes' are often drawn as a series of lines.) When the waves enter your ear, you hear them as **sound**.

Sound waves spread through air just as ripples spread across water. However, sound waves make the air vibrate backwards and forwards, not up and down.

Sound needs a material to travel through

Sound waves can travel through solids and liquids, as well as gases. But they cannot travel through a vacuum (empty space). If there is nothing to stretch and squash, sound waves cannot be made.

Sound is caused by vibrations

The vibrations can be produced in different ways. You can see some examples below:

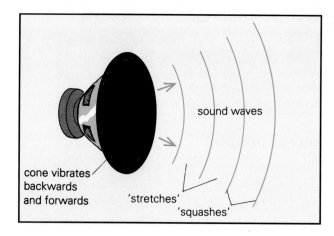

cone vibrates backwards and forwards

'stretches'

'squashes'

sound waves

The speed of sound

In air, the speed of sound is about 330 metres per second. The exact speed depends on the temperature.

Sound travels faster through water than it does through air, and even faster through most solids.

Sound is much slower than light, which travels at 300 000 *kilo*metres per second. That is why you see a flash of lightning before you hear it. The light reaches you almost instantly.

Sound on screen

If you whistle into a microphone connected to a **cathode ray oscilloscope (CRO)**, a wavy line appears on the screen of the CRO. However, you aren't really seeing sound waves. The up-and-down line is a graph showing how the air next to the microphone vibrates backwards and forwards with time.

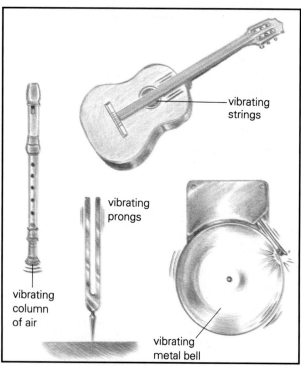

vibrating strings

vibrating prongs

vibrating column of air

vibrating metal bell

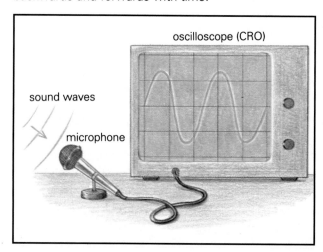

oscilloscope (CRO)

sound waves

microphone

Echoes

Hard surfaces, such as walls, reflect sound waves. When you hear an **echo**, you are hearing a reflected sound a short time after the original sound.

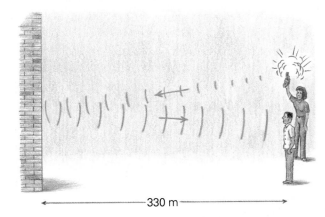

-330 m-

Finding the speed of sound You can use echoes to work out the speed of sound. The girl above is stood 330 metres from a wall. She fires a starting pistol. Her friend hears the echo 2 seconds later.

The sound has travelled a distance of 2 x 330 metres. The time taken is 2 seconds. So:

$$\text{speed of sound} = \frac{\text{distance travelled}}{\text{time taken}} = \frac{2 \times 330}{2}$$

$$= 330 \text{ m/s}$$

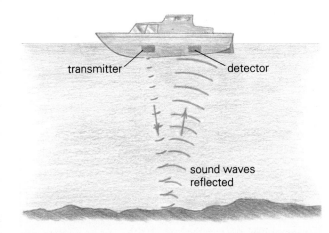

transmitter   detector

sound waves reflected

Echo-sounding Boats can use echo-sounding equipment to work out the depth of water beneath them. A sound pulse is sent down through the water. The time for the echo to return is measured. The longer the time, the deeper the water. A microchip can work out the depth and display it on a screen.

Absorbing sounds

Empty rooms sound echoey. The walls reflect the smallest sound, and it may take several seconds for the wave energy to be absorbed so that the sound dies away.

Echoes can be a nuisance in concert halls. Soft materials like carpets and curtains help to absorb sound waves, so do the clothes of the audience. Many large concert halls have specially-designed sound absorbers on the ceiling to make them less echoey.

The 'mushrooms' on the ceiling of this concert hall are sound absorbers to reduce unwanted echoes.

Assume that the speed of sound in air is 330 m/s.
1   Why cannot sound travel through a vacuum?
2   How could you show that sound travels in the form of waves?
3   Why do you hear lightning after you see it?
4   If you hear lightning 2 seconds after you see it, how far away is the lightning?
5   Chris shouts when he is 110 metres from a wall.
    a) What time does it take for the sound to reach the wall? b) When will Chris hear his echo?
6   What is *echo-sounding*? How does it work?
7   Why do some rooms sound echoey? What can be done to solve the problem?

Detecting sounds

By the end of this spread, you should be able to:
- *describe how the ear works*
- *explain how hearing can be damaged*
- *describe how sounds can differ*

The ear

Inside the ear, sound waves are detected and nerve impulses are sent to the brain for processing.

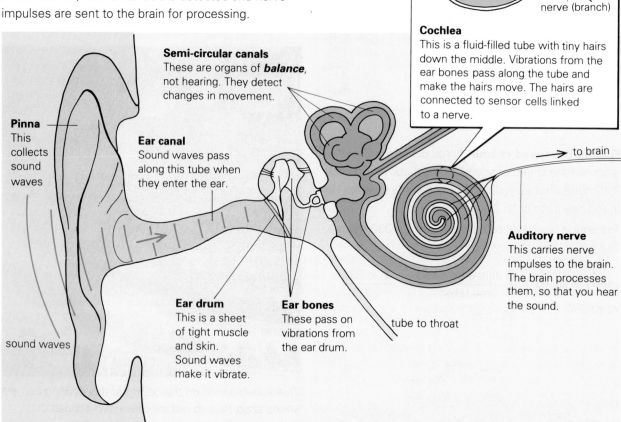

hair

sensor cells

nerve (branch)

Cochlea
This is a fluid-filled tube with tiny hairs down the middle. Vibrations from the ear bones pass along the tube and make the hairs move. The hairs are connected to sensor cells linked to a nerve.

Semi-circular canals
These are organs of *balance*, not hearing. They detect changes in movement.

Pinna
This collects sound waves

Ear canal
Sound waves pass along this tube when they enter the ear.

to brain

Auditory nerve
This carries nerve impulses to the brain. The brain processes them, so that you hear the sound.

sound waves

Ear drum
This is a sheet of tight muscle and skin. Sound waves make it vibrate.

Ear bones
These pass on vibrations from the ear drum.

tube to throat

Hearing problems

When sound waves enter the ear, the brain may not receive nerve impulses. Or the nerve impulses may be weak. Here are some of the problems that can cause deafness or poor hearing:
- The ear drum may be damaged.
- Bone growth may stop the ear bones moving.
- The cochlea or auditory nerve may be damaged.

The cochlea and auditory nerve can be damaged by very loud sounds. That is why you should not play a personal stereo at high volume. If you are exposed to loud sounds over a long period of time, the damage may be so gradual that you do not notice.

Noise

Unwanted sound is called *noise*. It can be annoying. It can also be damaging. Scientists check noise levels using meters marked in *decibels (dB)*.

	Noise level in dB
personal stereo, very loud	150
damage to ears	140
rock concert	110
some ear discomfort	90
telephone ringing	70
normal speech	60
whispering	40

Sounds different

Some sounds are louder than others. Some sounds are higher than others. To see how different sounds compare, you can use a microphone and CRO.

Amplitude and loudness The height of a peak or trough on the screen is called the **amplitude**. The higher the amplitude, the **louder** the sound will be.

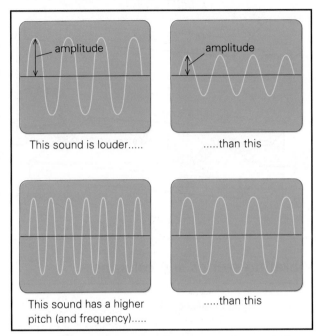

This sound is louder..... .....than this

This sound has a higher pitch (and frequency)..... .....than this

Frequency and pitch The **frequency** of a sound is the number of sound waves being sent out per second.

Frequency is measured in **hertz (Hz)**. If a sound has a frequency of, say, 100 Hz, then 100 sound waves are being sent out every second.

The higher the frequency, the higher the note sounds. Musicians say that it has a higher **pitch**.

If the frequency increases, you see more waves on the CRO screen. The peaks of the waves are closer together.

1 In the ear, what job is done by a) the ear drum b) the ear bones c) the cochlea?
2 Explain why a personal stereo played at high volume can damage your hearing.
3 A sound has a *frequency* of *200 Hz*. What does this tell you about the sound waves?
4 What difference will you hear in a sound if there is an increase in a) amplitude b) frequency?
5 In hospitals, why are sound waves sometimes used instead of X-rays? What are the sound waves used for?

Seeing with sound

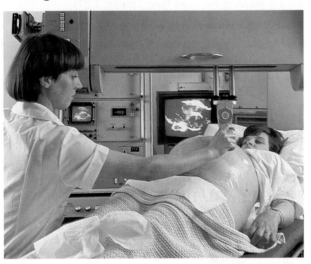

Sounds which are too high for the human ear to hear are called **ultrasonic sounds**, or **ultrasound**. Ultrasound can be used to check an unborn baby in the womb, as above. An ultrasound transmitter is moved over the mother's body. A detector picks up sound waves reflected from different layers inside the body. The signals are processed by a computer, which puts an image on a screen. The method is safer than using X-rays because X-rays damage body cells.

low frequency					high frequency
20 Hz	100 Hz	1 000 Hz	10 000 Hz	20 000 Hz	
					ultrasonic sounds
drum	low note from singer	high note from singer	whistle	highest note heard by human ear	
low pitch					high pitch

Waves and vibrations

By the end of this spread, you should be able to:
* *describe longitudinal and transverse waves*
* *link speed, frequency, and wavelength*
* *give examples of harmonics and resonance*

Longitudinal and transverse waves

There are two main types of waves. You can demonstrate both with a stretched spring.

Longitudinal waves have vibrations which are backwards and forwards. Sound waves are like this. So are seismic P-waves (see Spread 3.27).

Transverse waves have vibrations which are from side to side (or up and down). Radio waves and light waves are like this (see Spread 4.31). So are seismic S-waves (see Spread 3.27).

Speed, frequency, and wavelength

Below, transverse waves are travelling across water. The distance between the peaks is the **wavelength** (measured in metres). The number of waves passing per second is the **frequency** (measured in Hz):

These waves have a wavelength of 2 m and a frequency of 3 Hz

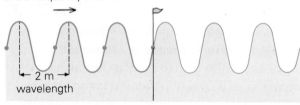

One second later...

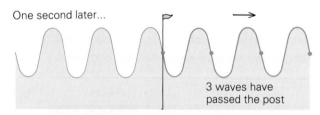

3 waves have passed the post

In this example, 3 waves pass every second. Each wave is 2 m long. So the waves travel 6 metres every second – their speed is 6 m/s. You could work out this result with an equation, which is true for all waves:

speed	=	frequency	×	wavelength
in m/s		in Hz		in m

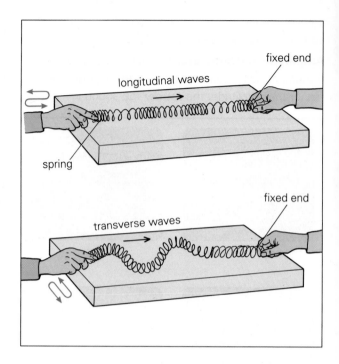

longitudinal waves

fixed end

spring

transverse waves

fixed end

Vibrating strings and columns

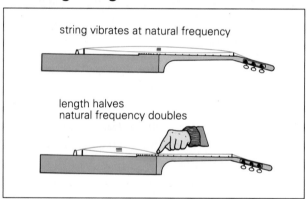

string vibrates at natural frequency

length halves
natural frequency doubles

If you pluck a stretched guitar string in the middle, it vibrates at a certain **natural frequency**.

The natural frequency is higher if
* the vibrating length of the string is shorter
* the string has more tension (it is tighter)
* the string has less mass.

If you halve the vibrating length of a string, its natural frequency doubles and the pitch of the note goes up by exactly one octave.

In the recorder on the right, the sound comes from a vibrating column of air. You cover or uncover holes to change the length of the vibrating column. The shorter the column, the higher the frequency.

Extra frequencies

A piano and a guitar sound different, even when playing the same note. The sounds have a different *quality*. They may have the same **fundamental** (basic) frequency, but they have different – higher – frequencies mixed in. These are called **harmonics**. They give each instrument its distinctive sound.

With a **synthesizer**, you can select which harmonics are added, and when. In this way, you can produce the sound of a piano, flute, or other instrument.

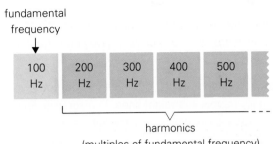

fundamental frequency

| 100 Hz | 200 Hz | 300 Hz | 400 Hz | 500 Hz | |

harmonics
(multiples of fundamental frequency)

Resonance

If a car wheel is out of balance, it will vibrate when the car reaches a certain speed. This 'wheel wobble' makes the steering wheel judder and can damage the suspension. To prevent it, each car wheel has to be balanced by fixing small lead masses to the rim.

In a washing machine, as on the right, there can be 'drum wobble' if the clothes aren't spread evenly. When the drum reaches a certain speed, severe vibrations start. These may damage the machine.

In both cases above, there is a source of vibration (such as the drum motor). And there is something with a natural frequency of vibration (such as the drum). If the frequency of the source matches this natural frequency, then the amplitude of the vibrations builds up to a peak. This effect is called **resonance**.

Resonance can be useful. Without it, most musical instruments would be too quiet to hear! When someone blows into a recorder, a wedge disturbs the airflow and sets off oscillations at a frequency which matches the natural frequency of the air column. The column resonates and produces a loud sound.

Resonance is used in a recorder

Larger units of frequency

1 kilohertz (kHz) = 1000 Hz

1 Megahertz (MHz) = 1 000 000 Hz (1 million Hz)

1. What is the difference between *longitudinal* and *transverse* waves? Give an example of each.
2. What is the effect on the natural frequency if a guitar string is a) shortened b) loosened?
3. Why does a clarinet sound different from a trumpet which is playing the same note?
4. What is resonance? Give an example of when it is a) useful b) a nuisance.
5. If a sound has a frequency of 110 Hz, what is its wavelength? (Speed of sound in air = 330 m/s)
6. The speed of radio waves is 300 000 000 m/s. If a VHF radio station broadcasts on a frequency of 100 MHz, what is the wavelength?

Rays of light

By the end of this spread, you should be able to:
* *explain how light can be reflected and refracted*

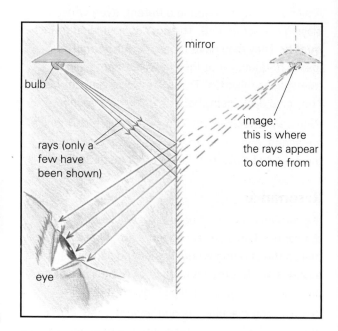

Light is radiation which your eyes can detect. It normally travels in straight lines. In diagrams, lines called **rays** show which way the light is going.

You see some things because they give off their own light: the Sun or a light bulb for example.

You see other things because daylight, or other light, bounces off them. They **reflect** light, and some goes into your eyes. That is why you can see this page.

The white parts of the page reflect light well, so they look bright. However, the black letters **absorb** most of the light striking them. They reflect very little. That is why they look so dark.

Transparent materials, like glass, let light pass through them. They **transmit** light.

Reflection and mirrors

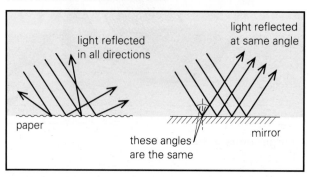

Most surfaces are uneven, or contain materials which scatter light. The light bounces off them in all directions. However, mirrors are smooth and shiny. They reflect light in a regular way.

In the diagram at the top on the right, light from a bulb is being reflected by a mirror. Some is reflected into the girl's eye. To the girl, the light seems to come from a point behind the mirror. She sees an **image** of the bulb in that position.

The image is the same size as the original bulb, and the same distance from the mirror. However its left and right sides are the wrong way round. It is **laterally inverted**, just like these letters:

ЯOЯЯIM A ИI SIHT Ǝ❘IꓘↃOOꟼↃ ꟼꟼↃↃↃↃↃↃ WRITING LOOKS LIKE THIS IN A MIRROR

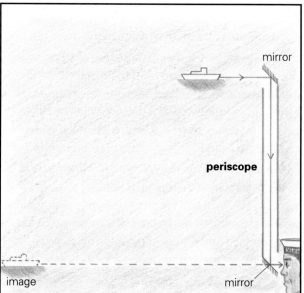

Periscope A periscope uses two mirrors to give you a higher view than normal. The image you see is the right way round because one mirror cancels out the lateral inversion of the other.

1 Hot, glowing things give off light. How can this page give off light if it isn't hot and glowing?
2 A wall reflects light. So does a mirror. What difference is there in the way they reflect light?
3 Why does a periscope need two mirrors?

Refraction

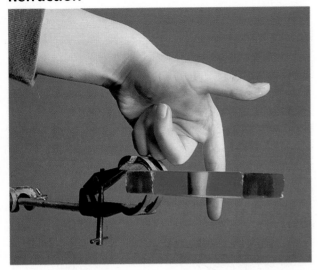

The light passing through the glass block above has been bent. The bending is called *refraction*: It happens with other transparent materials as well as glass.

Below, you can see how scientists explain refraction. Light is made up of tiny waves (see Spreads 4.31 and 4.33). These travel more slowly in glass than in air. One side of the light beam is slowed before the other. This makes the light waves bend.

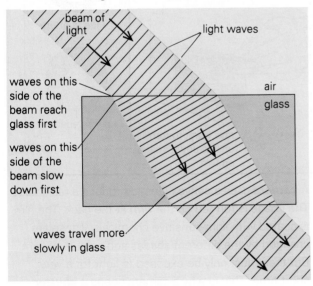

beam of light

light waves

waves on this side of the beam reach glass first

air

glass

waves on this side of the beam slow down first

waves travel more slowly in glass

4   What is *refraction*? Give an example.
5   Why does a beam of light bend when it enters glass at an angle? Why does it *not* bend if it enters the glass 'square on'.
6   What is an *optical fibre*? How does it work?

Reflection and fibres

The inside face of a glass block can act as a perfect mirror – provided light strikes it at a shallow enough angle. No light is refracted. All is reflected. Scientists call this **total internal reflection**.

Total internal reflection is used in **optical fibres**. These are thin, flexible strands of glass or plastic. When light enters one end of a fibre, it is reflected from side to side, until it comes out of the other end. (High-quality fibres have an outer layer of glass or plastic to protect the core which carries the light.)

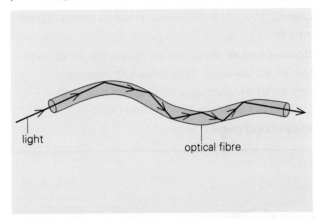

light

optical fibre

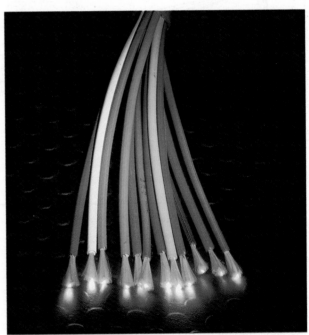

Optical fibres are used to carry telephone calls. Sound waves 'pulsate' the light from a tiny laser at one end of the fibre. At the other end, the light pulsations are detected and changed into electrical signals. These make the telephone give out sound.

Lenses at work

By the end of this spread, you should be able to:
- describe what different lenses do to light
- describe some uses of convex lenses
- explain how spectacles work

Lenses bend light and form images. There are two main types of lens:

Concave lenses these are thin in the middle and thickest round the edge. They bend light outwards. Looking through a concave lens makes things appear smaller.

Convex lenses these are thickest in the middle and thin round the edge. They bend light inwards. A convex lens makes *very close* things look bigger. Used in this way, the lens is often called a *magnifying glass*.

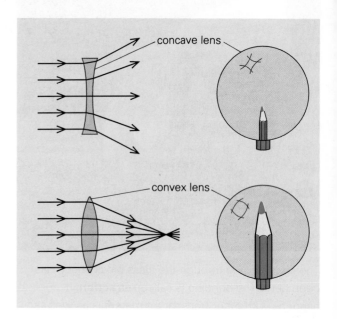

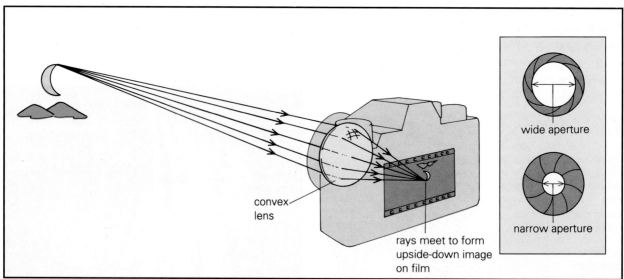

convex lens

rays meet to form upside-down image on film

wide aperture

narrow aperture

With *distant* things, a convex lens brings rays to a focus. The rays form a small, upside-down image which you can pick up on a screen. It is called a *real image* because the rays actually meet to produce it. (The image you see in a flat mirror isn't formed by rays meeting. It is called a *virtual image*.)

If a distant thing moves closer to a convex lens, the image moves further away. It also gets bigger. This idea is used in a *projector*. A brightly-lit piece of film is put fairly close to a convex lens. The result is a large, real image on a screen many metres away. For an upright image, the film must be upside-down.

A *camera* uses a convex lens to produce a real image. The image is formed on the *film* at the back. The film is coated with light-sensitive chemicals. These are changed by the different shades and colours of light. But they must only be exposed to light for a very short time. That is why a camera needs a *shutter* which opens and shuts very quickly.

To focus on things at different distances, the lens is moved in or out. This changes its distance from the film. Behind the lens, metals plates can alter the size of the *aperture* (hole) through which the light passes. A bigger aperture lets in more light.

The eye

Like a camera, the human eye uses a convex lens system to form a tiny, real, image at the back. The image is upside-down. However, the brain gets so used to this that it thinks the image is the right way up!

For focusing on things at different distances, tiny muscles make the eye lens thinner or fatter. However, many people can still not get a clearly-focused image. So they have to wear spectacles (or contact lenses) to help their eye lenses.

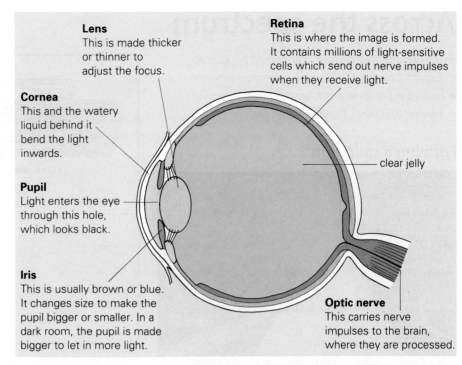

Lens
This is made thicker or thinner to adjust the focus.

Cornea
This and the watery liquid behind it bend the light inwards.

Pupil
Light enters the eye through this hole, which looks black.

Iris
This is usually brown or blue. It changes size to make the pupil bigger or smaller. In a dark room, the pupil is made bigger to let in more light.

Retina
This is where the image is formed. It contains millions of light-sensitive cells which send out nerve impulses when they receive light.

clear jelly

Optic nerve
This carries nerve impulses to the brain, where they are processed.

Short sight In a short-sighted eye, the eye lens cannot become thin enough for looking at distant things. So the rays are bent inwards too much. They meet before they reach the retina.

Long sight In a long-sighted eye, the eye lens cannot become thick enough for looking at close things. So the rays are not bent inwards enough. When they reach the retina, they have still not met.

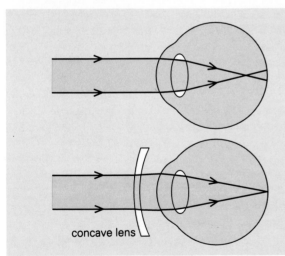

concave lens

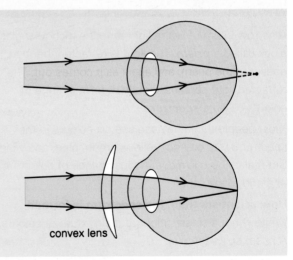

convex lens

A *concave* spectacle lens solves the problem. It bends the rays outwards a little before they enter the eye.

A *convex* spectacle lens solves the problem. It bends the rays inwards a little before they enter the eye.

---

1 How would a paper clip look if you saw it through a) a concave lens b) a convex lens? (Assume the paper clip is close to the lens.)

2 Name *three* things which make use of a convex lens. What job does the lens do in each one?

3 Give *three* ways in which the human eye is similar to a camera.

4 What is the difference between a short-sighted eye and a normal eye? What type of spectacle lens does a short-sighted person need? Why?

Across the spectrum

By the end of this spread, you should be able to:
- explain how a prism forms a spectrum
- describe the different types of electromagnetic waves, and what they are used for

Forming a spectrum

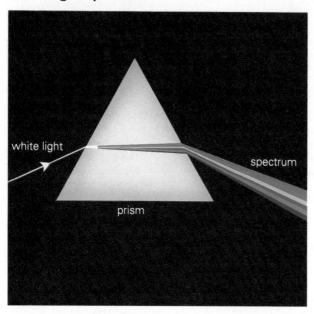

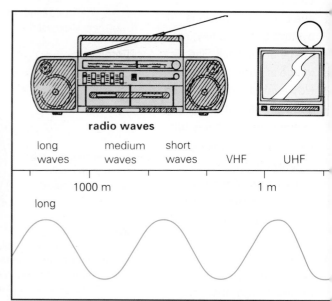

A narrow beam of white light enters a triangular glass block called a **prism**. The light is refracted (bent) as it goes into the prism, and again as it comes out. The refracted light spreads slightly to form a range of colours called a **spectrum**.

Most people think they can see six colours in the spectrum: red, orange, yellow, green, blue, and violet. But really, there is a continuous change of colour from one end to the other.

How scientists think the spectrum is formed

White is not a single colour, but a mixture of colours. A prism splits them up.

Light is made up of tiny waves. These have different **wavelengths**. The eyes and brain sense different wavelengths as different colours. Red waves are the longest and violet the shortest.

When light enters glass, it slows down and bends (see Spread 4.29). Waves of violet light slow down more than waves of red light. So they are bent more. That is why the different colours are spread out. The spreading effect is called **dispersion**.

Raindrops act like tiny prisms and split sunlight into its different colours.

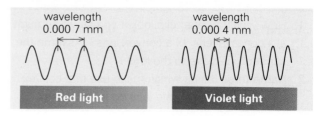

The electromagnetic spectrum

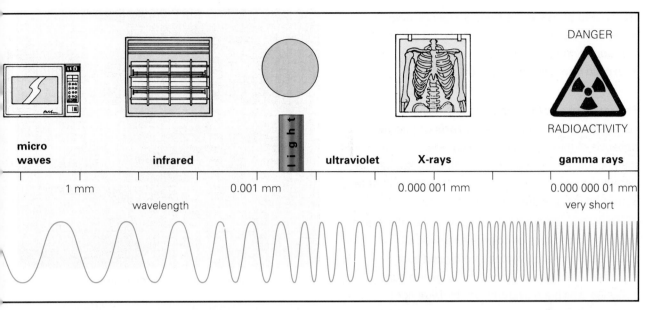

| micro waves | infrared | light | ultraviolet | X-rays | gamma rays |

DANGER

RADIOACTIVITY

| 1 mm | 0.001 mm | 0.000 001 mm | 0.000 000 01 mm |
| | wavelength | | very short |

Beyond the colours of the spectrum, there are types of radiation which the eye cannot see. Light is just one member of a much larger family of waves called the *electromagnetic spectrum*.

> Electromagnetic waves have these things in common:
> - They are electric and magnetic ripples, given off when electrons or other charged particles vibrate or lose energy.
> - They can travel though empty space.
> - Their speed through space is 300 000 km/s.

Radio waves These are produced by making electrons vibrate in an aerial. They cannot be seen or heard. But they can be sent out in a pattern which tells a radio or TV what sounds or pictures to make.

Microwaves These are radio waves of very short wavelength. They are used for radar, for satellite communication, and for beaming telephone and TV signals around the country.

Some microwaves are absorbed by food. This makes the food hot. The idea is used in microwave ovens.

Infrared Hot things like fires and radiators all give off infrared radiation. In fact, everything gives off some infrared. If you absorb it, it heats you up.

Light This is the visible part of the spectrum - the part which the eye can detect.

Ultraviolet The eye cannot detect ultraviolet, but there is lots of it in sunlight. This is the type of radiation which gives you a sun tan. Too much can damage your eyes and skin.

Fluorescent 'day glo' paints and inks absorb the ultraviolet in sunlight and change its energy into visible light. That is why they glow so brightly.

X-rays Shorter wavelengths can penetrate dense metals. Longer wavelengths can pass through flesh, but not bone. So they can be used to take 'shadow' photographs of bones. Only brief bursts of X-rays must be used for this. X-rays are very dangerous and damage living cells deep in the body.

Gamma rays These are given off by radioactive materials (see Spread 4.34). They have the same effects as X-rays and are very dangerous.

---

1 Which is refracted most by a prism, red light or violet light? Explain why.

The following questions are about these waves:
gamma radio micro X-rays light ultraviolet infrared

2 Put the waves in order of wavelength, starting with the longest wavelength.

3 Which of the waves a) can be detected by the eye b) are used for communications c) are used in cooking d) can pass through flesh e) can damage cells deep in the body?

Seeing colours

By the end of this spread, you should be able to:
- *describe how primary colours can be added to produce different colours*
- *explain how objects give their colours*

The retina of a human eye contains millions of light-sensitive cells. These are called **rods** and **cones** because of their shapes. There are many more rods than cones. Rods respond to weak light, but cannot detect colour differences. Cones need more light to start working, but are sensitive to colour.

Humans can see hundreds of colours. Yet the retina has only *three* types of colour-sensitive cell:
- Cones which are switched on by **red** light
- Cones which are switched on by **green** light
- Cones which are switched on by **blue** light

Each type is also sensitive to other colours in their part of the spectrum. So between them, they cover the full range. The brain senses *all* colours by how they affect each type of cone. So you see all colours in terms of **red**, **green**, and **blue**. These are the **primary colours**.

Adding colours

On the right, beams of red, green, and blue light are overlapping on a white screen.

White This is seen where all three primaries overlap. So:

> **red + green + blue = white**

Pure white contains all the colours of the rainbow. But a mixture of red, green, and blue is enough to give the eye the sensation of white. It switches on all three types of colour-sensitive cell, just as pure white would.

Secondary colours Where any two primary colours overlap, a new colour is seen:

> **red + green = yellow**
> **green + blue = cyan**
> **red + blue = magenta**

These colours, **yellow**, **cyan**, and **magenta,** are called the **secondary** colours. (They aren't really single colours. They just seem that way to the brain.)

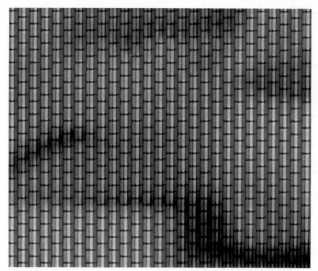

Part of a colour TV screen: magnification x3

By adding red, green, and blue light in different proportions, the brain can be given the sensation of almost any colour. The effect is used in colour television. The screen of a colour TV (like the one above) is covered with thousands of tiny red, green, and blue strips. These glow in different combinations to produce a full colour picture.

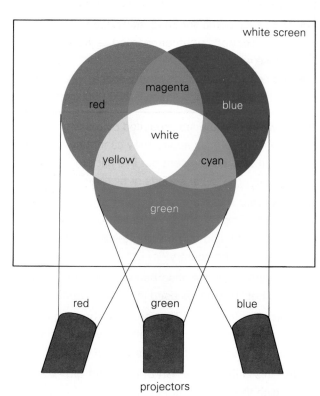

Taking colours away

The Sun gives out its own light, so does a TV screen. Most things are not like this. We see them because they reflect light from the Sun or some other source.

To the eye, white sunlight is a mixture of red, green, and blue. Things look coloured in sunlight because they *reflect* some colours only and *absorb* the rest. In other words, they take colours away from white.

In white light:

- A *red* cloth reflects red light but absorbs green and blue.
- A *yellow* cloth reflects red and green light but absorbs blue.
- A *white* cloth reflects red, green, and blue. It absorbs no colours.
- A *black* cloth reflects virtually no light. It absorbs red, green, and blue.

Paints, inks, and dyes reflect some colours and absorb others. For example, red paint reflects red light, but absorbs green and blue.

When you mix coloured paints (or inks or dyes), the final colour is not the same as that produced by overlapping light beams. With overlapping beams, colours are being *added*. When paints are mixed, more colours are *taken away*, so less light is reflected.

The pictures in this book were printed using inks of just three colours: yellow, cyan, and magenta (with some black added in places as well). For example the red area in the diagram on the left was produced by printing magenta ink on top of yellow. Red light is reflected because it is the only colour not absorbed by either the magenta ink or the yellow.

Filters are pieces of plastic or glass which let through certain colours only. For example, a red filter *transmits* red light but *absorbs* green and blue, as shown below.

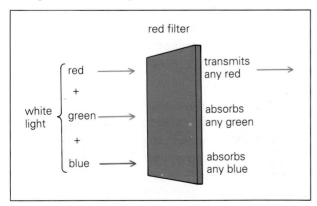

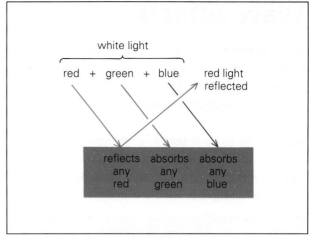

In white light, a red cloth looks red

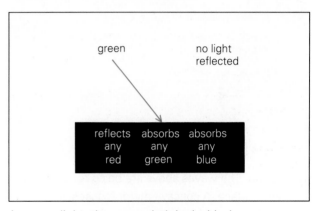

In green light, the same cloth looks black

If you shine coloured light on something, its colour may change. There is an example of this above. A cloth which looks red in white light, looks black when viewed in green light. If green light only is striking it, that is absorbed, so no light is reflected.

1 What are the three primary colours?
2 What colour is produced when the three primaries are added together?
3 What colour is produced when red and green light beams overlap on a white screen?
4 What colours does a white coat reflect?
5 What colours does a black coat absorb?
6 a) What colour does a blue filter transmit?
   b) What colours does it absorb?
7 a) What colour does a green coat reflect?
   b) What colours does it absorb?
8 What colour will a green coat appear in red light?

Wave effects

By the end of this spread, you should be able to:
• describe what happens to waves during these processes: reflection, refraction, diffraction, interference, and polarization

You can use a **ripple tank** to study how waves behave. Ripples are sent across the surface of some water in a shallow tank. Different shapes are placed in the water to reflect or bend the 'beam'.

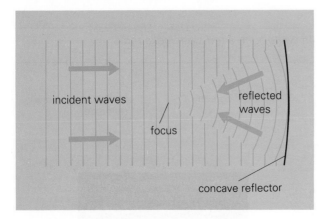

Reflection The waves above are being reflected by a concave surface. A concave mirror focuses light in the same way.

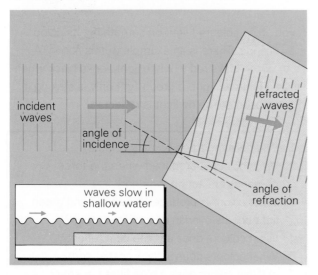

Refraction A flat piece of plastic makes the water less deep. This slows the waves down. As a result, they are refracted (bent). Scientists have found that:

$$\frac{\text{sine of angle of incidence}}{\text{sine of angle of refraction}} = \frac{\text{speed of incident waves}}{\text{speed of refracted waves}}$$

The effects of interference (see right)

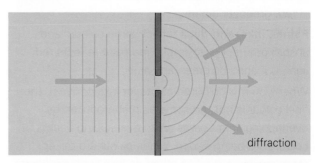

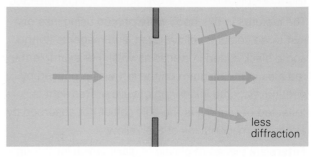

Diffraction Waves bend round the edges of a narrow gap. This is called **diffraction**. It works best if the width of the gap is about the same as the wavelength. Wider gaps cause less diffraction.

Sound waves diffract round large obstacles, which is why you hear round corners. Light waves are much shorter, so gaps must be very tiny to diffract them.

Long and medium wavelength radio waves are diffracted by hills, so you can still pick up a signal down in a valley. But with shorter VHF and UHF signals, the diffraction is much less. For good reception, there has to be an almost straight line between the transmitter and the receiving aerial.

Interference

If two identical sets of waves combine, they may either reinforce or cancel each other – depending on whether they are in **phase** ('in step') or out of phase ('out of step'). This effect is called **interference**.

Interference causes the colours on a soap bubble, as in the photograph on the left. Light reflected from the front of the soap film interferes with light reflected from the back. The light (white daylight) is a mixture of different colours (different wavelengths). Some are reinforced by the interference, so you see them. Others are cancelled out.

Polarization

Like ripples, light waves are transverse. However, most light is a mixture of waves which vibrate up-and-down, side-to-side, and all planes in between. Light like this is called **unpolarized** light.

Polaroid is a material which blocks vibrations in all planes except one. So, light leaving a piece of Polaroid has vibrations in one plane only (for example, up-and-down). Light like this is called **polarized** light.

If you put one piece of Polaroid over another and the planes of vibration match, light can pass through. But if you rotate one Polaroid through 90°, polarized light from the first is blocked by the second. The Polaroids are **crossed**. They look black.

Light reflected from water is partly polarized. Polaroid sunglasses block some of this light, which is why they reduce glare from wet surfaces.

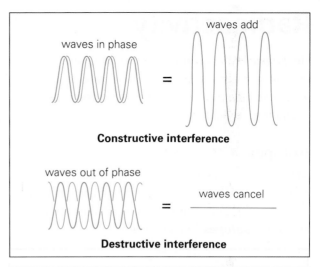

Constructive interference

Destructive interference

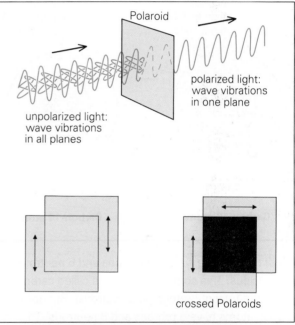

Polaroid

polarized light: wave vibrations in one plane

unpolarized light: wave vibrations in all planes

crossed Polaroids

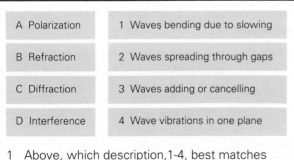

A Polarization	1 Waves bending due to slowing
B Refraction	2 Waves spreading through gaps
C Diffraction	3 Waves adding or cancelling
D Interference	4 Wave vibrations in one plane

1   Above, which description, 1-4, best matches each of the words A-D?
2   Down in a valley, why is long wave radio reception good, but VHF reception poor?
3   Why do two Polaroids let light through when covering each other one way, but not when one of them is rotated 90°?

In a 'liquid crystal' display (above), the liquid is sandwiched between two strips of Polaroid. These are crossed, but look clear because the liquid rotates the waves through 90°. If a tiny current is passed through the liquid, the rotation effect is stopped and the crossed Polaroids look black. By sending currents through different areas of the liquid, black strips can be produced. These form the numbers of the display.

Radioactivity

By the end of this spread, you should be able to:
- *explain why some substances are radioactive*
- *describe the three main types of nuclear radiation and their effects*

Isotopes

Atoms of the same element are not all alike. Elements can exist in different versions, with different numbers of neutrons in the nucleus. These different versions are called *isotopes*. For example:

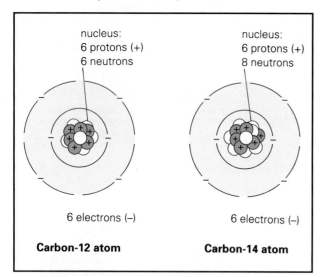

nucleus:
6 protons (+)
6 neutrons

nucleus:
6 protons (+)
8 neutrons

6 electrons (–)

6 electrons (–)

Carbon-12 atom

Carbon-14 atom

Most carbon atoms have 6 protons and 6 neutrons in the nucleus. This common isotope is called carbon-12 (12 is the total of protons plus neutrons). But some carbon atoms have 6 protons and 8 neutrons. This rare isotope is carbon-14.

Nuclear radiation

Some isotopes have unstable atoms. In time, the nucleus breaks up, and shoots out a tiny particle, or burst of wave energy, or both. This 'radiates' from the nucleus. It is called *nuclear radiation*. If a substance gives out nuclear radiation, scientists say that it is *radioactive*.

Some of the materials in nuclear power stations are highly radioactive. But nuclear radiation comes from many natural sources as well, as shown in the table on the right. This means that there is a small amount of nuclear radiation around us all the time. Scientists call it *background radiation*.

Containers for radioactive waste must be strong enough to withstand crashes like this.

Ionizing effect

Nuclear radiation can remove electrons from atoms in its path. In other words it can make ions: it has an *ionizing* effect. Ionizing radiation can be very dangerous. It may stop cells in vital organs working properly. It can also damage the chemical instructions in normal cells so that the cells grow abnormally and cause cancer. However, in *radiotherapy* treatment, carefully-directed radiation (gamma rays) is used to kill cancer cells.

Isotopes		
Stable	*Unstable, radioactive*	*Found in...*
carbon-12 carbon-13	carbon-14	air, plants, animals
potassium-39 potassium-41	potassium-40	rocks, plants, sea-water
	uranium-234 uranium-235 uranium-238	rocks

Alpha, beta, and gamma

There are three main types of nuclear radiation: **alpha** particles, **beta** particles, and **gamma** rays. They can be detected by a **Geiger-Müller tube (GM tube)**, connected to an electronic counter or meter.

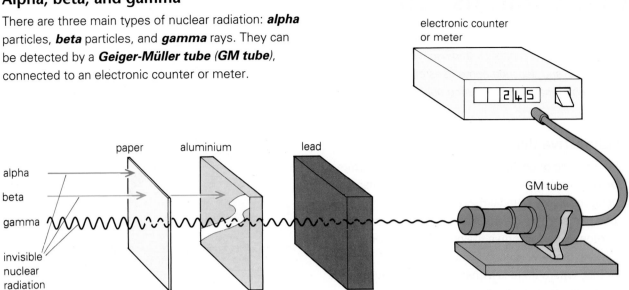

Nuclear radiation ⇨	Alpha particles	Beta particles	Gamma rays
	Each particle is 2 protons + 2 neutrons	Each particle is an electron (formed when the nucleus breaks up)	Electromagnetic waves similar to X-rays (see spread 4.31)
Electric charge	+	−	No charge
Ionizing effect	Strong	Weak	Very weak
Penetrating effect	Not very penetrating: stopped by thick sheet of paper, or skin	Penetrating: Stopped by thick sheet of aluminium	Highly penetrating: never completely stopped, though lead and very thick concrete reduce strength

1 Comparing atoms of *carbon-12* and *carbon-14*:
   a) What do the numbers '12' and '14' tell you?
   b) In what ways are the atoms the same?
   c) How are the atoms different?
2 If a substance is *radioactive*, what does this mean?
3 Nuclear radiation has an *ionizing effect*. What does this mean?

4 Why can ionizing radiation be dangerous?
5 What are the three main types of nuclear radiation?
6 Which type of radiation is stopped by skin or thick paper?
7 Which type of radiation can penetrate lead?
8 Which type of radiation is most ionizing?
9 Explain what is meant by *background radiation*.

4·35 Decay and fission

By the end of this spread, you should be able to:
- *explain what is meant by 'radioactive decay' and 'half-life' and describe some uses of radioactivity*
- *describe what happens during nuclear fission*

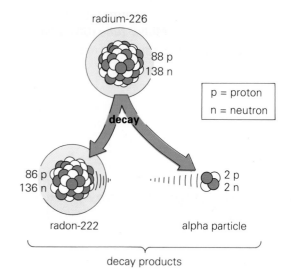

radium-226

88 p
138 n

p = proton
n = neutron

decay

86 p
136 n

radon-222

2 p
2 n

alpha particle

decay products

Radioactive decay

The break up of unstable nuclei is called **radioactive decay**. The diagram on the right shows what happens during the decay of radium-226. The nucleus emits an alpha particle. This means that it loses 2 neutrons and 2 protons. So it becomes the nucleus of a different element, the new isotope being radon-222. A process like this, where there is a change in the nucleus, is called a **nuclear reaction**. Radon-222 and the alpha particle are the **products** of the reaction.

In radioactive decay, energy is released, and the products move faster than the original atoms. For example, it is the decay of radioactive materials in the rocks which keeps temperatures high underground.

Half-life

Radioactive decay is a random process. You cannot tell which nucleus is going to break up next, or when. But some types of nuclei are more unstable than others. They decay at a faster rate.

The graph on the right shows the decay of a sample of iodine-128. The number of nuclei decaying per second is called the **activity**. As time goes on, there are fewer and fewer unstable nuclei left to decay, so the activity gets less and less. After 25 minutes, half the unstable nuclei have decayed, so the activity has halved. After another 25 minutes, the activity has halved again .....and so on. Scientists say that iodine-128 has a **half-life** of 25 minutes.

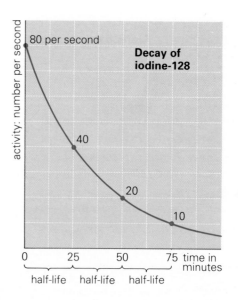

Decay of iodine-128

80 per second

40

20

10

0   25   50   75   time in minutes

half-life half-life half-life

Isotope	Half-life
radon-222	3.8 days
strontium-90	28 years
radium-226	1602 years
carbon-14	5730 years
plutonium-239	24 400 years
uranium-235	710 000 000 years

Fission

Natural uranium is a dense, radioactive metal. It is mainly a mixture of two isotopes: uranium-238 (over 99%) and uranium-235 (less than 1%). Both isotopes decay slowly. However, nuclei of uranium-235 can be split by neutrons. This process is called **fission**. It can release energy very quickly, like this:

A neutron strikes a uranium-235 nucleus, making it split into two roughly equal parts. Two or three neutrons are shot out as well. If these hit other uranium-235 nuclei, they split and give out more neutrons...... and so on in a **chain reaction**.

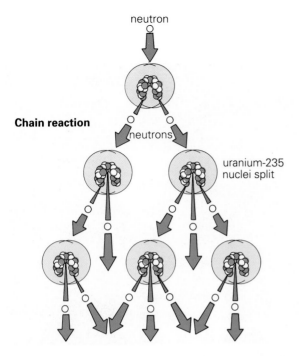

Chain reaction

neutron

neutrons

uranium-235
nuclei split

In an *uncontrolled* chain reaction, huge numbers of nuclei are split in a fraction of a second. The heat builds up so rapidly that the material bursts apart in an explosion. This happens in a nuclear bomb.

In a *controlled* chain reaction, the flow of neutrons is regulated so that there is a steady output of heat. This happens in a **nuclear reactor**. The power station below uses a nuclear reactor as the heat source for its boilers (see Spread 4.14). There is no burning fuel to pollute the atmosphere. But a small amount of radioactive waste is produced. Some of this waste will need to be stored for hundreds of years before its activity falls to a safe level.

Using radioactivity

Radioactive dating can be used to find the age of rocks. When rocks are formed, natural radioactive isotopes become trapped in them. As these decay, new products are formed – and trapped. For example, in mica rock, over millions of years, the amount of radioactive potassium-40 becomes less and less, while the amount of argon-40 decay product becomes more and more. By measuring the ratio of potassium to argon, the age of the rock can be estimated.

Smoke detectors contain a tiny radioactive source which emits alpha particles. These ionize the air in a small chamber, so that it conducts an electric current. Incoming smoke particles attract ions and reduce the current. The drop in current is detected by an electronic circuit which triggers the alarm.

1 Radium-226 decays by emitting an alpha particle. a) What happens during decay? b) Why is a completely different element formed as a result?
2 Strontium-90 has a *half-life* of 28 years. What does this mean?
3 Here are some measurements of the activity of a small sample of iodine-131:

Time in days	0	4	8	12
Activities: Number/s	240	170	120	85

   a) What is the half-life of iodine-131? b) After how many days would you expect the activity of the sample to be 30 per second?
4 What happens to a nucleus of uranium-235 during fission?
5 Give an example of a *chain reaction*. Where is a controlled chain reaction used?

Sun, Earth, and Moon

By the end of this spread, you should be able to:
- *explain why the Earth has seasons*
- *explain why the Moon has phases*
- *describe some of the effects of gravity*
- *describe some of the uses of satellites*

The Sun

The Sun is a huge, hot, brightly glowing ball of gas, called a **star**. It is 150 000 000 kilometres away from us. Its diameter, 1.4 million kilometres, is more than a hundred times that of the Earth. The Sun is extremely hot: 6000 °C on the surface, rising to 15 000 000 °C in the centre. The heat comes from nuclear reactions deep in its core.

Earth, orbiting and spinning

The Earth moves round the Sun in a path called an **orbit**. One orbit takes just over 365 days, which is the length of our year. As it moves through space, the Earth spins slowly on its axis once a day. This gives us day and night as we move from the sunny side facing the Sun to the dark side away from it.

The Earth's axis is tilted by 23.5°. This means that in Britain, for example, the Sun seems to climb higher in the sky in June than it does in December. Also, there are more hours of daylight in June than there are in December. That is why there are different seasons.

When you look at the moon, some of it is usually in shadow. You only see the sunlit part.

A view of the Moon

The Moon is in orbit around the Earth, and 380 000 kilometres away from us. It is smaller than the Earth, and has a rocky, cratered surface. We only see the Moon because its surface reflects sunlight.

The Moon orbits the Earth once every 27 days. It also spins on its axis once every 27 days. That is why it always keeps the same face toward us.

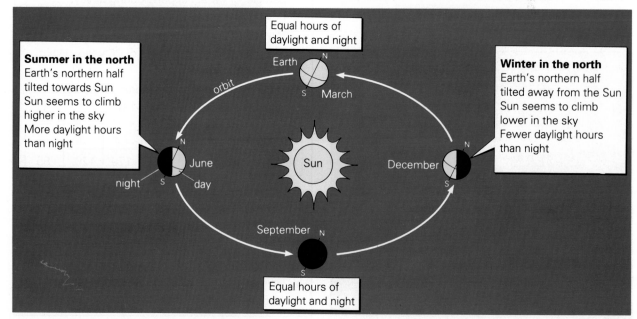

Equal hours of daylight and night

Earth

N

S March

orbit

Summer in the north
Earth's northern half tilted towards Sun
Sun seems to climb higher in the sky
More daylight hours than night

N

night S day

June

Sun

December

N

S

Winter in the north
Earth's northern half tilted away from the Sun
Sun seems to climb lower in the sky
Fewer daylight hours than night

September N

S

Equal hours of daylight and night

As the Moon orbits the Earth, we see different amounts of its surface depending on the position of the Sun. Sometimes we see the whole face (a full Moon). Sometimes we see less than half the face (a crescent Moon), because the rest is in shadow. And sometimes we see almost no face (a new Moon). These different views of the Moon are called **phases**. A complete sequence of phases takes 29.5 days, and not 27. That is because the Earth also changes position as it slowly orbits the Sun.

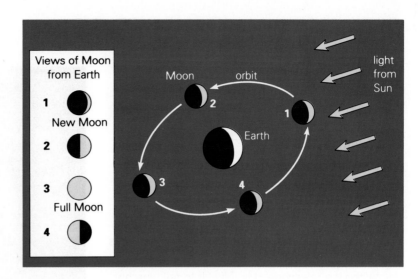

Gravity in action

We are pulled to the Earth by the force of gravity. No one knows what causes gravity. But scientists know that there is a gravitational pull between *all* masses:

- small masses have a weaker pull than large masses
- distant masses have a weaker pull than close masses.

The pull between everyday things is far too weak to detect. It only becomes strong if one of the things has a huge mass, like the Earth.

The gravitational force between the Earth and the Sun holds the Earth in orbit around the Sun. The gravitational force between the Moon and the Earth holds the Moon in orbit around the Earth.

---

1 How long does it take for a) the Moon to orbit the Earth? b) the Earth to orbit the Sun?
2 In the north, why does the Sun seem to climb higher in the sky in June than in December?
3 Why do we always see the same side of the Moon?
4 We can see the Sun because it is glowing. How are we able to see the Moon?
5 Why do we sometimes see the Moon as a crescent rather than a full disc?
6 If the Moon and Earth were further apart, how would this affect the gravitational pull between them?
7 Communications satellites are in orbit, and moving. Yet satellites dishes on the ground point in a fixed direction. How is this is possible?

Satellites in orbit

There are hundreds of satellites in orbit around the Earth. Some carry cameras for surveying the Earth's surface. Some have telescopes for observing distant stars. Telescopes in space can pick up light or other radiation before it is disturbed by the Earth's atmosphere. Some satellites give out navigation signals. And some are used for communications. They relay TV pictures and telephone messages between different places on Earth.

Communications and navigation satellites are normally in **geostationary** orbits. This means that the orbit has been carefully chosen so that the satellite orbits at the same rate as the Earth turns. From the ground, the satellite appears to be in a fixed position in the sky.

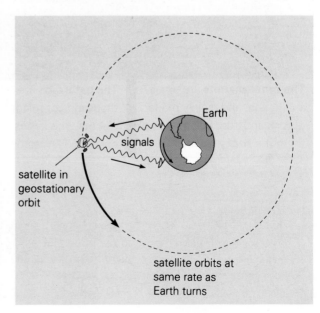

Planets, stars, and galaxies

By the end of this spread, you should be able to:
- explain what the Solar System is, and its place in the Universe.

The Solar System

The Earth is one of many **planets** in orbit around the Sun. The Sun, planets, and other objects in orbit, are together known as the **Solar System**.

Planets are not hot enough to give off their own light. We can only see them because they reflect the Sun's light. From Earth, they look like tiny dots in the night sky. Without a telescope, it is difficult to tell whether you are looking at a star or a planet.

Most of the planets move in near-circular orbits around the Sun. Many have smaller **moons** in orbit around them.

Comets are collections of ice, gas, and dust which orbit the Sun and reflect its light. They have highly elliptical orbits which bring them close to the Sun and then far out in the Solar System.

Saturn is a gassy giant. Its 'rings' are billions of orbiting bits of ice which reflect light.

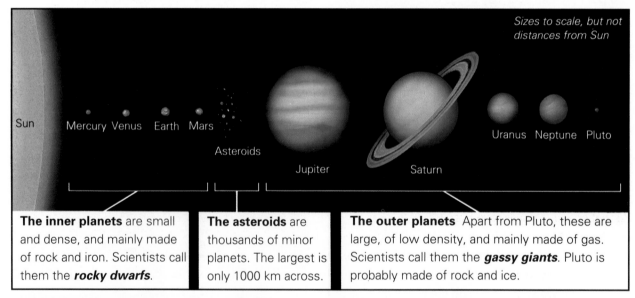

Sizes to scale, but not distances from Sun

Sun — Mercury — Venus — Earth — Mars — Asteroids — Jupiter — Saturn — Uranus — Neptune — Pluto

The inner planets are small and dense, and mainly made of rock and iron. Scientists call them the **rocky dwarfs**.

The asteroids are thousands of minor planets. The largest is only 1000 km across.

The outer planets Apart from Pluto, these are large, of low density, and mainly made of gas. Scientists call them the **gassy giants**. Pluto is probably made of rock and ice.

	Mercury	Venus	Earth	Mars	Jupiter	Saturn	Uranus	Neptune	Pluto
Average distance from Sun in million km	58	108	150	228	778	1427	2870	4497	5900
Time for one orbit in years	0.24	0.62	1	1.88	11.86	29.46	84.01	164.8	247
Diameter in km	4900	12 100	12 800	6800	143 000	120 000	51 000	49 000	3900
Average surface temperature	350 °C	480 °C	22 °C	-23 °C	-150 °C	-180 °C	-210 °C	-220 °C	-230 °C
Number of moons	0	0	1	2	16	23	15	8	1

Stars and galaxies

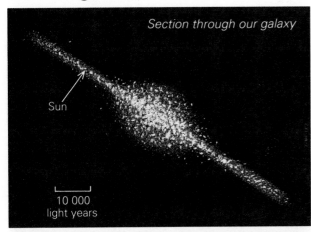
Section through our galaxy

Sun

10 000
light years

Our Sun is just one star in a huge star system called a **galaxy**. This contains over 100 billion stars. It is so big that a beam of light, travelling at 300 000 kilometres *per second*, would take 100 000 years to cross it! Scientists say that the galaxy is 100 000 **light years** across.

Ours is not the only galaxy. In the whole **Universe**, there are over 100 billion galaxies.

Our galaxy is called the **Milky Way**. You can see the edge of its disc as a bright band of stars across the night sky. The Milky Way is a member of a local cluster of about 30 galaxies. The other major member is the **Andromeda Galaxy**.

Exploring space

People have stood on the Moon, unmanned spacecraft have landed on Mars and Venus, and space probes have passed close to most of the outer planets. But travelling further into space is a problem. The *Voyager 2* probe took 12 years to reach Neptune. At that speed, it would take over 100 000 years to reach the nearest star! To find out more about stars and galaxies, we have to rely on the light and other forms of radiation picked up by telescopes.

The Andromeda Galaxy is 2 million light years away.

Models of the Universe

Scientists create descriptions called **models** to explain what they observe. Over the centuries, various models of the Universe have been proposed (put forward). The models have been improved as new instruments have given better observations.

Century	
2nd BC	**Ptolemy** proposes that the Earth is a sphere at the centre of the Universe. The Sun, Moon, planets, and stars move around it.
16th	**Copernicus** proposes that the Sun is at the centre of the Universe, with the Earth and planets moving around it.
18th	**Herschel** proposes that the Sun is in a huge, disc-shaped galaxy of stars.
20th	**Hubble** proposes that our galaxy is just one of billions, and that the Universe is expanding.

1 Which is the largest planet in the Solar System?
2 Which planets are smaller than the Earth?
3 Which planets are colder than the Earth? Why?
4 Name the planets known as *gassy giants*.
5 Why do planets give off light?
6 What link can you see between the time for a planet's orbit and its distance from the Sun?

7 Carbon dioxide in Venus' atmosphere produces a greenhouse effect (global warming). What clues are there for this in the table on the left?
8 What is a) *galaxy* b) a *light year*?
9 What other large galaxy belongs to the same cluster as our own? How long does its light take to reach us? Why are humans unlikely to visit it?

Action in orbit

By the end of this spread, you should be able to:
* *describe the orbit of a comet*
* *explain the causes of tides, eclipses, and craters*

Orbits and beyond

Gravity holds the planets in their orbits around the Sun. But the pull of gravity weakens with distance:

If two masses *double* their distance apart, the gravitational pull between them drops to a *quarter*, and so on. Scientists call this an **inverse square law**.

Most planets have near-circular orbits. However, the orbits of comets are highly elliptical. A comet has least speed when it is furthest from the Sun. That is also when the gravitational pull on it is weakest. As the comet moves closer to the Sun, the force of gravity increases. And the comet speeds up as some of its potential energy is changed into kinetic energy.

Most satellites have circular orbits (see also Spread 4.23). They are launched by rockets whose engines are so powerful that they can only work for ten minutes or so before running out of fuel.

A satellite travels fastest in a low orbit. In a higher orbit, it travels more slowly. However, to put a satellite into a higher orbit the launch rocket must leave the Earth at a higher speed, otherwise it will not be able to 'coast' far enough out into space when its engines shut down.

If a rocket leaves the Earth at more than 11 200 m/s (25 000 mph), it will 'coast' so far out into space that it is never pulled back to Earth again. This speed is called the **escape velocity** for the Earth.

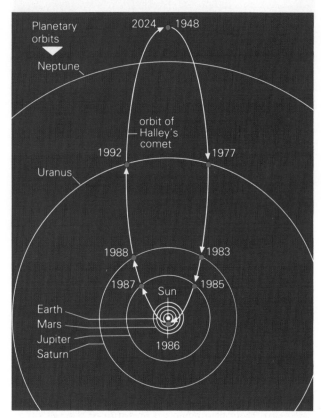

Orbit of Halley's Comet (1948–2024)

Eclipses

The Moon is much smaller and closer than the Sun, but it *looks* the same size from Earth. As the Moon orbits the Earth, it sometimes passes exactly between us and the Sun. Then, the Sun's disc is blotted out – there is an **eclipse of the Sun.** However, this does not happen very often because the Moon's orbit is tilted.

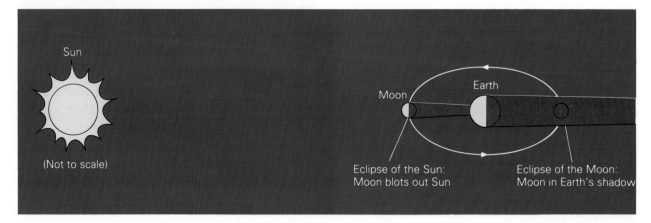

More frequently, the Moon's orbit takes it into the Earth's shadow, where sunlight cannot reach it (apart from some light bent by the Earth's atmosphere). The Moon darkens – there is an **eclipse of the Moon**.

Tides

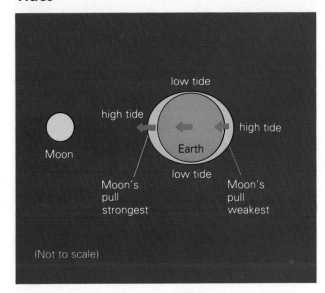

(Not to scale)

Tides are mainly caused by the Moon's gravitational pull. The pull is stronger than average on the side of the Earth nearest the Moon. This makes the water bulge slightly on that side. On the opposite side, the pull is weaker than average, so water is 'left behind' in another bulge. As the Earth rotates, each place passes in and out of a bulge about twice a day. So the sea level rises and falls.

The Sun's gravitational pull also affects the tides. Sometimes the Earth, Moon, and Sun are lined up so that the Sun's pull makes the bulges even bigger. These *highest* high tides are called **spring tides**. However, in some positions, the Sun's pull weakens the effect of the Moon's pull. This gives smaller bulges. The *lowest* high tides are called **neap tides**.

Bombarded from space

Millions of pieces of rock, ice, and dust orbit the Sun. Some have elliptical orbits which can bring them close to planets. When high-speed dust particles hit a planet's atmosphere, they burn up. On Earth, we call them **meteors** ('shooting stars'). Bigger lumps of material may reach the surface as **meteorites**.

A large meteorite can cause a huge **impact crater** like the one above in Arizona, USA. This one was probably formed about 50 000 years ago. It is 180 metres deep and 1220 metres across.

Today, strikes by large meteorites are very rare. The bombardment was at its greatest about 4000 million years ago, when the Solar System was young.

The Moon's surface is covered with craters. Most were caused by meteorites, though some were the result of volcanic activity. The Moon has no atmosphere or oceans, so its craters have not been eroded away like those on Earth. Mercury is a planet with virtually no atmosphere. It too has a cratered surface.

---

1 Look at the orbit of Halley's comet on the opposite page. Where in its orbit is a) the gravitational pull on the comet strongest b) the gravitational pull weakest c) its speed greatest d) its speed least? (You can answer these by giving a year for each position.)

2 If two masses halve their distance apart, what happens to the gravitational pull between them?

3 Describe what happens during a) an eclipse of the Sun b) an eclipse of the Moon.

4 What causes tides? Why are there two high tides per day?

5 What evidence is there that planets and moons in the Solar System were once under heavy bombardment by meteorites? Why is there little visible evidence of this on Earth?

Birth and death

By the end of this spread, you should be able to:
- describe the life cycle of a star
- explain why scientists think that the Universe is expanding, and started with the big bang

Birth of a star

The Sun started to shine about 4500 million years ago. Hydrogen is its 'fuel'. Deep in its core, the intense heat and pressure make hydrogen nuclei fuse (join) together to form helium nuclei, releasing energy as they do so. The process is called **nuclear fusion** (see also Spread 4.16).

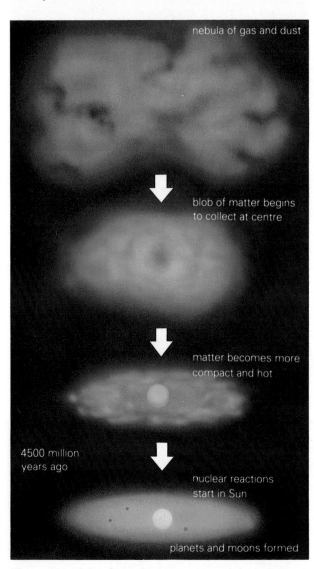

Formation of the Solar System

(labels within diagram:)
nebula of gas and dust

blob of matter begins to collect at centre

matter becomes more compact and hot

4500 million years ago

nuclear reactions start in Sun

planets and moons formed

The Great Nebula in the Constellation of Orion

The Sun formed in a huge cloud of gas and dust called a **nebula**, like the one above. Gravity pulled more and more material into a blob, compacting it until it was hot enough for fusion to start. Smaller blobs also formed, but these did not heat up enough for fusion. In time, they cooled to become planets and moons.

Death of a star

In about 6000 million years time, the Sun will have converted all its hydrogen to helium. Then it will swell and its outer layer will cool to a red glow. It will have become a **red giant**. Eventually, its outer layer will drift into space, exposing a hot, dense core called a **white dwarf**. This tiny star will use helium as its nuclear fuel. When this runs out, the star will cool and fade for ever.

In each galaxy, new stars are forming and old ones are dying. The most massive stars have a different fate from that of the Sun. Eventually, they blow up in a gigantic nuclear explosion called a **supernova**, leaving a dense core called a **neutron star**. If this has enough mass, it continues to collapse under its own gravity. Nothing can resist the pull. Even light cannot escape. The star becomes a **black hole**.

Like the Earth, other planets and moons are active beneath the surface. This photo shows a volcano erupting on Io, a moon of Jupiter.

Cosmic radiation

The Earth and other planets are continually being bombarded by small amounts of **cosmic radiation**. This consists of fast-moving atomic nuclei, electrons, and gamma rays. Some come from the Sun. But some come from other parts of our galaxy, probably from supernovae explosions.

1 By what process does the Sun get its energy?
2 The Sun was formed from a blob of matter in a *nebula*. a) What is a nebula? b) What made matter in the nebula collect together in a blob? c) About how long ago was the Sun formed?
3 What is a) a red giant b) a white dwarf?
4 How is a *black hole* formed?
5 What is *cosmic radiation*?
6 What evidence is there that the Universe may have started with a *big bang*?
7 The value of the Hubble constant is uncertain. If its value is 1/10 000 km per year per million km separation, how old is the Universe?

The expanding Universe

The light waves we receive from distant galaxies are 'stretched out' – their wavelengths are longer. This is called the **Doppler effect**. Scientists think that it occurs because the galaxies seem to be rushing apart at high speed. We are living in an expanding Universe.

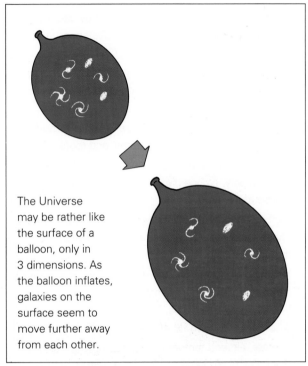

The Universe may be rather like the surface of a balloon, only in 3 dimensions. As the balloon inflates, galaxies on the surface seem to move further away from each other.

The Universe may have been created in a gigantic explosion called the **big bang**. Here are two pieces of evidence which support this idea:

- Radio telescopes have picked up background microwave radiation coming from every direction in space. This may be an 'echo' of the big bang.
- As the galaxies seem to be moving apart, they may all have come from the same tiny volume of space.

Scientists have tried to estimate the rate at which the galaxies seem to be moving apart. The value has not been agreed, but is thought to be about 1/15 000 km per year for each million km of separation. They call this the **Hubble constant**. Using this value, it is possible to work out that the galaxies must have started to separate about 15 000 million years ago. If so, that is when the big bang occurred.

The gravitational pull between galaxies is gradually slowing the expansion of the Universe. But no one yet knows whether the expansion will ever stop. That will depend on how much mass there is in the Universe.

Summary

The spread number in brackets tells you where to find more information.

- Animals and plants feed, respire, excrete, grow, move, reproduce, show sensitivity, and are made of cells. *(2.1)*

- Plant cells absorb the Sun's energy. They use it to make their own food from simple substances. The process is called photosynthesis. *(2.2)*

- Respiration is the process in which cells get energy from their food. Usually, the food is combined with oxygen. *(2.2)*

- Photosynthesis produces glucose which is turned into starch for storage in leaves, stems, and roots. *(2.3)*

- The rate of photosynthesis depends on light intensity, water supply, carbon dioxide concentration, and temperature. *(2.3)*

- For healthy growth, plants need minerals from the soil. These enter roots by diffusion and are pushed up through the plant by active transport. *(2.3)*

- Insects or the wind can carry pollen from one flower to another. Pollen contains male sex cells which can fertilize female sex cells. Fertilized cells become seeds, which are scattered. *(2.4)*

- If water, air, and temperature conditions are right, a seed may begin to grow. This is called germination. *(2.4)*

- The skeleton supports the body, protects internal organs, and has joints for movement. Joints are moved by pairs of muscles. *(2.5)*

- The body is controlled by the central nervous system (brain and spinal cord). *(2.5)*

- As food passes along the gut, it is digested and then absorbed into the blood. *(2.6)*

- Food contains five main types of nutrient: carbohydrates, fats, proteins, minerals, and vitamins. *(2.6)*

- Your blood absorbs digested food through villi on the inner surface of the small intestine. *(2.7)*

- During aerobic respiration, oxygen is used up. However, muscles can deliver energy for short periods without oxygen. In this case, the respiration is anaerobic. *(2.7)*

- Blood carries oxygen, digested food, water, waste products, heat, and hormones. It also carries antibodies, which are used to fight disease. *(2.8)*

- The heart is really two pumps. One circulates blood through the lungs. The other circulates blood round the rest of the body. *(2.8)*

- In the lungs, oxygen passes into the blood, and carbon dioxide and water are removed. *(2.9)*

- One of the liver's jobs is to keep the blood topped up with the right amount of 'fuel' (glucose). *(2.9)*

- The kidneys filter unwanted substances from the blood. These pass out of the body as urine. *(2.9)*

- A woman's ovaries release an ovum about once every 28 days. If the ovum is fertilized by a sperm from a man, it may embed itself in the uterus wall and develop into an embryo. If not, the uterus lining will break up and pass out of the woman when she has her period. *(2.10)*

- In the uterus, a developing baby gets food and oxygen from its mother's blood through the placenta and umbilical cord. *(2.11)*

- Things which affect the mother's blood, such as smoking and disease, can also affect the baby. *(2.11)*

- Your body has two methods of co-ordinating the activities of different organs. These are by nerve impulses and by chemical messengers called hormones. Hormones are made in the endocrine glands. *(2.12)*

- Sensory nerve cells carry information to the central nervous system, motor nerve cells carry instructions from it. *(2.12)*

- Plants use only hormones for co-ordination. For example, auxin is a hormone which stimulates growth. *(2.12)*

- In your body, temperature, amount of water, and blood sugar are three factors which must be kept steady. Maintaining the balance is called homeostasis. *(2.13)*

- In the kidneys, nephrons remove unwanted substances from the blood and maintain water balance. *(2.13)*

- Insulin is a hormone which controls how much glucose the liver changes into glycogen for storage. *(2.13)*

- Microbes which cause disease are known as germs. They can be transferred by air, contact, animals, and contaminated food. *(2.14)*

- Defending against disease is the job of your immune system. The defenders are the white blood cells. *(2.14)*

- Skin is an oily, waterproof barrier which makes it difficult for germs to get into the body. *(2.15)*
- Some white blood cells (lymphocytes) deal with invading germs by making antibodies. These stick to chemicals called antigens on the germs. *(2.15)*
- Some drugs are based on hormones: for example, the contraceptive pill, fertility drugs, and growth drugs. Growth drugs such as anabolic steroids can be very dangerous. *(2.15)*
- Animals with backbones are called vertebrates. The five main groups of vertebrates are fish, amphibians, reptiles, birds, and mammals. *(2.16)*
- Some of your characteristics you inherit. Others depend on your environment. *(2.17)*
- The chemical instructions for your inherited characteristics are called genes. Genes are small sections of the chromosomes in your cells. *(2.17)*
- By selecting the parents carefully, animals and plants can be bred to give the characteristics that breeders want. *(2.17)*
- Alleles are different versions of a gene. Alleles operate in pairs. If one is dominant and the other recessive, the dominant allele controls the characteristic. *(2.18)*
- A characteristic you can see is called a phenotype, the combination of alleles producing it is the genotype. *(2.18)*
- Sex cells (sperms and ova) are formed by a type of cell division called meiosis. Each has half the number of chromosomes in the original cell. *(2.18)*
- Human cells each have two sex chromosomes: XX in females and XY in males. *(2.18)*
- For growth, cells must multiply. They do this by a type of cell division called mitosis. *(2.19)*
- In every cell, there are long, spiral molecules of DNA. These carry genetic information in the form of a chemical code that controls which proteins are made. *(2.19)*
- In asexual reproduction, cells divide to form a new organism genetically identical to the parent. *(2.19)*
- If a plant or animal is homozygous (pure bred) for a characteristic, the two alleles are the same. If it is heterozygous (hybrid), they are different. *(2.20)*
- Crossing two pure bred organisms produces the F_1 generation. Crossing their hybrid offspring produces the F_2 generation. *(2.20)*
- Making genetically identical copies of a plant (or animal) is called cloning. *(2.20)*
- According to Darwin's theory of natural selection, animals (or plants) of a species show variation. Some variations help in the struggle for survival. Survivors reproduce and pass on their characteristics to later generations. So the species becomes adapted to its environment. *(2.21)*
- Mutations are chance genetic changes. They produce variation, and so contribute to natural selection. *(2.21)*
- Animals and plants are affected by non-living and living factors in their environment. Conditions can change daily or seasonally, and habitats may be shared with other organisms. These factors affect population sizes. *(2.22)*
- Humans grow crops, take materials from the ground, and burn fuels. These activities affect other populations of animals and plants, and are often a cause of pollution. *(2.23)*
- Where different organisms live in different zones, as on a sea-shore, the zonation can be studied by means of a line or belt transect. *(2.24)*
- Using a quadrat to sample small areas of ground, it is possible to estimate plant populations in a larger area. *(2.24)*
- The burning of fossil fuels is putting extra carbon dioxide into the atmosphere. This is trapping more of the Sun's heat and may be causing global warming (the greenhouse effect). *(2.25)*
- Other environmental problems caused by human industrial and commercial activity include acid rain, destruction of the ozone layer, forest destruction, and river pollution. *(2.25)*
- Plants are food for animals, which are food for other animals, and so on in a food chain. Energy is lost from the chain at every stage. *(2.26)*
- Decomposers are microbes which feed on the remains of dead plants and animals. They put useful chemicals back into the soil. *(2.26)*
- Living things are made of atoms. Carbon and nitrogen are two types of atom which are recycled by living things. *(2.27)*
- The rate at which plant or animal matter decomposes depends on temperature, and the availability of water and air for the microbes. *(2.28)*
- In a sewage treatment works, microbe action produces useful products such as methane and fertilizer. *(2.28)*
- Crop yields can be increased by the use of chemicals but these can cause pollution. *(2.28)*

Summary

The spread number in brackets tells you where to find more information.

- Materials can be solid, liquid, or gas. *(3.1)*
- Density can be measured in kg/m^3:

$$\text{density} = \frac{\text{mass}}{\text{volume}} \qquad (3.1)$$

- Solids, liquids, and gases are made up of tiny particles which are constantly on the move. *(3.2)*
- Everything is made from about 90 simple substances called elements. Atoms of different elements can join together in chemical reactions to form new substances called compounds. *(3.3)*
- The reactivity series tells you how reactive metals are compared with each other. *(3.3)*
- If one substance (the solute) dissolves in another (the solvent), the result is a solution. *(3.4)*
- Unlike compounds, mixtures have components which can be separated easily. *(3.5)*
- Composites are solid mixtures of different substances. Often, these substances give either compressive strength or tensile strength to the material. *(3.5)*
- All acids contain hydrogen. If an acid reacts with a metal, hydrogen gas is given off. *(3.6)*
- A base will neutralize an acid. The result is a solution containing a salt. *(3.6)*
- Acids turn litmus red, alkalis turn it blue. *(3.6)*
- The strength of an acid or alkali is measured on the pH scale. pH1 is a very strong acid, pH14 is a very strong alkali, pH7 is neutral. *(3.6)*
- In the periodic table, elements in the same column have similar properties and similar arrangements of outer shell electrons. *(3.7)*
- Atoms have a nucleus of protons (+ charge) and neutrons (no charge), with electrons (− charge) moving around it. *(3.8)*
- Some atoms bond together by sharing electrons. This is called covalent bonding. A molecule is a group of atoms joined by covalent bonds. *(3.8)*
- Charged atoms are called ions. They are atoms which have gained or lost electrons. *(3.8)*
- In ionic crystals, such as sodium chloride, strong forces of attraction bind positive and negative ions tightly together. In molecular crystals, such as iodine, weak forces bind one molecule to another. *(3.9)*

- In giant molecules, such as diamond, the atoms are rigidly fixed by strong covalent bonds. *(3.9)*
- Metals are composed of rafts of positive ions surrounded by a sea of electrons. *(3.9)*
- Some chemical reactions are exothermic: they give out energy (heat). Others are endothermic: they take in energy. *(3.10)*
- The rate of a reaction depends on the size of the bits, concentration, temperature, and presence of a catalyst. *(3.10)*
- When an element burns, it combines with oxygen and an oxide is produced. *(3.11)*
- Most fuels are compounds of hydrogen and carbon. When they burn, the main products are carbon dioxide and water. *(3.11)*
- Three things are needed for combustion (burning): fuel, oxygen, and heat. *(3.11)*
- If a metal's surface becomes oxidized, the result is called corrosion. *(3.11)*
- Balanced chemical equations show how atoms change partners during reactions. *(3.12)*
- The relative atomic mass scale compares the masses of atoms with each other. The standard is that one atom of carbon-12 has a mass of 12.000 units. *(3.12)*
- One mole of any gas contains 6 $\times$ 10^{23} particles (e.g. molecules), and occupies 24 dm^3 at normal room temperature and pressure. *(3.12)*
- The more reactive a metal, the more difficult it is to separate from its ore. Iron is separated from its ore by smelting. But electrolysis is needed to produce aluminium. *(3.13)*
- Common salt (sodium chloride) is an important source of other chemicals, including chlorine, and sodium hydroxide. *(3.14)*
- Limestone is used to make cement and concrete. It is also needed for steel-making. *(3.14)*
- Ionic substances split up into separate ions in solution or when melted. Ionic equations show how these ions change during reactions. *(3.15)*
- Half-reaction equations are used to show what substances are formed at the anode and cathode during electrolysis. *(3.15)*

- Electroplating is the transfer of a metal from anode to cathode by electrolysis. *(3.15)*
- The atoms of the elements in any group of the periodic table get bigger and become more metallic down the group. Across a period the atoms get smaller and more nonmetallic. *(3.16)*
- The oxides of the elements in Groups I and II are basic. The oxides become increasingly acidic from left to right across a period. *(3.16)*
- Chlorine will bleach damp litmus paper. *(3.17)*
- Chlorine is used to kill germs in water. It is also used in making many other substances. *(3.17)*
- If an acid reacts with a carbonate, the products are a salt, water, and carbon dioxide. *(3.17)*
- Many of the transition metals have similar properties. Most are hard, dense, and strong, form more than one type of ion, and have coloured compounds. *(3.17)*
- Transition metals and their compounds are often used as catalysts. *(3.17)*
- In redox reactions, electrons pass from a reducing agent to an oxidizing agent. *(3.18)*
- Some metals can form more than one type of ion. These ions can be changed from one to another by oxidation or reduction. *(3.18)*
- The products of some reactions can be recombined to reform the original substances. These are reversible reactions. *(3.18)*
- Ammonia is made by a reversible reaction. Manufacturers of ammonia have to use conditions which give a reasonable compromise between yield and cost. *(3.18)*
- In any chemical reaction, energy is absorbed in order to break down the bonds between the atoms in the reacting substances. Energy is released by the formation of new bonds in the products. *(3.19)*
- You can calculate the net change of energy during a chemical reaction if you know the bond energies of all the links being broken or made. *(3.19)*
- The fractions (parts) of crude oil can be separated by distillation. Some are used as fuels. Others are used in making plastics. *(3.20)*
- Air is a mixture of gases. It is mainly nitrogen (78%) and oxygen (21%). *(3.20)*
- Addition polymerization is the joining up of large numbers of small unsaturated hydrocarbon molecules to form a very long chain molecule. *(3.21)*
- Plants make starch by joining up chains of glucose molecules with the elimination of molecules of water. Starch is a condensation polymer. *(3.21)*
- The long polymer chains of nylon 66 can be stretched parallel to each other to form fibres. *(3.21)*
- Most fertilizers are made from ammonia. Ammonia is manufactured by the Haber process. *(3.22)*
- Ammonium nitrate is mixed with ammonium phosphate and potassium chloride to produce NPK compound fertilizers. *(3.22)*
- To produce fertilizers competitively, the individual processes take place on one site. This must be chosen to take account of economic and environmental costs. *(3.22)*
- Some microbes make food rot. Methods of slowing the process include pasteurizing, canning, drying, and refrigerating. *(3.23)*
- Some enzymes are useful. They are used in making bread, cheese, and alcohol. *(3.23)*
- The gases in the Earth's early atmosphere mostly came from volcanoes. The main gas was carbon dioxide. The atmosphere changed to its present composition because of the activities of microbes, plants, and animals. *(3.24)*
- The weakening of a rock's surface is called weathering. Causes include wind, the acid effect of rain, and the cracking produced by frost. Frost (frozen dew) causes cracking because water expands when it freezes. *(3.24)*
- Weathered rock is eroded, transported, and then deposited. Eventually, it can form part of new rock. This process is called the rock cycle. *(3.25)*
- On Earth, water evaporates, condenses to form clouds, and then falls as rain. This is the water cycle. *(3.25)*
- Igneous rocks are formed when molten magma cools. *(3.26)*
- Sedimentary rocks are formed from layers of deposited sediment. *(3.26)*
- Metamorphic rocks are igneous or sedimentary rocks which have been changed by heat or pressure. *(3.26)*
- The Earth's crust and upper mantle is made up of huge sections called plates which move very slowly. Plate movements cause earthquakes, volcanoes, and mountain-building, and contribute to rock recycling. *(3.27)*
- Seismic waves provide evidence that the Earth has a layered structure, with a partly-liquid core. *(3.27)*

Summary

The spread number in brackets tells you where to find more information.

- A current is a flow of electrons. *(4.1)*

- Metals and carbon are good conductors of electricity. Most nonmetals are insulators. *(4.1)*

- Like charges repel. Unlike charges attract. *(4.1)*

- Current is measured in amperes (A). Voltage is measured in volts (V). *(4.2)*

- Bulbs (or other components) can be connected in series or in parallel. *(4.2)*

- When a current flows through a resistance, energy is given off as heat. *(4.3)*

- 1 kW h is the energy supplied to a 1 kilowatt appliance in 1 hour. *(4.3)*

- Circuits can be controlled by logic gates, such as AND, OR, and NOT gates. The possible input and output settings are given in truth tables. *(4.4)*

- Automatic control systems rely on feedback. *(4.5)*

- A bistable has two possible output states when both inputs are OFF. *(4.5)*

- Metals obey Ohm's law. At constant temperature, the current through them is proportional to the voltage across them. *(4.6)*

- Resistance $= \dfrac{\text{voltage}}{\text{current}}$ resistance in Ω (ohms)
  voltage in V
  current in A

- Power = voltage x current   power in W (watts)
  (4.6)

- Like poles of a magnet repel, unlike poles attract. *(4.7)*

- Electromagnets are used in relays, and loudspeakers. *(4.7)*

- Electric motors use a current and magnetism to produce motion. Generators use motion and magnetism to produce a current. *(4.8)*

- Transformers step AC voltages up or down. *(4.8)*

- In UK mains circuits, wires in plugs are coloured brown (live), blue (neutral), and yellow/green (earth). *(4.9)*

- Switches and fuses are fitted in the live wire. *(4.9)*

- Transformers work with AC only. For a transformer:
  $$\dfrac{\text{output voltage}}{\text{input voltage}} = \dfrac{\text{output turns}}{\text{input turns}}$$
  (4.10)

- Mains power is transmitted across country at high voltage to reduce the current in the cable. *(4.10)*

- Charge is measured in coulombs (C). *(4.11)*

- Charge = current x time *(4.11)*

- A 12 V battery gives 12 joules of energy (see *4.12*) to each coulomb of charge it pushes out. *(4.11)*

- X-rays are produced by stopping fast electrons. *(4.11)*

- Energy is measured in joules (J). *(4.12)*

- Energy can change into different forms, but it cannot be made or destroyed. This is called the law of conservation of energy. *(4.12)*

- Heat can travel by conduction, convection, or radiation. *(4.13)*

- Fuels like coal, oil, and natural gas are non-renewable. Energy sources like the wind, and water behind dams, are renewable. *(4.14)*

- If an engine has an efficiency of 30%, then 30% of its fuel's energy is changed into movement energy. The rest is wasted as heat. *(4.14)*

- In one way or another, nearly all of our energy originally came from the Sun. *(4.15)*

- If the particles in a material move faster, the internal energy is more and the temperature is higher. *(4.16)*

- $\dfrac{\text{Heat}}{\text{input}} = \text{mass} \times \dfrac{\text{specific heat}}{\text{capacity}} \times \dfrac{\text{temperature}}{\text{rise}}$ *(4.16)*

- Heat energy becomes less useful when it spreads. *(4.16)*

- Force is measured in newtons (N). *(4.17)*

- Pressure $= \dfrac{\text{force}}{\text{area}}$ *(4.17)*

- For a fixed mass of gas, if the pressure (P), volume (V) and Kelvin temperature (T) change, then:
  $$\dfrac{P_1 \times V_1}{T_1} = \dfrac{P_2 \times V_2}{T_2} \quad (4.18)$$

- Moment = force x distance from turning point. *(4.19)*

- If something is balanced, the total left-turning moment is equal to the total right-turning moment. This is the law of moments. *(4.19)*

- If a material obeys Hooke's law, then its extension is proportional to the stretching force. *(4.20)*

- If a material is stretched beyond its elastic limit, then it will not return to its original shape when the stretching force is removed. *(4.20)*

- Vectors, such as force, have direction and 'size'. *(4.20)*

- Average speed = $\dfrac{\text{distance travelled}}{\text{time taken}}$ *(4.21)*

- The force of friction provides grip. But in machinery, it wastes energy. *(4.21)*

- Acceleration = $\dfrac{\text{gain in velocity}}{\text{time taken}}$ *(4.22)*

- Force = mass × acceleration *(4.22)*

- Wherever there is a force (action), there is an equal but opposite force (reaction) acting on something else. *(4.22)*

- Momentum = mass × velocity *(4.22)*

- If there is no outside force, the total momentum of a system stays the same. This is the law of conservation of momentum. *(4.23)*

- On Earth, the acceleration of free fall, g, is 10 m/s^2. g is also the gravitational field strength: 10 N/kg. *(4.23)*

- A centripetal (inward) force is needed to keep something moving in a circle. *(4.23)*

- Some machines are force magnifiers, others are movement magnifiers. *(4.24)*

- Work, like energy, can be measured in joules (J): Work done = force × distance moved *(4.24)*

- Power can be measured in watts (W):

  Power = $\dfrac{\text{work done}}{\text{time taken}}$ or $\dfrac{\text{energy spent}}{\text{time taken}}$ *(4.24)*

- Hydraulic machines use trapped liquids to transmit pressure. Liquids are virtually incompressible. *(4.25)*

- Gravitational potential energy = mass × g × height lifted *(4.25)*

- Kinetic energy = $\frac{1}{2}$ × mass × velocity^2 *(4.25)*

- Sound waves can travel through solids, liquids, and gases, but not through a vacuum. *(4.26)*

- Echoes are reflected sounds which you hear a short time after the original sound. *(4.26)*

- Frequency is measured in hertz (Hz). 1 Hz means 1 vibration per second or 1 wave per second. *(4.27)*

- The higher the amplitude, the louder the sound. The higher the frequency, the higher the pitch. *(4.27)*

- Longitudinal waves vibrate up and down. Transverse waves vibrate from side to side (or up and down). *(4.28)*

- For waves: speed = frequency × wavelength *(4.28)*

- Resonance is the strong vibration which builds up when an incoming frequency matches the natural frequency of vibration. *(4.28)*

- You see this page because it reflects light. A mirror reflects light in a regular way. *(4.29)*

- Light bends when it enters glass or water. This is called refraction. *(4.29)*

- Convex lenses are used in the eye, camera, and projector to form images. *(4.30)*

- White light is a mixture of all the colours of the rainbow. *(4.31)*

- The electromagnetic spectrum is made up of radio waves, microwaves, infrared, light, ultraviolet, X-rays, and gamma rays. *(4.31)*

- To the human eye: red + green + blue = white Red, green, and blue are the primary colours. *(4.32)*

- Most things appear coloured because they reflect some colours only. Others are absorbed. *(4.32)*

- Diffraction is the bending of waves round obstacles. *(4.33)*

- Two sets of waves may reinforce each other or cancel each other out. This is called interference. *(4.33)*

- Radioactive materials give out nuclear radiation. The main types of radiation are alpha particles, beta particles, and gamma rays (waves). *(4.34)*

- The atoms of some isotopes have unstable nuclei. The break-up of unstable nuclei is called radioactive decay. The half-life is the time it takes for half the unstable nuclei to decay. *(4.35)*

- The splitting of nuclei (such as uranium-235) by neutrons is called fission. It releases energy, and can produce a chain reaction. *(4.35)*

- The Earth orbits the Sun, held by the force of gravity. The Moon orbits the Earth. *(4.36)*

- We see the Moon because it reflects the Sun's light. But part of it is often in shadow. *(4.36)*

- The Solar System is mainly made up of the Sun and its planets. The Sun is one star in a vast galaxy of 100 billion stars. There are more than 100 billion galaxies in the whole Universe. *(4.37)*

- A comet has most speed when nearest the Sun and least when furthest from it. *(4.38)*

- The Moon's gravitational pull causes water bulges (high tides) on opposite sides of the Earth. *(4.38)*

- The Sun and planets formed in a huge cloud of gas and dust called a nebula. *(4.39)*

- The Sun is powered by nuclear fusion. *(4.39)*

- There is evidence to suggest that the Universe is expanding. *(4.39)*

GCSE questions

1 a It is sometimes necessary for a person with heart disease to have an operation on their heart. During this operation the heart is stopped and their blood is passed through a heart-lung machine.

  i) Suggest why the heart is stopped during the operation.

  ii) Describe *two* jobs that the heart-lung machine will do for the person during the operation.

 b Medical instruments can be used to record heart rates on graph paper. The line drawn is called an ECG. The diagram below shows an ECG.

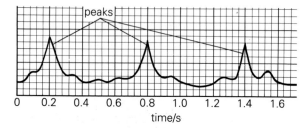

The distance between any two peaks is the time taken for one heart beat. Work out the heart rate shown in this ECG. (Give your answer in beats per minute.) Show your working.

(ULEAC)

2 The diagram below shows a plant.

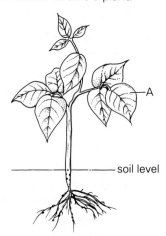

 a Outline the job of structure A.

 b A cell from the leaf of this plant is shown below. How does the structure of this cell enable it to make food for the plant?

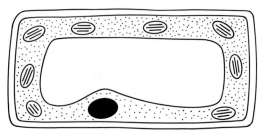

 c i) Copy and complete the following word equation showing what happens during photosynthesis:

$$\text{carbon dioxide} + \text{----} \xrightarrow[\text{chlorophyll}]{\text{sunlight}} \text{carbohydrate} + \text{----}$$

  ii) How does carbon dioxide enter a leaf for photosynthesis?

 d In Autumn many plants die. Describe the role of microbes in re-converting the carbohydrate from the plant into carbon dioxide.

 e Sugar is a word which can be used to describe several carbohydrates. Two examples are given below.

  glucose – chemical formula $C_6H_{12}O_6$
  maltose – chemical formula $C_{12}H_{22}O_{11}$

  i) Name the elements contained in sugars.

  ii) When sugars are heated they melt at low temperature. When sodium chloride is heated, it does not melt until a much higher temperature. Explain this in terms of the structures of these compounds.

(MEG)

3 a The diagram below shows a cell with four chromosomes. Explain, using diagrams to aid your answer, how this cell can divide by mitosis.

b The black panther is a black variety of the spotted leopard. It occurs quite commonly in dense tropical rain forests. However, it is much rarer in areas of open grassland where the normal (spotted) form is much more common.

The diagram at the top of the next column shows the results of a cross between a spotted leopard and a black panther, and it also shows the results of a cross between two of their offspring (the F_1 generation).

i) Which *one* of the alleles H (dominant) or h (recessive) controls black coat colour? Explain your answer.

ii) Write hh, Hh or HH in the spaces between each of the brackets in your own copy of the diagram to show the possible alleles possessed by each of the animals illustrated.

iii) What is the expected ratio of homozygous to heterozygous individuals in the F_2 generation?

iv) Black panthers are far more common in the rain forests than in open grassland. Explain how natural selection could bring this about.

(MEG)

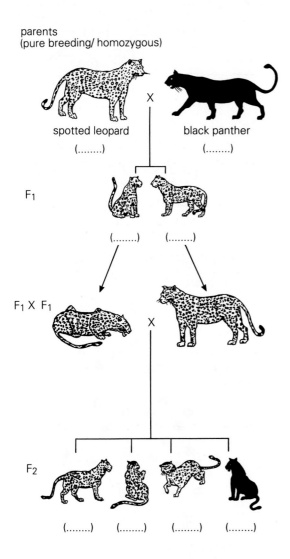

parents
(pure breeding/ homozygous)

X

spotted leopard   black panther
(........)   (........)

F_1

(........)   (........)

F_1 X F_1

X

F_2

(........)   (........)   (........)   (........)

Assume that coat colour is controlled by a single gene with two alleles (H and h), one being responsible for the spotted coat and the other for the black coat.

4 'Beanies' are small chocolate sweets covered in brightly coloured sugar coating. The colourings used for the coatings were investigated as below.

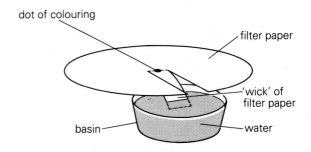

dot of colouring   filter paper

'wick' of filter paper

basin   water

a i) What is the name given to this method of investigating different colourings?
  ii) Why is the paper used often filter paper?
  iii) What is the solvent used in this investigation?

b Explain how the method used for the investigation makes the colourings separate so that they can be identified.

c The results of the investigation are shown below.

Green Beanie   Red Beanie   Brown Beanie
experiment   experiment   experiment

What do these results tell you about the dyes in
i) the green colouring and ii) the brown colouring?

5 Ammonium sulphate is made for use as a fertilizer.

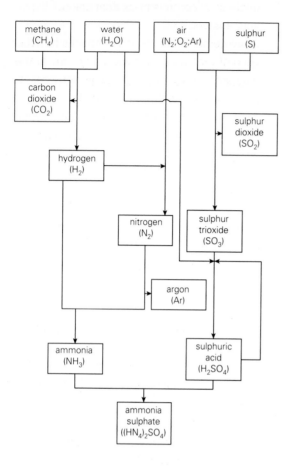

a Several stages in the flow diagram use a catalyst. The use of catalysts is economical. Explain why.

b The by-products from this process include carbon dioxide, sulphur dioxide and argon. Which of these by-products is harmful and which is useful? Explain your answer.

c A company wants to build a chemical factory to make ammonium sulphate. They have to consider costs, both economic and environmental. Explain what this means.
In your answer use examples of *three economic costs* and *three environmental costs*.

d i) Give a balanced symbolic equation for the reaction between ammonia and sulphuric acid.

ii) How many tonnes of sulphuric acid are needed to exactly neutralize 340 tonnes of ammonia? (The relative atomic masses are H 1, N 14, O 16 and S 32.)
Show clearly how you obtain your answer.

(SEG)

6 The diagram shows a section through a volcano.

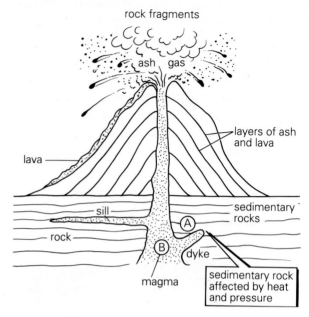

a Name a type of rock you would expect to find at (A).

b i) What type of rock will eventually be formed at (B)?

ii) Explain how this type of rock is formed.

(NEAB)

7 Sand is silicon(IV) oxide. It has a structure similar to that of diamond. Part of its structure is shown in the diagram below.

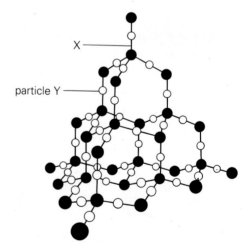

a i) What does X represent?

ii) What is particle Y?

iii) What type of structure is shown by the diagram? Select one of the following:
giant ionic solid   *giant molecular solid*
simple ionic solid   *simple molecular solid*

b Predict one physical property of silicon(IV) oxide and explain how the property you have predicted is due to its structure.

c i) A mixture of silicon(IV) oxide and calcium oxide is known as 'Roman mortar'. It is used to lay paving stones instead of concrete. When water is added to the mixture, a reaction takes place and a solid network of calcium silicate crystals is formed. *From this description*, is silicon(IV) oxide a neutral, acidic or basic oxide? *Explain* the reasons for your answer.

ii) Suggest one reason why straw is sometimes added to the mortar.

(SEG)

8 The diagram below represents the Earth and Sun.

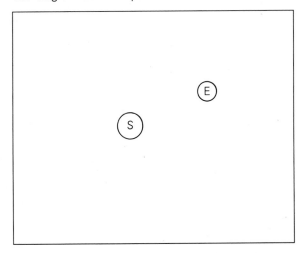

a On a copy of the diagram, draw a line to show how the Earth will move in the next six months.

b The orbit time of Venus is 0.6 years and that of Mars is 1.9 years. Add a 'V' and an 'M' to your diagram to show the approximate positions of Venus and Mars.

(MEG)

9 a The diagram below shows a circuit with a lamp and buzzer.

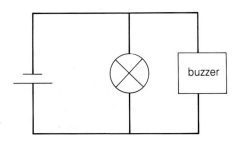

i) Draw the circuit with a single switch which controls both the lamp and the buzzer.

ii) Draw the circuit with two switches. One switch should control only the lamp and the second switch should control only the buzzer.

b i) A student wants to be able to control the brightness of a lamp. Draw and label a circuit diagram to show how this can be done.

The student adds an ammeter and a voltmeter to the circuit. He predicts that to double the current he will need to double the voltage. The table below shows the readings he takes.

lamp	voltage/V	current/A
dim	4.0	1.0
normal	7.0	1.5
bright	11.0	2.0

ii) Use the data in the table to explain whether his prediction is correct.

iii) Compare the resistance of the bright filament to that of the dim filament. What do you observe?

(MEG)

10 a The diagram below shows the position of a hydroelectric power station.

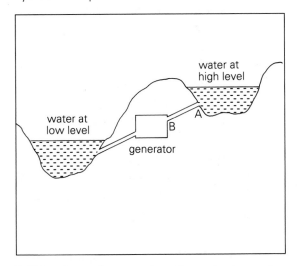

i) What form of energy does the water have at the position marked A on the diagram?

ii) What forms of energy does the water have at the position marked B on the diagram?

iii) Give three advantages of a hydroelectric power station over a coal-fired power station.

b The diagram below shows an electrically heated hot water storage tank.

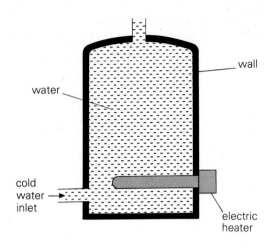

i) Explain why the heater is placed at the bottom of the tank rather than at the top.

ii) Explain how you would reduce the heat energy loss through the walls of the tank, naming any materials you might use.

c The diagram below shows a microwave oven.

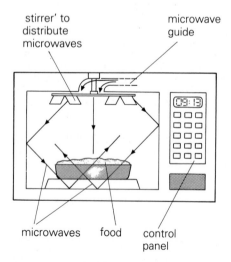

Microwaves are absorbed by water in the food. The specific heat capacity of water is 4.2 kJ/(kg °C).

i) A plastic jug containing 500 g of water at 20 °C was placed in the microwave oven. The oven was switched on at full power. After two minutes in the oven, the temperature of the water had risen to 44 °C. Calculate how much energy had been transferred to the water in two minutes.

ii) The output power of the oven is rated at 650 W. How much energy does the cooker transfer from the electricity supply in two minutes?

iii) Compare the amounts of energy you have calculated in i) and ii). Account for any difference.

iv) The microwaves produced by the oven have a frequency of 2450 MHz and a velocity of 300 000 km per second. Calculate their wavelength.

(NEAB)

11 The graph below represents the motion of a bicycle and rider rolling down a ramp onto level ground and then being stopped by the brakes.

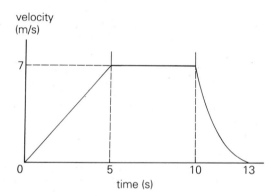

a Calculate
   i) the acceleration during the first 5 seconds.
   ii) the distance travelled in the first 10 seconds.

b The total mass of the bicycle and rider is 90 kg. The gravitational field strength of the Earth is 10 N/kg [10 N weight per kg].

Calculate
   i) the accelerating force on the bicycle and rider during the first 5 seconds.
   ii) the kinetic energy of the bicycle and rider after 5 seconds.
   iii) the heat produced in the brakes between 10 seconds and 13 seconds.
   iv) the average power developed in the brakes.

(NEAB)

Answers to questions on spreads

2.1
1 Living things feed, respire, excrete, grow, move, reproduce, show sensitivity, are made of cells **2** Plants make own food, animals move to find food; cells different (see 5) **3** Plants growing towards light **4** Both have a nucleus, cytoplasm, and cell membrane **5** Plant cells have cellulose wall, chloroplasts, cell sap **6** Contain chlorophyll which absorbs energy in sunlight **7** Control centre of cell **8** Releasing energy from food; takes place in cells **9** Group of similar cells; organ

2.2
1 a) Carbon dioxide b) Oxygen **2** Sugar **3** No light **4** Healthy growth (making body proteins) **5** Stoma **6** Stream of water (and dissolved minerals) moving up through plant **7** a) Oxygen b) Carbon dioxide **8** Plants make oxygen

2.3
1 a) No change b) Rate of photosynthesis limited by amount of light available **2** Osmosis **3** Control stomata size, hence water loss and gas flow in/out of leaf; swell up by osmosis **4** Used in respiration, changed into starch, used in making proteins

2.4
1 a) Ovules (in carpels) b) Pollen (in stamens) **2** In cross-pollination, pollen transferred to flower on different plant **3** By wind, by insects **4** To attract insects **5** Tube grows down to ovary, nucleus passes down tube **6** Fruit **7** Wind, hooks, eaten by animals, flicked from pods **8** Seed starting to grow into plant **9** Protection **10** Plants growing toward light

2.5
1 a) Brain b) Heart and lungs c) Spinal cord **2** Allow bending, absorb jolts **3** Support, allowing movement **4** Calcium; collagen fibres **5** a) Fibres attaching muscles to bones b) Fibres holding joints together **6** Muscles can only contract; antagonistic pairs. **7** Ears send nerve impulses to brain, brain sends nerve impulses to muscles

2.6
1 Broken down into substances which will dissolve **2** Stomach and small intestine **3** Biological catalysts (speed up reactions) **4** Churned, mixed with juice containing enzyme and acid **5** Absorbed into blood **6** Leaves body through anus **7** Carbohydrates, fats, proteins, minerals, vitamins **8** Carbohydrates, fats **9** a) Growth b) Bones and teeth; a) Fish, bread b) Cheese, milk **10** To speed up some chemical reactions **11** Helps food pass along the gut

2.7
1 a) 2200 kJ b) 950 kJ c) 1650 kJ **2** If energy not needed, food turned into fat **3** Bumps on surface of small intestine; absorb digested food into blood **4** Not enough oxygen available; oxygen not used in anaerobic respiration **5** In mitochondria; storage of energy for rapid release **6** See diagram on page 29

2.8
1 a) Arteries b) Veins **2** Fine tubes; carry blood near cells **3** To get food and oxygen, and get rid of waste products **4** Plasma **5** White **6** Red; haemoglobin **7** Lungs **8** So blood only flows one way **9** Passes through lungs, heart, other parts of body, heart

2.9
1 a) Oxygen b) Carbon dioxide (+ water) **2** For blood to absorb/release gases **3** Ribs out, diaphragm down **4** Glycogen, iron, vitamins **5** Removes old red blood cells, produces heat **6** Filtering/cleaning blood **7** Go to bladder **8** They remove unwanted substances from body **9** Lungs

2.10
1 Egg cell; release of egg cell; cycle of egg cell release, uterus lining growth, period **2** 28 days **3** Passes out of uterus **4** Must meet sperm **5** In testicles **6** Condom, diaphragm **7** a) Can cause heart, liver, breast disease b) Not very reliable

2.11
1 Chemical instructions needed from both parents for full set **2** Bag of watery liquid **3** Organ which grows into uterus lining where substances can pass between mother's blood and baby's blood **4 & 5** Through placenta and umbilical cord **6** Turns head down; for exit from uterus **7** Substances in mother's blood can get into baby's blood

2.12
1 Carry signals a) from receptors to central nervous system b) from central nervous system to muscles/other organs **2** Blinking, coughing, sneezing **3** In the blood **4** HGH stimulates growth; ADH reduces kidneys' water output **5** Adrenal glands; prepares body for rapid energy output **6** Auxin collects away from light, stimulates growth that side, so shoot bends

2.13
1 a) Drink, food, respiration b) Urine, sweat **2** Filter liquid from blood, then cause useful substances and water to be reabsorbed **3** Reduces nephrons' water output by increasing reabsorption **4** Kidneys not working properly; same job as nephrons **5** Makes liver change glucose (sugar) into glycogen **6** Glands in pancreas produce more insulin which affects liver as in Q5. **7** a) Increased b) Decreased **8** Sweating

2.14
1 Contact, animals, droplets in air **2** To avoid contaminating food **3** Some white blood cells digest germs, others make antibodies which kill germs **4** Contain dead or harmless germs which make immune system produce antibodies **5** Exercise, good diet, avoid smoking **6** Stops it working **7** Sexual contact, blood-to-blood contact, infected mother to unborn child

2.15
1 a) Chemicals on microbes b) Chemicals, made by antibodies, which stick to antigens **2** a) Barrier, with oils that kill germs b) Traps dust and germs c) Engulf and digest microbes **3** Anabolic steroids damage heart, liver, kidneys; pill increases risk of heart and liver disease and breast cancer **4** Nicotine, heroin; body becomes dependent on them

2.16
1 Fish, amphibians, reptiles, birds, mammals; backbones **2** All except most mammals **3** Feathers, steady body temperature, lay eggs **4** Mammals; live young which feed on milk **5** A Daisy B Plantain C Yarrow D Rye

2.17
1 Height, weight **2** Tongue-rolling, blood group **3** Chemical instructions for a characteristic; in nucleus **4** One from each parent **5** Same genes **6** Features depend on environment **7** Racehorses, varieties of wheat **8** Preserve genes

2.18
1 Phenotype is characteristic which is seen (e.g. black hair), genotype is combination of alleles producing it (e.g. Hh) 2 a) Meiosis b) Alleles c) Zygote 3 a) 23 b) 46 4 a) Female b) Male 5 1 in 2

2.19
1 Cell from mitosis is like original, cell from meiosis has only half the chromosomes 2 In chromosomes; carrying genetic information 3 a) Sequence of three bases b) Protein 4 A-T 5 'Unzips', then unattached bases join on to produce two identical molecules 6 Genetically a) different b) the same

2.20
1 The same 2 Making genetically identical copies; growing plants from cuttings 3 Females have two X chromosomes, so chances of both having harmful allele are low; mother can pass on harmful allele to child 4 Pieces of DNA from human cells inserted into DNA of bacteria 5 All F_1 are Ss, no wrinkled seeds; F_2 can be SS, Ss, or ss, 1/4 have wrinkled seeds

2.21
1 Reptiles, dinosaurs, birds, mammals 2 Height, weight 3 Help in struggle for survival, so animals live to reproduce 4 Chance change in genes; dark wing colouring (peppered moth) 5 Radiation; inaccurate DNA copying 6 Dark one; better camouflage 7 Less dark moths eaten by birds, so more reproduce 8 Members start to live and breed in separate groups

2.22
1 Place where organism lives; group of same organisms; all organisms in one habitat; animal which feeds on other animals 2 Tides cover/uncover beach 3 Temperature change from summer to winter 4 For light and water 5 Has features which help its survival; bear's fur for winter warmth 6 a) Eaten by toads b) Toads have died off, more plants 7 Fewer toads because fewer slugs for food

2.23
1 A Bigger crops, healthier crops B Timber, more crop space C More crop space, easier to harvest D Concrete, steelmaking; A Encourages algae, harms wildlife B Destroys habitats, exposes soil C Destroys habitats, encourages pests D Spoils landscape, produces waste 2 Gases from burning fuels 3 Damages stonework, plants, steel 4 Fertilizers, sewage, chemical waste 5 Oil spillages cause pollution

2.24
1 Conditions change further from water's edge, different conditions suit different organisms 2 a) Transect b) Capture-recapture 3 80 4 120

2.25
1 More from burning fossil fuels 2 Heat trapped as in a greenhouse 3 Stops ultraviolet 4 Sulphur dioxide and nitrogen oxides from burning fossil fuels; attacks stone & steelwork, harms plants and water life 5 Chemicals cause poisoning; nutrients in sewage encourages algae growth which uses up oxygen; warm water discharge lessens oxygen, encourages weed growth 6 Releases more carbon dioxide; less plants to absorb carbon dioxide 7 Leads to erosion; deprives soil of nutrients

2.26
1 Producers make food, consumers eat it; leaf, snail 2 Materials which rot; leaves, paper 3 Octopus, crab, seal, seagull; populations would fall 4 & 5 See pyramid examples on page 66 (For question 5, biomasses are: frogs 200 g, worms 10 000 g, leaves 500 000 g)

2.27
1 Photosynthesis 2 Respiration, burning 3 Burning coal makes carbon dioxide which is absorbed by plants, which are eaten by animals 4 For making proteins 5 From nitrates in soil 6 By eating plants 7 By microbes taking nitrogen from air and dead organisms, by the effect of lightning

2.28
1 Herbivore feeds on plants, carnivore feeds on animals; herbivore; plants are at 1st trophic level 2 Energy lost at each level, so not enough left for more 3 Plenty of moisture, air, warmth 4 Return vital elements to soil 5 In aeration tank & sludge digester to feed on polluting matter and sludge 6 Land needed to produce beef for one person can produce wheat for 20 7 Too many young fish caught, so not enough left to breed

3.1
1 a) Liquid has no definite shape b) Gas can have any volume 2 a) 1 m^3 of water has a mass of 1000 kg b) 5000 kg 3 Too brittle 4 a) Transparent or translucent b) Hard, strong c) Strong, good conductor (heat) d) Insulator (heat) e) Flexible, insulator (electricity)

3.2
1 a) Particles in liquid can change positions b) Particles in gas not held together, can move about freely 2 Move faster 3 a) 0 °C b) 100 °C 4 Energy needed for evaporation, so heat absorbed 5 Particles wander, jostled by other particles; diffusion 6 Particles vibrate more, push each other apart 7 To allow for contraction ('shrinking') when temperature falls

3.3
1 Metals, nonmetals 2 Al Fe Ca Na K Mg 3 Hydrogen 4 Compounds are new substances made when elements combine 5 Molecule made from carbon atom and two oxygen atoms 6 Iron reactive, so forms compounds easily, gold unreactive 7 No; reactive, so would have formed compounds

3.4
1 Single substance with nothing mixed in 2 Will dissolve; substance which dissolves; substance it dissolves in; mixture of solvent and solute 3 Mixture of metals 4 Can have best properties of several metals 5 a) Dissolving b) Filtering or distilling c) Chromatography 6 Tea-bag (flavoured water, tea leaves), vacuum-cleaner bag (dust, air)

3.5
1 Mixtures have various melting or boiling points; keep properties of components which vary in proportion; are separated easily 2 a) Cannot be separated by filtering, clear b) Settle out, opaque c) Cannot be filtered, scatter light 3 Droplets of one liquid dispersed in another; salad cream 4 a) Gel b) Sol c) Foam 5 Made of two (or more) components contributing their own best properties 6 a) Concrete b) Steel rods 7 Bone is collagen + calcium phosphate; wood is cellulose fibres + lignin 8 a) Glass fibres + plastic resin, in canoes b) Carbon fibres + nylon, in tennis rackets

3.6
1 Dilute acid has more water in it 2 Strong acid more corrosive, lower pH 3 Hydrogen 4 Hydrogen; air/hydrogen mixture explodes with pop when lit 5 Salt and water 6 Acidic 7 Slightly alkaline 8 pH7 9 Indigestion tablet in stomach, toothpaste on teeth

3.7
1 Metals, reactive, one outer shell electron 2 Gases, unreactive, full outer shells 3 a) 2 b) 6 4 Kr is unreactive gas, 36 electrons in full shells; Cs is reactive metal, 55 electrons, one in outer shell; Co is magnetic metal, 27 electrons 5 Neon has full outer shell, sodium has one outer shell electron

3.8

1 a) Proton b) Electron c) Neutron **2** 5 **3** Charged atoms **4** Covalent bonds (shared electrons) **5** Bonds more easily broken **6** Ions separate and spread between water molecules

3.9

1 a) Attractions between oppositely charged ions b) Weak bonds between molecules c) 'Sea' of free electrons **2** Weak bonds between molecules easily broken by heat **3** Each carbon atom strongly bonded to four others **4** Flat layers of atoms slide over each other **5** Mixture not compound **6** Different sizes of atoms resist sliding of layers

3.10

1 Reversible, no new substance formed **2** a) Magnesium oxide b) Exothermic; gives out heat **3** Powdered magnesium; bigger surface area for reaction **4** a) Decomposition b) Substance which speeds up reaction without being used up

c) glucose $\xrightarrow{\text{yeast}}$ ethanol + carbon dioxide

3.11

1 Heat, air (oxygen), fuel **2** An oxide **3** Carbon dioxide and water **4** a) Turns lime water milky b) Makes smouldering splint burst into flames **5** Air (oxygen) and water **6** Makes fats rancid; refrigerating, keeping out oxygen

3.12

1 a) 2; so that equation balances b) Solid and gas **2** Relative atomic mass, relative molecular mass; 18 **3** 6×10^{23} molecules a) 16 g b) 24 dm^3 **4** 3 moles of solute in 1 dm^3 solution **5** $CH_4(g) + 2O_2(g) \rightarrow CO_2(g) + 2H_2O(l)$; a) 36 g b) 48 dm^3

3.13

1 To produce carbon monoxide for reaction which releases iron from ore **2** Electrolysis **3** Copper ions (+) attracted to cathode (−) **4** Impurities burnt off, then carbon added **5** a) Aluminium b) Gold; very unreactive c) Aluminium; most readily forms compounds, so most difficult to remove from compounds

3.14

1 a) Treating icy roads, flavouring food, preserving food b) Sodium hydroxide, sodium, chlorine **2** a) Water b) Chlorine c) Purifying water, making PVC, bleach, pesticides, solvents **3** Chippings, making cement

3.15

1 a) Sodium, chloride, hydrogen, and hydroxide ions + water molecules b) Sodium, hydrogen, and hydroxide ions + water molecules **2** $H^+(aq) + OH^-(aq) \rightarrow H_2O(l)$ **3** Negative electrode (cathode); positively charged **4** Metal atoms leave anode as positive ions, travel to cathode, pick up electrons, deposit as layers of atoms **5** a) Chlorine; sodium b) Chlorine; hydrogen c) Oxygen; hydrogen **6** 32 g

3.16

1 a) Atoms smaller, lose electrons less easily b) Atoms bigger **2** Ionic; turn it blue (alkaline) **3** Diagrams to show outer shell with 7 electrons becoming full by gaining 1 electron (inner shell has 2 electrons) **4** Form positive ions, ionic chlorides, and ionic (basic) oxides **5** High melting point, semiconductor, oxide both acidic and basic; shows some properties of metals as well as nonmetals

3.17

1 Bleaches it (removes colour) **2** Making bleach, chlorates, hydrochloric acid **3** Iron (in steel, for construction), tungsten (bulb filaments), copper (electrical wires) **4** Strong, more than one type of ion, coloured compounds

3.18

1 Reactions in which electrons pass from reducing agent to oxidizing agent; electron supplier **2** a) Zinc b) Calcium c) Iron **3** a) Iron(III) sulphate b) Pale green to yellow **4** a) Products recombine to give original substances b) Heating in sealed container; $CaCO_3(s) \rightarrow CaO(s) + CO_2(g)$ **5** a) 150 atm, 450 °C b) Compromise between speed and good yield c) 17% d) 500 atm, 380 °C

3.19

1 Oxygen; 4 shared electrons **2** Energy needed to start reaction **3** More energy released in making new bonds than absorbed in breaking existing bonds **4** Reverse of 3 **5** Energy needed to break a bond (or energy released when bond is made) **6** 2054 kJ

3.20

1 Compounds of hydrogen and carbon **2** Petrol, diesel oil, kerosene **3** Breaking long molecules into shorter molecules; to match supply of different oil fractions to demand **4** Nitrogen; preserving food, quickfreezing food **5** Passing methane and steam over catalysts, electrolysing sodium chloride solution, electrolysing acidified water **6** Hydrogen, helium; helium; does not burn **7** Distillation (different substances boiled off at different temperatures)

3.21

1 Breaking down large hydrocarbon molecules **2** Alkanes – hydrocarbons with single bonds, alkenes – hydrocarbons with double bonds **3** Join up when a) double bonds break open b) water molecules are eliminated **4** Mixing solutions of 1,6 diaminohexane and hexanedioic acid **5** Starch and protein; break down easily **6** Polymer chains stretched parallel

3.22

1 Nitrogen from air and hydrogen from methane + steam **2** Iron **3** Ammonium nitrate; neutralizing nitric acid with ammonia **4** Nitrogen, phosphorus, potassium **5** Six; make ammonia, nitric acid, Nitram, sulphuric acid, phosphoric acid, NPK blends **6** Anywhere near a port with road/rail links and close to supplies of natural gas and potassium chloride

3.23

1 Disease, decomposing food (harmful); making bread, alcohol (useful) **2** Microbe growth stopped by low temperature, lack of liquid **3** If parts undercooked, microbes not killed **4** Keep out microbes in air, low temperature slows microbe growth **5** Making cheese, yoghurt **6** Reaction which changes sugar (glucose) into alcohol (ethanol) and carbon dioxide **7** Gas bubbles from fermentation **8** Biological catalysts (speed up reactions)

3.24

1 Millions of tiny water droplets; water vapour condenses when temperature falls **2** Water vapour in air condenses and freezes; water expands when it freezes **3** Damage to surfaces caused by weather; frost cracking rock, acid rain eating away stonework **4** a) Condensed to form oceans b) Carbon became locked up in sedimentary rocks c) Given off by plants when these appeared **5** Act as reservoir for dissolved carbon dioxide

3.25

1 Water goes from drains to sea, evaporates to form clouds, rain falls over reservoir **2** Building reservoirs changes landscape, destroys habitats, taking water from ground can dry it out **3** Wearing away of surfaces **4** Particles transported, deposited as sediments, crushed to form new rock **5** Rock underneath; rock gets broken up by frost, rain, expansion due to Sun's heat

3.26

1 Molten rock from under Earth's surface **2** Magma cools, solidifies **3** Quick cooling gives smaller crystals **4** Layers of sediment crushed, then set hard **5** a) Can form from sediments containing remains of dead organisms b) Formed from very hot, molten material **6** Metamorphic; limestone, changed by heat **7** No advantages; disadvantages a) Not easy to split into layers b) Not so hard, attacked by acid rain

3.27

1 Crust movements occur there, also heat released **2** Plates move together at destructive boundary, apart at constructive boundary **3** P-waves; faster **4** S-waves cannot travel through liquids, no S-waves travel through Earth's core

4.1

1 Metals, carbon **2** negative (–) **3** Like charges repel **4** a) Positive (+) b) Negative (–) **5** Break in conducting path, so circuit not complete

4.2

1 Ammeter; 2.0 **2** Voltmeter **3** a) Brighter b) Higher c) Higher (approx double) **4** a) Reduced to previous brightness b) Reduced to previous value (2.0) **5** Brightness not reduced; one bulb keeps working if other bulb removed

4.3

1 Lower resistance; resistance too high, heat given off, current reduced **2** Heating elements; because high resistance gives heating effect **3** Brighter; less resistance, so higher current **4** 2 kW h; 20p **5** a) 80p b) 10p **6** 160p

4.4

1 AND gate **2** Both OFF **3** Output is always opposite of input **4** a) AND b) OR gate

4.5

1 Thermostat switches power off if too much heat fedback, switches power on again if too little heat fedback **2** a) 9 V b) 4.5 V **3** R = S = 0, Q changes to 1, both 1s change to 0s, and remaining 0 to 1 **4** Retains last output state until input changed **5** ON, OFF, ON, ON, OFF, ON, ON **6** Truth table rows from top ABPQ, 0010, 0101, 1001, 1101; OR

4.6

1 a) 2 A b) 3 A c) 0.5 A **2** a) 3 Ω b) 12 W c) 48 W **3** a) 18 Ω b) 1.33 A **4** a) 4 A (through 6 Ω), 2 A (through 12 Ω) b) 6 A c) 4 Ω

4.7

1 With a compass **2** More turns on coil, higher current **3** Wrap coil round nail, connect coil to battery **4** Circles round wire, becoming more spaced out further out **5** Small current switches on electromagnet in relay, relay switches on motor circuit **6** Cone must vibrate to give out sound, so magnetic force must be backwards, forwards .. and so on

4.8

1 a) Connecting outside circuit to coil b) Reversing current through coil every half turn **2** Stronger magnet, more turns on coil, higher current **3** AC keeps changing direction; a) DC b) AC c) AC **4** a) By turning coil in magnetic field b) To connect coil to outside circuit **5** Changing voltage; AC

4.9

1 a) Live, so that wire in flex/appliance is not live when switch is off b) Safety, takes current from metal body to Earth so that fuse blows c) Two conducting routes to each socket, so thinner cable needed **2** a) 2 A b) 3 A c) Lamp current small, so any increase might cause overheating without blowing fuse

4.10

1 Faster rotation, stronger magnet, more turns on coil **2** a) Step-down b) 23 V c) 46 W d) 46 W e) 2 A **3** To reduce current in cables **4** a) 100 A b) 1 A

4.11

1 a) 12 C b) 72 J **2** Downwards; negative charge repelled by negative, attracted by positive **3** Faster electrons, so shorter wavelength X-rays **4** Downwards

4.12

1 a) Moving car b) Battery c) Stretched spring **2** 10 000 J **3** Chemical; changed to heat + kinetic energy **4** Kinetic → heat **5** Chemical → kinetic → potential → kinetic → heat **6** Energy can change forms, but total amount stays the same

4.13

1 Conduction and convection need particles to carry energy, space empty; radiation **2** Hot air rises, cooler air replaces it and is heated **3** a) Air very poor conductor b) To reflect Sun's radiation c) Poor radiators of heat **4** a) Part-vacuum b) Stopper c) Shiny surfaces; reduces heat flow in either direction

4.14 and 4.15

1 Cannot be replaced; coal, oil **2** Global warming (carbon dioxide), acid rain (sulphur dioxide) **3** Hydroelectric scheme, aerogenerators **4** Ancient sea plants absorbed Sun's energy, ancient sea creatures fed on plants, remains of plants and creatures trapped and crushed by sediment to form oil, petrol extracted from oil **5** 25% of fuel's energy changed into kinetic energy, rest wasted as heat **6** Less fuel burnt, so supplies last longer and less pollution

4.16

1 Energy of atoms and molecules because of their motion and position **2** 800 J of energy needed to heat 1 kg through 1 °C **3** a) 12 600 000 J b) 4200 s (70 minutes) **4** a) B b) E c) 4800 W d) Some heat cannot be used as energy source for turbine, so it is wasted e) No fuel used, no polluting gases f) Wind farm produces noise, tidal scheme destroys habitats, both alter landscape **5** a) Low fuel costs, no polluting gases b) Expensive to build and decommission, hazardous waste **6** a) Middle east b) Natural gas c) Russia + East Europe d) Europe, N America

4.17

1 500 N **2** Forces are weight (500 N downwards), air resistance (500 N upwards); resultant 0 **3** a) Force spread over larger area so pressure less b) Pressure from water produces upward force which balances weight **4** 200 Pa

4.18

1 a) 273 K b) 373 K c) 300 K d) 200 K **2** a) P proportional to T b) V proportional to T c) P increases if V decreases d) P proportional to $1/V$ **3** a) Particles packed into smaller space, so more strike each mm^2 of balloon b) Temperature rises, particles hit sides of canister faster **4** 12 m^3

4.19

1 To give turning effect which matches turning effect of load, so that centre of mass of crane and load is over base **2** When load is changed, turning effect of counterbalance must be changed **3** 200 N m **4** 200 N m **5** 0.5 m **6** 200 N (counterbalance is then at max distance) **7** Wider base, heavier weight low down on base

4.20

1 a) Extensions are (in mm) 0, 9, 18, 27, 39, 59 b) Graph is straight line through origin c) Up to 27 mm extension d) 2.3 N **2** a) 8 N m b) 4 N c) 9 N

4.21
1 10 m/s 2 Head-down position, shaped helmet, smooth & tight-fitting oufit, streamlined bike (e.g no spokes) 3 a) Brakes, tyres, steering wheel b) Wheel bearings, moving parts of engine and gearbox, car body moving through air 4 a) 15 m b) 18 m; at higher speed, car travels further in same time 5 a) 50 m b) 99 m

4.22
1 a) Increasing by 3 m/s every s b) Decreasing by 3 m/s every s 2 a) 25 m/s b) 2.5 m/s^2 c) 1.25 m/s^2 3 Mass x velocity 4 a) 12 N b) 15 m/s c) 60 kg m/s 5 12 N; yes

4.23
1 a) −12 kg m/s b) +12 kg m/s c) 6 m/s 2 a) 50 N b) 10 m/s^2 downwards c) Double the force, but double the mass to be accelerated 3 10 m/s^2 downwards 4 Inward force needed to keep object moving in a circle; gravity on an orbiting satellite

4.24
1 Pliers, nutcrackers, can opener 2 Energy output would be greater than energy input, which breaks law of conservation of energy 3 100 J 4 10 W 5 100 W

4.25
1 a) 200 Pa b) 100 N c) Greater 2 a) 600 J b) 300 J c) 300 J d) 600 J e) 20 m/s f) 20 m/s

4.26
1 Solid, liquid, or gas needed to carry vibrations 2 Microphone + CRO, seeing wave trace on screen 3 Sound much slower than light 4 660 m 5 a) $^1/_3$ s b) $^2/_3$ s after he shouts 6 Using echo to measure depth of water; sound reflected from sea-bed, echo time measured, longer time means greater depth of water 7 Sound keeps reflecting from walls; putting sound-absorbing materials (curtains, carpet) in room

4.27
1 a) Vibrates when sound waves strike it b) Transmit vibrations to cochlea c) Sensor cells respond to vibrations and send nerve impulses to brain 2 Very high amplitude sound waves can damage ear drum, cochlea, or auditory nerve 3 200 sound waves every second 4 a) Louder b) Higher pitch 5 Safer (do not damage/destroy body cells); checking unborn baby in womb

4.28
1 Longitudinal - backwards-forwards vibrations e.g. sound, transverse - side-to-side vibrations e.g. light 2 a) Higher b) Lower 3 Different harmonics present 4 Vibration build up when incoming frequency matches natural frequency; a) Wind instruments b) Wheel wobble 5 3 m 6 3 m

4.29
1 Reflects daylight or other lighting 2 Wall scatters light, mirror reflects light in regular way 3 For straight-ahead view and image which is right way round 4 Bending of light when it enters/leaves transparent material; light entering glass block 5 Light waves on one side of beam reach glass first and slow before those on other side, so beam bends; both sides of beam reach glass at same time and slow together 6 Thin, flexible, rod of glass/plastic which transmits light; light zig-zags along fibre as it reflects from side to side

4.30
1 a) Smaller, upright b) Larger, upright 2 Camera (forms image on film, eye (forms image on retina), projector (forms image on screen) 3 Convex lens system, aperture control, upside-down image on retina/film 4 For distant object, short-sighted eye focuses light in front of retina, not on it; concave; to spread rays before they enter eye

4.31
1 Violet; shorter wavelength, slowed more by glass 2 Radio, micro, infrared, light, ultraviolet, X-rays, gamma 3 a) Light b) radio, micro, light (+ infrared in remote controllers) c) infrared, micro d) X-rays, gamma e) X-rays, gamma

4.32
1 Red, green, blue 2 White 3 Yellow 4 All (red, green, blue) 5 All (red, green, blue) 6 a) Blue b) Red, green 7 a) Green b) Red, blue 8 Black

4.33
1 A4, B1, C2, D3 2 Long waves diffract round hills, but VHF does not because of shorter wavelength 3 First Polaroid lets through wave vibrations in one plane only. If plane matches second Polaroid, waves get through. If not, waves stopped

4.34
1 a) Total of protons + neutrons b) Same number of protons (and electrons) c) Different numbers of neutrons 2 Has atoms with unstable nuclei 3 Removes electrons from atoms 4 Can kill or damage cells 5 Alpha, beta, gamma 6 Alpha 7 Gamma 8 Alpha 9 Small amount of radiation always present from natural sources

4.35
1 a) Nucleus breaks up b) Change in number of protons in nucleus 2 Takes 28 years for half strontium-90 nuclei to decay 3 a) 8 days b) 24 days 4 Hit by neutron, splits into two smaller nuclei plus neutrons 5 Neutrons from fission of uranium-235 causing further fission, and so on; nuclear reactor

4.36
1 a) 27 days b) Just over 365 days 2 Earth's axis tilted so that north angled towards Sun in June, away from Sun in December 3 Time for Moon's orbit same as time for rotation 4 Reflects Sun's light 5 Crescent is sunlit part, rest is in shadow 6 Less 7 Earth turning at same rate as satellite orbiting

4.37
1 Jupiter 2 Mercury, Venus, Mars, Pluto 3 Mars, Jupiter, Saturn, Uranus, Neptune, Pluto; further from Sun, so receive less heat 4 Jupiter, Saturn, Uranus, Neptune 5 Reflect Sun's light 6 Greater distance, longer orbit time 7 Venus hotter than Mercury, yet further from Sun 8 a) Star system with billions of stars b) Distance travelled by light in one year 9 Andromeda; 2 million years; take too long as nothing can travel faster than light

4.38
1 a) 1986 b) 2024 c) 1986 d) 2024 2 Reduce to 1/4 3 a) Moon comes between Sun and Earth, so part of Earth in Moon's shadow b) Moon in Earth's shadow 4 Gravitational pull of Moon (and Sun); during one rotation of Earth, each place moves in and out of two water bulges (towards and away from Moon) 5 Impact craters; oceans and atmosphere have worn craters away

4.39
1 Fusion 2 a) Huge cloud of gas and dust b) Gravity c) 4500 million years 3 a) Expanded, cooled star b) Hot core exposed after red giant loses outer layer 4 Collapse of very massive star's core after supernova 5 Atomic particles and gamma rays from Sun and space 6 Galaxies moving apart, background microwave radiation 7 10 000 million years

Answers to GCSE questions (pages 210-214)

1
a i) Prevent loss of blood ii) Supply blood with oxygen; maintain blood circulation **b** 100 beats per minute

2
a Making food (glucose) **b** Light needed for food-making can pass through cell walls and be absorbed by chlorophyll in chloroplasts **c** i) First space, water; second space, oxygen ii) Through stomata **d** Microbes are decomposers which digest carbohydrate and release carbon dioxide as a product **e** i) Carbon, hydrogen, oxygen ii) Sodium chloride has strong ionic bonds, sugars have much weaker covalent bonds

3
a See page 52 **b** i) h; Both F_1 offspring spotted despite one parent with black coat, so black coat must be recessive ii) Parents are (from left to right) HH hh, F_1 are Hh Hh, F_2 are HH Hh Hh hh iii) 1:1 iv) Black better camouflage in forest than in grassland, so survival more likely in forest

4
a i) Chromatography ii) Porous iii) Water **b** Solution of colourings penetrates pores of paper, colours eventually sticking to fibres in different places **c** i) Single dye ii) Mixture of red and green dyes

5
a Speeds up reactions **b** Harmful – sulphur dioxide (acid rain); useful – argon (lighting), carbon dioxide (coolant) **c** Economic – availability of raw materials, transport, efficiency of factory; environmental – destruction of farmland, impact on wildlife, pollution **d** i) $2NH_3(g) + H_2SO_4(aq) \rightarrow (NH_4)_2SO_4(aq)$ ii) M_rs are $NH_3 = 17$, $H_2SO_4 = 98$. From equation, $2 \times 17 = 34$ tonnes ammonia are neutralized by 98 tonnes sulphuric acid. So 340 tonnes ammonia needs 980 tonnes sulphuric acid

6
a Metamorphic **b** i) Igneous ii) Liquid magma cools to form solid made up of interlocking crystals

7
a i) Covalent bond ii) Oxygen atom iii) Giant molecular solid **b** Very hard, high melting point; strongly bonded **c** i) Acidic; reacts with base giving salt ii) Adds tensile strength to composite

8
a Semicircle round Sun **b** V should be between S and E, M should be beyond E

9
a i) Switch in connecting wire next to battery ii) One switch in connecting wire next to buzzer, other switch in connecting wire next to lamp **b** i) Circuit should have battery, lamp, and variable resistor in series ii) No, because value of voltage divided by current changes iii) Bright filament has higher resistance

10
a i) Potential ii) Potential and kinetic iii) No fuel to buy, no fuel to tranport, no polluting gases **b** i) Hot water rises. If element were at top, bottom would stay cool ii) Insulation (lagging) round tank, using glass wool or plastic foam **c** i) 50 400 J ii) 78 000 J iii) Not all electrical energy is converted into microwave energy because of heat losses in circuits iv) 0.12 m

11
a i) 1.4 m/s^2 ii) 52.5 m **b** i) 126 N ii) 2205 J iii) 2205 J iv) 735 W

Units and symbols

Quantity	Unit	Symbol
mass	kilogram	kg
length	metre	m
time	second	s
force	newton	N
weight	newton	N
pressure	pascal	Pa
energy	joule	J
work	joule	J
power	watt	W
voltage	volt	V
current	ampere	A
resistance	ohm	Ω
temperature {	degree Celsius	^{o}C
	kelvin	K

Bigger or smaller

To make units bigger or smaller, prefixes are put in front of them:

micro (μ)	= 1 millionth	= 0.000 001	= 10^{-6}
milli (m)	= 1 thousandth	= 0.001	= 10^{-3}
kilo (k)	= 1 thousand	= 1000	= 10^3
mega (M)	= 1 million	= 1 000 000	= 10^6

For example

1 micrometre	= 1 μm	= 0.000 001 m
1 millisecond	= 1 ms	= 0.001 s
1 milliampere	= 1 mA	= 0.001 A
1 kilometre	= 1 km	= 1000 m
1 kilojoule	= 1 kJ	= 1000 J
1 megatonne	= 1 Mt	= 1 000 000 t

Index

Periodic table

Group

Period	Group 1	Group 2								transition metals							Group 3	Group 4	Group 5	Group 6	Group 7	Group 0
1	H hydrogen 1																					He helium 2
2	Li lithium 3	Be beryllium 4															B boron 5	C carbon 6	N nitrogen 7	O oxygen 8	F fluorine 9	Ne neon 10
3	Na sodium 11	Mg magnesium 12															Al aluminium 13	Si silicon 14	P phosphorus 15	S sulphur 16	Cl chlorine 17	Ar argon 18
4	K potassium 19	Ca calcium 20	Sc scandium 21	Ti titanium 22	V vandium 23	Cr chromium 24	Mn manganese 25	Fe iron 26	Co cobalt 27	Ni nickel 28	Cu copper 29	Zn zinc 30	Ga gallium 31	Ge germanium 32	As arsenic 33	Se selenium 34	Br bromine 35	Kr krypton 36
5	Rb rubidium 37	Sr strontium 38	Y yttrium 39	Zr zirconium 40	Nb niobium 41	Mo molybdenum 42	Tc technetium 43	Ru ruthenium 44	Rh rhodium 45	Pd palladium 46	Ag silver 47	Cd cadmium 48	In indium 49	Sn tin 50	Sb antimony 51	Te tellurium 52	I iodine 53	Xe xenon 54
6	Cs caesium 55	Ba barium 56	La lanthanum 57	Hf hafnium 72	Ta tantalum 73	W tungsten 74	Re rhenium 75	Os osmium 76	Ir iridium 77	Pt platinum 78	Au gold 79	Hg mercury 80	Tl thallium 81	Pb lead 82	Bi bismuth 83	Po polonium 84	At astatine 85	Rn radon 86
7	Fr francium 87	Ra radium 88	Ac actinium 89															

Ce cerium 58	Pr praseodymium 59	Nd neodymium 60	Pm promethium 61	Sm samarium 62	Eu europium 63	Gd gadolinium 64	Tb terbium 65	Dy dysprosium 66	Ho holmium 67	Er erbium 68	Tm thulium 69	Yb ytterbium 70	Lu lutetium 71
Th thorium 90	Pa protactinium 91	U uranium 92	Np neptunium 93	Pu plutonium 94	Am americium 95	Cm curium 96	Bk berkelium 97	Cf californium 98	Es einsteinium 99	Fm fermium 100	Md mendelevium 101	No nobelium 102	Lr lawrencium 103

Table of approximate relative atomic masses (A_r) for calculations

Element	Symbol	A_r	Element	Symbol	A_r	Element	Symbol	A_r
aluminium	Al	27	iodine	I	127	oxygen	O	16
bromine	Br	80	iron	Fe	56	phosphorus	P	31
calcium	Ca	40	lead	Pb	207	potassium	K	39
carbon	C	12	lithium	Li	7	silicon	Si	28
chlorine	Cl	35.5	magnesium	Mg	24	silver	Ag	108
copper	Cu	64	manganese	Mn	55	sodium	Na	23
helium	He	4	neon	Ne	20	sulphur	S	32
hydrogen	H	1	nitrogen	N	14	zinc	Zn	65